LIFE VISION

Student Book

A1/A2

Elementary

Carla Leonard

CONTENTS

INTRODUCTION p.4	LESSON 0.1	LESSON 0.2	LESSON 0.3	LESSON 0.4
	Vocabulary: An English exam; countries and nationalities; the alphabet **Grammar** Present simple the verb *be*: affirmative, negative and questions	**Vocabulary:** Everyday objects **Grammar:** Singular and plural nouns *This / that / these / those* Imperatives	**Vocabulary:** Families **Grammar:** *Have got* Possessive *'s*	**Vocabulary:** School subjects **Grammar** *Can* Object pronouns

UNIT	VOCABULARY 1	GRAMMAR 1	READING (R) / LISTENING (L)	GLOBAL SKILLS
1 Vlog your day! p.8	**Daily routines** **Vocabulary:** Daily routines ▶ Vlog	**Present simple: affirmative** **Pronunciation:** Third person singular verbs ▶ Grammar animation	(L) **Vlogging** **Strategy:** Predicting before you listen	**Managing your time** **Vocabulary:** How to manage your time
	Review p.18 **Exam skills** p.19: **Reading** *Missing sentences*; **Speaking** *Answering questions*			
2 Healthy living p.22	**Crazy about sport** **Vocabulary:** Staying fit ▶ Vlog	**Adverbs of frequency, question words** ▶ Grammar animation	(L) **An athlete's schedule** **Strategy:** Recognising common collocations	**Food labels** **Phrasebook:** Talking about labels
	Review p.32 **Exam skills** p.33: **Listening** *Multiple choice photos*; **Use of English** *Missing words*;			
3 Looking good p.34	**What's your style?** **Vocabulary:** Clothes from around the world ▶ Vlog	**Present continuous** **Pronunciation:** /ŋ/ ▶ Grammar animation	(L) **Costumes** **Strategy:** Identifying examples	**Being safe online** **Vocabulary:** Sharing information safely
	Review p.44 **Exam skills** p.45: **Reading** *True or false*; **Speaking** *Describing a photo*			
4 Where we live p.48	**Come on in** **Vocabulary:** Houses and rooms ▶ Vlog	**Comparative adjectives** **Pronunciation:** The schwa /ə/ ▶ Grammar animation	(L) **Unusual houses** **Strategy:** Recognising prepositions of place	**Designing a better classroom** **Phrasebook:** Problem-solving
	Review p.58 **Exam skills** p.59: **Listening** *Multiple matching*; **Use of English** *Multiple choice texts*;			
5 Time out p.60	**I'm into art** **Vocabulary:** Entertainment ▶ Vlog	**Past simple: regular verbs** **Pronunciation:** -ed ▶ Grammar animation	(R) **Street art** **Vocabulary:** Adjectives **Strategy:** Scanning for information	**Researching and evaluating information** **Vocabulary:** Finding information online
	Review p.70 **Exam skills** p.71: **Reading** *Multiple choice in short texts*; **Speaking** *Making suggestions*			
6 Digital detox p.74	**Phone zombies** **Vocabulary:** Technology ▶ Vlog	**Past simple affirmative: irregular verbs** **Pronunciation:** /ɔː/ and /e/ ▶ Grammar animation	(R) **Goodbye to technology** **Vocabulary:** Living without technology **Strategy:** Understanding linking words: reasons and results	**Social media etiquette** Rules for online behaviour
	Review p.84 **Exam skills** p.85: **Listening** *True or False*; **Use of English** *Missing words*;			
7 A bright future p.86	**Dream big** **Vocabulary:** Life goals ▶ Vlog	**Be going to** ▶ Grammar animation	(L) **New Year celebrations** **Strategy:** Recognising different speakers	**My dreams** **Phrasebook:** Giving a presentation
	Review p.96 **Exam skills** p.97: **Reading** *Multiple matching*; **Speaking** *Comparing and contrasting*			
8 A ticket to ride p.100	**Getting around** **Vocabulary:** Travel and tourism ▶ Vlog	**Present perfect: affirmative** ▶ Grammar animation	(L) **Adventures on the road** **Strategy:** Recognising phrasal verbs for travel	**Difficult situations** Dealing with a travel problem
	Review p.110 **Exam skills** p.111: **Listening** *Missing information*; **Use of English** *Multiple choice text*;			

VOCABULARY BOOSTER	p.112
GRAMMAR BOOSTER	p.128
IRREGULAR VERB LIST	p.148

VOCABULARY 2	GRAMMAR 2	READING ®/ LISTENING ⓛ	SPEAKING	WRITING
Free-time activities Vocabulary: Hobbies	**Present simple: negative and yes / no questions** ▶ Grammar animation	® **Teenage stress** Strategy: Identifying main ideas	**Likes and dislikes** Strategy: Consonant-vowel linking Phrasebook: Talking about likes and dislikes	**A personal profile** Strategy: Using pronouns or adverbs to avoid repetition Language focus: Conjunctions: *and*, *but*, *or*

Vision 360 p.20–21

| **How to eat well** Vocabulary: Food and drink Pronunciation: /ɪ/ and /iː/ | **There is / There are, some, any, a lot of, much and many** ▶ Grammar animation | ® **Healthy eating habits** Strategy: Using general knowledge to predict content | **Ordering food and drink** Strategy: Rating your performance Phrasebook: Ordering food and drink Paying for your meal | **Completing a form** Strategy: Using capital letters Language focus: Abbreviations |

Writing *Replying to a letter / email* ▶ **Documentary** *Soccer in Soweto*

| **Describing character** Vocabulary: Character types | **Present simple and present continuous** ▶ Grammar animation | ® **Perfect selfies** Vocabulary: Describing appearance Strategy: Dealing with unknown words | **Describing photos** Strategy: Brainstorming useful vocabulary Phrasebook: Describing photos | **An informal email** Strategy: Writing informal emails / letters Language focus: *like* |

Vision 360 p.46–47

| **Places in the world** Vocabulary: Places and geographical features | **Superlative adjectives** ▶ Grammar animation | ® **Favourite countries** Strategy: Recognising different word forms | **Asking for and giving directions** Strategy: Asking for clarification Phrasebook: Directions | **A description of a place** Strategy: Making your descriptions more interesting |

Writing *Using adjectives* ▶ **Documentary** *Fairytale house*

| **Entertainment** Vocabulary: Film and TV | **Past simple: the verb *be* and *can*** ▶ Grammar animation | ⓛ **The life of Frida Kahlo** Strategy: Understanding the structure of a listening text | **Telling a personal story** Strategy: Showing interest Phrasebook: Telling a personal story | **A diary entry** Strategy: Organising your writing Language focus: Time sequencers |

Speaking *Responding to suggestions, agreeing and disagreeing*   **Vision 360** p.72–73

| **Everyday items** Vocabulary: Things you can't live without | **Past simple: negative and questions: irregular verbs** ▶ Grammar animation | ⓛ **Past events** Strategy: Recognising specific information | **Shopping** Strategy: Asking questions politely Phrasebook: Shopping How to talk about prices | **A product review** Strategy: Writing product reviews Language focus: Adverbs |

Writing *A formal letter* ▶ **Documentary** *TV time travellers*

| **Career choices** Vocabulary: Jobs Pronunciation: /ə/ and /ɜː/ | **Will** ▶ Grammar animation | ® **Teens changing the world** Strategy: Recognising proper nouns | **Comparing and contrasting** Strategy: Following a structure Phrasebook: Comparing and contrasting photos | **An informal invitation email** Strategy: Using appropriate tenses Language focus: Contractions |

Vision 360 p.98–99

| **Holidays and places to stay** Vocabulary: Types of holidays Pronunciation: /æ/ and /eɪ/ | **Present perfect: negative and questions** ▶ Grammar animation | ® **A travel photographer** Strategy: Understanding topic sentences Vocabulary: Describing a career | **Asking for information** Strategy: Preparing to talk Phrasebook: Talking about numbers | **A postcard** Strategy: Deciding what to include Language focus: Postcards |

Writing *Making notes* ▶ **Documentary** *Sky Lodge: an unusual hotel*

Contents 3

0.1 INTRODUCTION
Talk about personal information and nationalities.

An English exam

1 🔊 **0.01** Read and listen to the dialogue. Does Margot know Rodrigo and Tomek?

Margot Hi, are you here for the English exam?
Rodrigo Yes, we are.
Margot I'm Margot. What's your name?
Rodrigo My name's Rodrigo and this is Tomek.
Margot Where are you from? Are you Spanish?
Rodrigo No, we aren't. We're from Portugal.
Tomek But my dad isn't Portuguese. He's Polish. Are you French?
Margot No, I'm not. I'm from Switzerland.
Rodrigo I'm eighteen and he's seventeen years old. How old are you, Margot?
Margot I'm sixteen.
Tomek Rodrigo! The exam is in ten minutes! Is it in room eleven?
Margot No, it isn't. It's in room fifteen.
Rodrigo Thanks, Margot!
Margot Good luck!

2 Read the dialogue again. Find all the numbers. Write them in number form.

3 Work in pairs. Count from 0 to 50, and then back to 0.

4 **VOCABULARY** 🔊 **0.02** How do you say the numbers below?

| 11   12   46   56   64   72   88   99   100   150

5 Read the rules. Then underline sentences with present simple and the verb *be* in the dialogue and complete the table.

Present simple + the verb *be*: affirmative, negative and questions

We can use present simple + the verb *be* to talk about our name, age and nationality.
I _____ Lucy.
Our cat _____ two years old.
Jan and Marek _____ Czech.
We form the negative with the verb *be* + *not*.
He _____ Hungarian – he's German.
They _____ from Peru – they're from Mexico.
To answer questions with the verb *be*, we use short answers.
Are you English? No, I _____.
Is she Chinese? Yes, she _____.
Are they from Slovakia? No, they _____.
What's his name? It _____ Dan.

GRAMMAR BOOSTER P128

6 Complete the text with the affirmative (+) or negative (–) form of the verb *be*.
My name [1]_____ (+) Margot and I [2]_____ (+) sixteen years old. I [3]_____ (+) a student, but I [4]_____ (–) at school now. My dad [5]_____ (–) Swiss. He [6]_____ (+) German. He and my mum [7]_____ (+) 42. Our teacher [8]_____ (–) in the classroom now. My friends [9]_____ (+) at home because it [10]_____ (–) Monday today – it [11]_____ Sunday!

7 Complete the questions with the correct form of *be*.
1 What _____ your name?
2 Where _____ you from?
3 _____ you sixteen years old?
4 _____ our teacher Czech?
5 _____ your best friend in this class?
6 _____ it Tuesday today?

8 💬 Work in pairs. Ask and answer the questions in Ex 7.

9 **VOCABULARY** Find all the countries and nationalities in the dialogue and Ex 5. Use them to help you complete the table.

Country	Nationality
France	[1]_____
the UK	[2]_____
Poland	[3]_____
[4]_____	Portuguese
Spain	[5]_____
[6]_____	Swiss
[7]_____	Slovak
the Czech Republic	[8]_____
[9]_____	Peruvian
Hungary	[10]_____
[11]_____	Mexican
China	[12]_____

10 💬 Work in pairs. Can you think of more countries or nationalities?

11 💬 **VOCABULARY** 🔊 **0.03** Listen and repeat the alphabet. Work in pairs. How fast can you say it?

12 🔊 **0.04** Listen to the English exam. How many people are in the exam room? What is the woman's name?

13 🔊 **0.04** Listen again. Write the names.

	First name	Surname
Candidate 1	Rodrigo	[1]_____
Candidate 2	Tomek	[2]_____

14 💬 Work in groups of four. Take turns to be the two examiners and Candidates 1 and 2 in the English exam. Use the phrases below.

- Good morning / afternoon.
- I'm … and this is …
- He/She is here to listen to us.
- What's your name / surname?
- How do you spell it?

4 Introduction

Use nouns, pronouns and imperatives to talk about everyday objects.

0.2 INTRODUCTION

Everyday objects

1 Look at the poster. Answer the questions.
1 Where's it from?
2 What things are on it?
3 Which things are/aren't OK for people to take?

2 🔊 **0.05** Listen to a security guard and a boy at the stadium. What colours do you hear?

3 🔊 **0.05** Listen again. Tick (✓) the things you hear on the poster.

4 **VOCABULARY** Complete the table with the words below.

| blue   books   box   chair   diaries   drink |
| fast   food   headphones   keys   mobile phone   new |
| old   orange   purple   slow   sunglasses   umbrella |

Technology	video game, ¹_____, ²_____
Other objects	bag, ³_____, ⁴_____, ⁵_____, ⁶_____, ⁷_____, ⁸_____, ⁹_____, ¹⁰_____, ¹¹_____
Colours	yellow, ¹²_____, ¹³_____, ¹⁴_____
Adjectives	big, ¹⁵_____, ¹⁶_____, ¹⁷_____, ¹⁸_____

5 Read the rules and complete the table.

Singular and plural nouns

We use *a* before singular nouns that start with a consonant. If the noun starts with a vowel, we use *an*.
____ bag
____ orange
We add ____ to form most plural nouns, but sometimes we add *–es* or *–ies*.
book → books   box → boxes   diary → diaries
Some plural nouns are irregular.
woman → women   child → children

GRAMMAR BOOSTER P129

6 Work in pairs. Make singular and plural nouns using objects from Ex 4.

drink   drinks!   orange   oranges!

7 Write the plural form of these nouns.
1 a boy _____   7 a person _____
2 a class _____   8 a phone _____
3 a country _____   9 a watch _____
4 a family _____   10 a woman _____
5 a half _____   11 an apple _____
6 a man _____   12 an exam _____

8 💬 Work in pairs. Look at the bag. Write a list of the things in it.

9 Read the table. Then complete the rules.

This / that / these / those

	near	not near
Singular	This is a bag.	That is a computer.
Plural	These are pens.	Those are books.

We use _____ or _____ with *is/are* to talk about things or people that are near us.
We use _____ or _____ with *is/are* to talk about things or people that aren't near us.

GRAMMAR BOOSTER P129

10 Read the rules. Then complete the sentences with the correct form of the verb *be*, *listen*, *open*, *sit*.

Imperatives

We use imperatives to tell someone to do something.
We form the affirmative imperative with the infinitive without *to*.
_____ to the teacher.   _____ your books.
We form the negative imperative with *don't* + the infinitive without *to*.
_____ _____ on that chair.
_____ _____ late for the exam.

GRAMMAR BOOSTER P129

11 Write some instructions for your home, your school and another place (e.g. a stadium). Use the imperative. Then, in pairs, share your ideas.

Don't forget the test on Monday!

Introduction   5

0.3 INTRODUCTION
Use *have got* and possessive *'s* to talk about family and possessions.

Families

1 💬 Work in pairs. Look at the photo of the family video call. What do you think is the relationship between them?

This is my family

I'm Cora. I'm fifteen years old. I'm from Dublin, and this is my family video call!

In this call, I'm with my <mark>dad</mark>, Mark, my <mark>mum</mark>, Anna, and my <mark>brother</mark>, Charlie. We're <mark>twins</mark>. I've got a little <mark>sister</mark> too. My sister's name's Chloe. She's ten. Today, she's in Cork at our <mark>grandmother</mark> Agnes's house. Our grandmother's got <mark>pets</mark>. She's got two cats, four rabbits and a bird!

We've got <mark>grandparents</mark> in Australia too. My dad's parents' names are Conrad and Mary. My <mark>grandfather</mark>'s got a new mobile phone for video calls!

Dad's got a sister in Wales too. That's my <mark>aunt</mark> Rachel and my <mark>uncle</mark> James – they've got two little <mark>children</mark>. Their names are Olly and <mark>baby</mark> Archie. Mum hasn't got any brothers or sisters; she's an <mark>only child</mark>. Have you got <mark>cousins</mark> too?

2 🔊 0.06 💬 Work in pairs. Read and listen to the text. Ask and answer the questions.
  1 What are the names of the people in each photo?
  2 Where are they?

3 **VOCABULARY** Look at the diagram. Write the highlighted words in the text in the correct part.

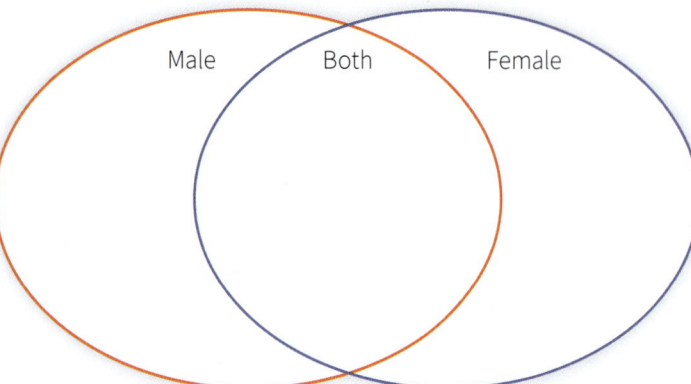

4 Read the rules. <u>Underline</u> examples in the text and complete the sentences.

Have got
We use *have got* and *has got* to talk about things that people have or own. The form for the third person singular is *has got*. The short forms are *'ve got* and *'s got*.
I _____ a little sister.
Our grandmother _____ pets.
They _____ two little children.
We form the negative by adding *not* between *have/has* and *got*.
Mum _____ any brothers or sisters.
We form questions by placing *have/has* before the subject.
_____ you _____ cousins too?

GRAMMAR BOOSTER P130

5 💬 Work in pairs. Find out if your partner has got the people below in their family.

a baby a brother a pet a sister an aunt
an uncle cousins grandparents twins

> Have you got cousins in your family?
>> Yes, I have. I've got five cousins.

6 Read the rules. <u>Underline</u> examples in the text and complete the table.

Possessive *'s*
With singular nouns we add *'s* to show possession.
Blanca is Jorge's sister.
_____
With plural nouns and nouns ending in –s we sometimes only add ', but *'s* is more common.
This is my cousins' house.
Those are Thomas's keys.
_____

GRAMMAR BOOSTER P130

7 💬 Work in pairs. Look at the sentences. Decide if the *'s* is possessive *'s* (P), *is* (I) or *has* (H).
  1 My dad**'s** name**'s** Simran. ___ ___
  2 She**'s** got her sister**'s** keys. ___ ___
  3 That**'s** my mum**'s** umbrella. ___ ___
  4 Oh no! The dog**'s** got the baby**'s** toy! ___ ___
  5 It**'s** Zahra**'s** brother**'s** bag. ___ ___ ___
  6 Jack**'s** sister**'s** got Abi**'s** book. ___ ___ ___

8 💬 Work in pairs. Draw Cora's family tree. Then take turns to ask and answer questions about her family.
> Who's Mary?
>> She's Cora's dad's mother.

9 💬 Write down the names of at least six people in your family. Then work in pairs and take turns to ask and answer two questions about each person.
> Is Oscar your dad?
>> No, he isn't. He's my uncle.
> Has he got children?
>> No, he hasn't.

6 Introduction

Use *can* and pronouns to talk about school subjects.

0.4 INTRODUCTION

School subjects

1 💬 Work in pairs. Look at the picture. Find all the school subjects. You have got two minutes.

2 🔊 0.07 Look at the photo. What family members are in it? Read and listen to the article and check your answers.

Are subjects like geography, history and art easy for you? Can you speak six foreign languages? Can you solve difficult maths problems without a computer? Most people can't do it all, but Anne-Marie can. She's in Britain's most intelligent family: the Imafidons!

Anne-Marie's got a degree in computer science from Oxford University and the STEM subjects (science, technology, engineering and maths) are very easy for her too. Her brother and sisters, Christiana, Samantha and the twins, Peter and Paula, are all amazing at maths. The twins also love P.E. and can run very fast! And Peter's sister plays music with him. She can play the violin and he can play the guitar.

The Imafidons can do many things when they work as a team, but is it true for us too? Can we be like them? Yes, we can! Repeat after me: 'Can I do it? Yes, I can!'

3 **VOCABULARY** Put the highlighted words in the article in the correct categories. Then work in pairs and add any other words that you know.

School subjects and abilities
STEM: ¹_____, ²_____, ³_____, ⁴_____, ⁵_____, ⁶_____ maths problems
Arts: ⁷_____ the violin / guitar
Humanities: ⁸_____, ⁹_____, speak foreign ¹⁰_____
Sport: ¹¹_____, ¹²_____ fast

4 💬 Put the school subjects in the order you like/dislike them. Work in pairs. Which are your favourite subjects? Why?

5 Read the rules. Then underline examples in the text and complete the sentences. What can the family in the text do?

Can

We use *can* to talk about abilities. It has only one form for *I, you, he*, etc.

The Imafidons _____ do many things.
She _____ play the violin and he _____ play the guitar.

The negative form of *can* is cannot. In spoken or informal written English, we use *can't*.

Most people _____ do it all.

We form questions by placing *can* before the subject.
_____ you speak six foreign languages?

We don't repeat the other verb in short answers.
_____ I do it? Yes, I _____!

GRAMMAR BOOSTER P131

6 Write three sentences about your abilities: two true and one false.

7 💬 Work in pairs. Share your sentences. Try and guess which one is false. Change pairs and repeat.

> I can dance. I can swim fast. I can play the piano.

> I think you can swim fast and you can dance, but you can't play the piano.

8 Read the table. Then underline examples in the text and complete the table.

Object pronouns

Subject pronoun	Object pronoun
I	¹_____
you	you
he	²_____
she	³_____
it	⁴_____
you	you
we	⁵_____
they	⁶_____

GRAMMAR BOOSTER P131

9 Change the words in **bold** to an object pronoun.
1 Can you play **the piano**?
2 She can't speak **French or Spanish**.
3 Can we see **Lara** now?
4 She's got a box for **me and you**.
5 I can draw **my uncle**.
6 I like **you and your dad**.

10 💬 Make questions with *can* and the prompts below. Find two people in your class who can do these things.
1 speak three languages
2 solve 40 + 40 x 0 + 1 = ?
3 play the violin, piano or guitar
4 run very fast
5 swim well
6 draw a woman's face

> Can you speak three languages?

11 Write a paragraph about yourself for your school website. Write about …
• your favourite school subjects.
• what you can do well.
• what you want to do one day.

12 💬 **THINK & SHARE** Work in pairs. Share your paragraphs. Ask each other questions about them.

Introduction 7

1 Vlog your day!

- **VOCABULARY** Daily routines / Hobbies
- **GRAMMAR** Present simple: affirmative / Present simple: negative and *yes/no* questions
- **READING** Teenage stress
- **LISTENING** Vlogging
- **GLOBAL SKILLS** Managing your time
- **SPEAKING** Likes and dislikes
- **WRITING** A personal profile
- **VISION 360** Another world

VOCABULARY BOOSTER P112–113
GRAMMAR BOOSTER P132–133

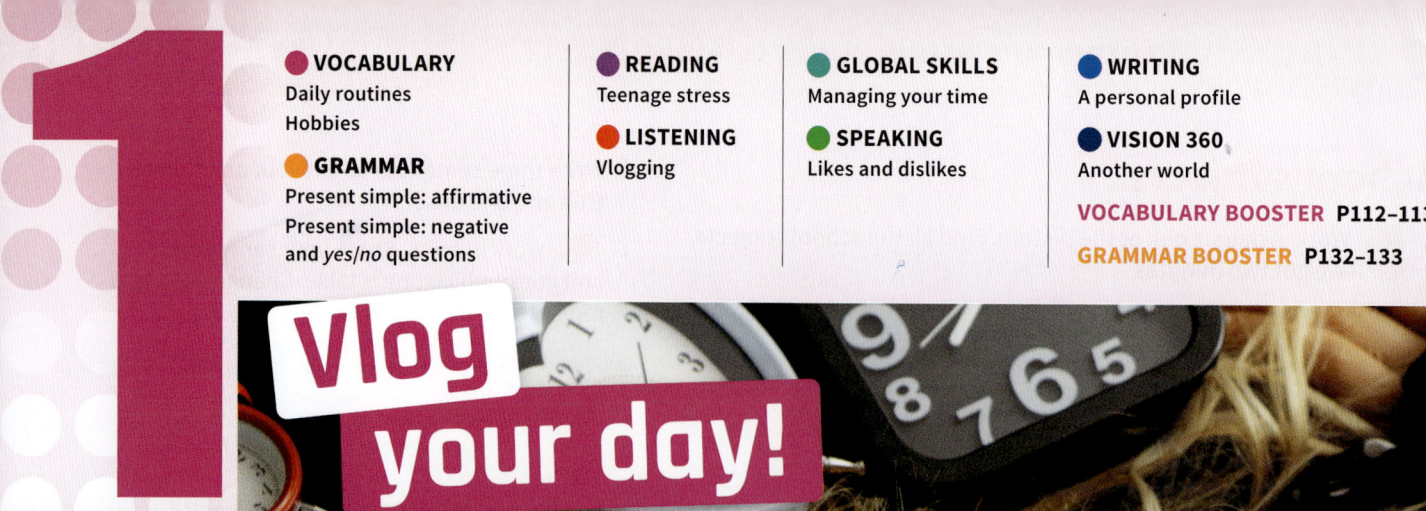

Daily routines

1 **THINK & SHARE** Look at the photo. Work in pairs. Ask and answer the questions about the photo.
   1 What time of day is it? Why do you think this?
   2 What is your favourite time of day? Why?

2 ▶ 🔊 **1.01** Watch or listen. How old are Callum and Zara? What relation are they to each other?

3 ▶ 🔊 **1.01** Watch or listen again. Choose the correct alternative.
   1 Zara and Callum are from **London** / **Edinburgh**.
   2 Their vlog is called *Born in* **Scotland** / **the UK**.
   3 They've got a **daily** / **weekly** vlog.
   4 Callum vlogs up to **15** / **50** minutes every morning.
   5 His lunch is at **12.30** / **1.30**.
   6 Callum can play the **violin** / **guitar**.
   7 In step 4, Callum makes a video in the **afternoon** / **evening**.
   8 He finishes his video at **dinnertime** / **bedtime**.

8   Unit 1

Talk about daily routines. **1.1 VOCABULARY**

4 Work in pairs. Ask and answer the questions.
1 Where are you from?
2 Have you got a vlog? What's its name?
3 What time is your breakfast / lunch / dinner?
4 Can you play a musical instrument?
5 When is your bedtime?

> I'm from Zagreb in Croatia.

5 **REAL ENGLISH** Match the highlighted phrases to their meaning.
1 Hi guys. I'm Zara!
2 Why not try something like this?
3 But don't worry about it – just do what's natural!
4 So congratulations – you're now a vlogger, like us!
5 Lots of you want to know how we do it.
6 And this is our awesome vlog.

A It's a good idea.
B Well done!
C many
D a group of people
E amazing
F It's OK.

6 **VOCABULARY** Complete the phrases with the verbs below.

| brush do get go have |
| relax take watch |

1 _____ home / to school / to bed
2 _____ my teeth / hair
3 _____ the bus
4 _____ my homework
5 _____ TV / music videos
6 _____ with my sister
7 _____ up / dressed
8 _____ a shower / breakfast / lunch / dinner / guitar lessons

7 Work in pairs. Take turns to act out the activities in Ex 6. Can you guess which one it is?

> Is it 'go to school'?
>> No, it isn't.

8 🔊 **1.02** Complete the text. Then listen and check.

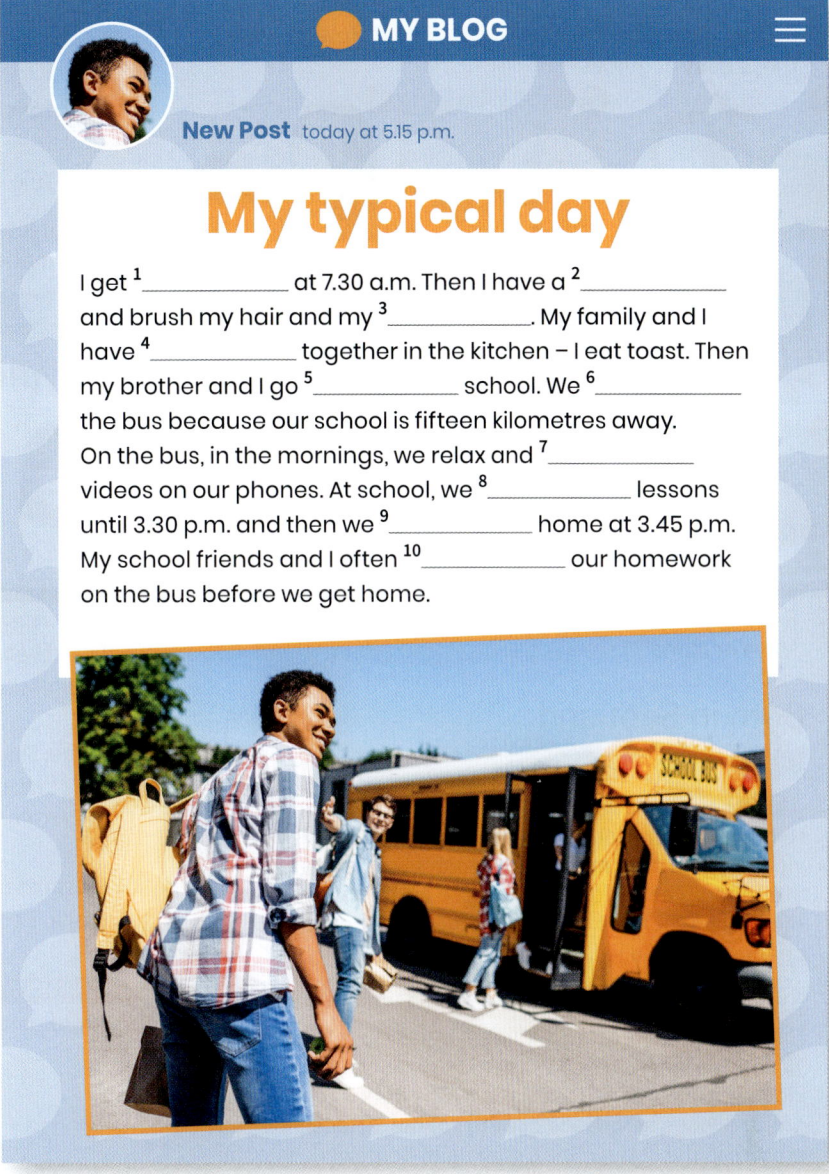

MY BLOG
New Post today at 5.15 p.m.

My typical day

I get ¹_____ at 7.30 a.m. Then I have a ²_____ and brush my hair and my ³_____. My family and I have ⁴_____ together in the kitchen – I eat toast. Then my brother and I go ⁵_____ school. We ⁶_____ the bus because our school is fifteen kilometres away. On the bus, in the mornings, we relax and ⁷_____ videos on our phones. At school, we ⁸_____ lessons until 3.30 p.m. and then we ⁹_____ home at 3.45 p.m. My school friends and I often ¹⁰_____ our homework on the bus before we get home.

9 Tick (✓) the activities in Ex 6 that you do every day. Then use them to complete the table.

In the morning	In the afternoon and evening	At night

10 Number the activities in the order that you do them. Then tell your partner about your daily routine.

> I get up at 7 a.m. Then I brush my teeth ...

VOCABULARY BOOSTER Unit 1

1.2 GRAMMAR   Use the present simple affirmative to talk about my school day.

Present simple: affirmative

1 Do you remember how to vlog your day? How do you say these daily activities?

2 Read the comments. Who is similar to Callum: Anita, Maya or Jamal?

Born in Scotland

💬 Comments

Jamal 36 minutes ago
Hi guys! Callum, you get up very early! 😱 I'm a daily vlogger, but I hate mornings. I make my videos in the afternoon. Then I do my homework and I have a shower in the evening before I go to bed ... Please subscribe to my channel – it's called *My Life*! 👍 👎 REPLY

Anita one hour ago
Hello Callum and Zara! Congratulations! I love your videos!!! 😍 I watch them every day after I have dinner. I'm not a vlogger, but my big sister Maya is. She gets up at 6 a.m. and she vlogs before she goes to school. After school, she studies in the library. She's got lots of homework, but she relaxes with me in the evening. See you. 👍 👎 REPLY

3 <u>Underline</u> all the examples of the present simple in the comments in Ex 2. Then complete the rules.

Present simple: affirmative
▶ Grammar animation

A We use the present simple to talk about regular activities, daily routines and facts.
B We form the present simple affirmative with the infinitive without *to* for *I / you / we / they*.
C We add *-s* or *-es* to the end of the verb for third-person singular, *he / she / it*.
D We add *-es* when a verb ends with: *-o, -ss, -x, -ch, -sh*.
   She vlogs before she ¹_____ to school.
   She ²_____ with me in the evening.
E The consonant + *-y* changes to *-ies*.
   She ³_____ in the library.
F The verb *have* is irregular.
   He has dinner.

GRAMMAR BOOSTER P132

4 Choose the correct alternative.
1 You and Alona **takes** / **take** the train to school.
2 His sister **goes** / **go** to the same school as me.
3 My friends **gets** / **get** dressed in the morning.
4 I **does** / **do** my homework after school.
5 My cousin and I **has** / **have** music lessons together.
6 Paulo **watches** / **watch** TV every evening.

5 Complete the blog entry with the present simple affirmative form of the verbs in brackets.

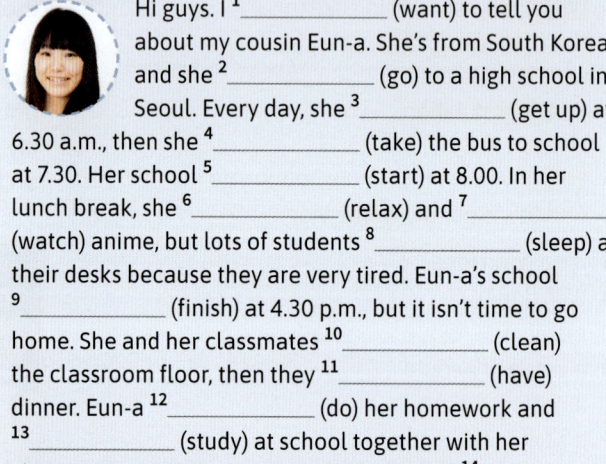

Posted 4 hours ago

A typical school day in South Korea

Hi guys. I ¹_____ (want) to tell you about my cousin Eun-a. She's from South Korea and she ²_____ (go) to a high school in Seoul. Every day, she ³_____ (get up) at 6.30 a.m., then she ⁴_____ (take) the bus to school at 7.30. Her school ⁵_____ (start) at 8.00. In her lunch break, she ⁶_____ (relax) and ⁷_____ (watch) anime, but lots of students ⁸_____ (sleep) at their desks because they are very tired. Eun-a's school ⁹_____ (finish) at 4.30 p.m., but it isn't time to go home. She and her classmates ¹⁰_____ (clean) the classroom floor, then they ¹¹_____ (have) dinner. Eun-a ¹²_____ (do) her homework and ¹³_____ (study) at school together with her classmates until 11 p.m. She and her friends ¹⁴_____ (go) to bed after 1 a.m. every night! Zzzzzzzzzzz!

6 **PRONUNCIATION** How do you pronounce the *-s* in the third person singular verbs below? Complete the table.

brushes   cooks   does   eats   finishes   gets
goes   likes   lives   relaxes   studies   watches

1	/s/	takes
2	/z/	has
3	/ɪz/	uses

7 🔊 **1.05** Listen and check your answers to Ex 6. Then listen again and repeat.

8 💬 Work in pairs. Compare your school day to Eun-a's.
   She goes to school in Seoul, but we go to school in Hanoi.

9 💬 **THINK & SHARE** Work in small groups. You want to make a 30-second vlog about your daily routines. Write a plan. Use these ideas to help you.
• Start your vlog – say hello.
• Talk about your daily activities.
• Finish your video – say goodbye.
• Give it a title.

10 💬 Share your group's ideas with the class.
   Lars gets up at half past six because he takes the train to school.

Predict before you listen. **1.3 LISTENING**

Vlogging

1 **THINK & SHARE** Work in pairs. Discuss the questions. Use the ideas below or your own ideas.

| art   beauty products   fashion   language |
| music and dance   sport   video games |

1 Who are your favourite vloggers?
2 What type of vloggers are they?

STRATEGY Predicting before you listen

Before you listen, read the title and look at the photos of people, objects and activities. Guess what words you think you will hear. This helps you understand better.

2 Read the strategy. You are going to listen to some vloggers.
1 Look at the title and photos and try to guess what it's about.
2 Write 6–8 words that you think you will hear.
3 Write down what you know about the typical day of a vlogger.

3 🔊 1.06 Listen to the people talk about vlogging. Match photos A–D to the speakers. Write the names. What words or phrases in the listening helped you? Are any of these in your list in Ex 2?

4 🔊 1.06 Listen again. Are the sentences true (T) or false (F)? Correct the false ones.
1 Sam makes videos about money.
2 He goes to school at 11 a.m.
3 Lukas and Hanna make videos every day.
4 They relax at the weekend.
5 Lots of people like Demi's vlog.
6 Nobody knows her in the town where she lives.
7 Megan plays the piano in her videos.
8 She hates vlogging now.

5 **MEDIATION** Larisa's friend Ruben wants to start his own vlog. Complete Larisa's email to Ruben with information from the podcast. Write one or two words in each gap.

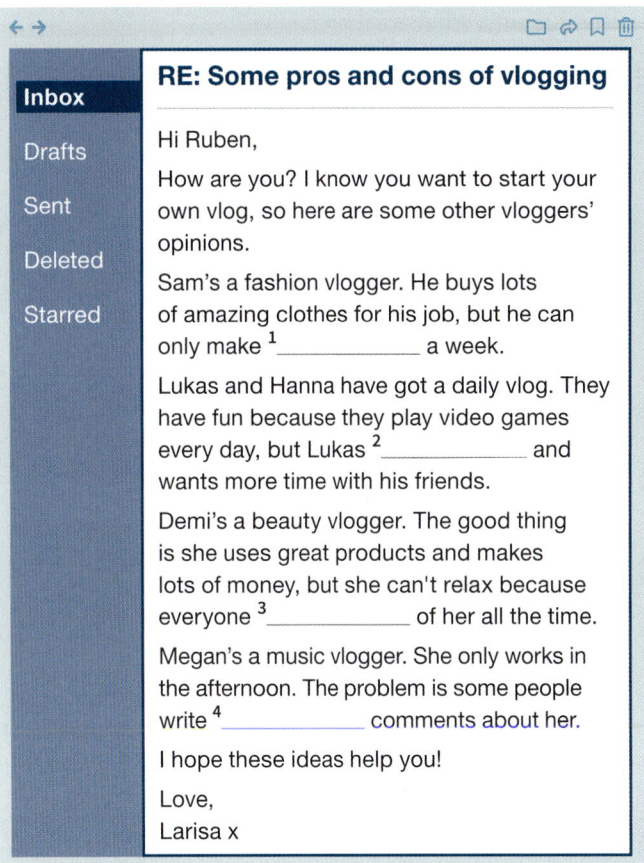

RE: Some pros and cons of vlogging

Hi Ruben,

How are you? I know you want to start your own vlog, so here are some other vloggers' opinions.

Sam's a fashion vlogger. He buys lots of amazing clothes for his job, but he can only make ¹_____ a week.

Lukas and Hanna have got a daily vlog. They have fun because they play video games every day, but Lukas ²_____ and wants more time with his friends.

Demi's a beauty vlogger. The good thing is she uses great products and makes lots of money, but she can't relax because everyone ³_____ of her all the time.

Megan's a music vlogger. She only works in the afternoon. The problem is some people write ⁴_____ comments about her.

I hope these ideas help you!

Love,
Larisa x

6 💬 Work in pairs. Make a list of all the pros (good things) or cons (bad things) about vlogging. Use the information in the email to help you. Can you think of any more pros and cons of vlogging?

Pros +	Cons –

7 💬 Work in pairs. Compare your ideas. Do you want to be a vlogger? Why? / Why not?

Unit 1   11

1.4 GLOBAL SKILLS — Understand how to manage your time.

Managing your time

1 How much time do you spend doing these activities? Complete the sentences, then compare with a partner.
1 I go to school for _____ a day.
2 I do my homework for _____ a day.
3 I relax for _____ a day.
4 I watch TV or videos, look at my phone or play video games for _____ a day.
5 I spend time with friends for _____ a day.
6 I have a shower, brush my teeth and get dressed for _____ a day.
7 I help at home for _____ a day.
8 I eat for _____ a day.

> I go to school for about five hours and 30 minutes a day. And you?

2 🔊 1.07 Listen to a conversation between students. Count the students. What are their names?

3 **VOCABULARY** 🔊 1.07 Listen again and complete the tips on how to manage your time with the words below.

| daily | homework | minutes | notes |
| routine | tasks | week |

How to manage your time

1. Every Sunday, plan your _____.
2. Make a list of the important tasks you need to do, e.g. your _____.
3. Find out how much time you spend on each _____ activity.
4. Make _____ on your phone or in a diary.
5. Break your big projects into small _____.
6. Plan study breaks: every two hours, relax for fifteen _____.
7. Have the same _____ every day.

break (v) – separate into smaller pieces
a break (n) – a short rest or stop

4 Look at the examples. Complete the box with *at*, *on* or *in*.

Prepositions of time
We use the following prepositions of time:
1 _____: parts of the day, months, seasons, years
   I go back to school in September.
2 _____: dates, days, parts of a day of the week
   We have art classes on Mondays.
3 _____: times, night, weekend, special occasions lasting more than a day
   I relax at the weekend.

GRAMMAR BOOSTER P132

5 Look at the diagram and complete it with the examples below. Can you think of any others?

> 2 a.m.   January   midnight   Monday   the afternoon
> the summer   23rd August   2018

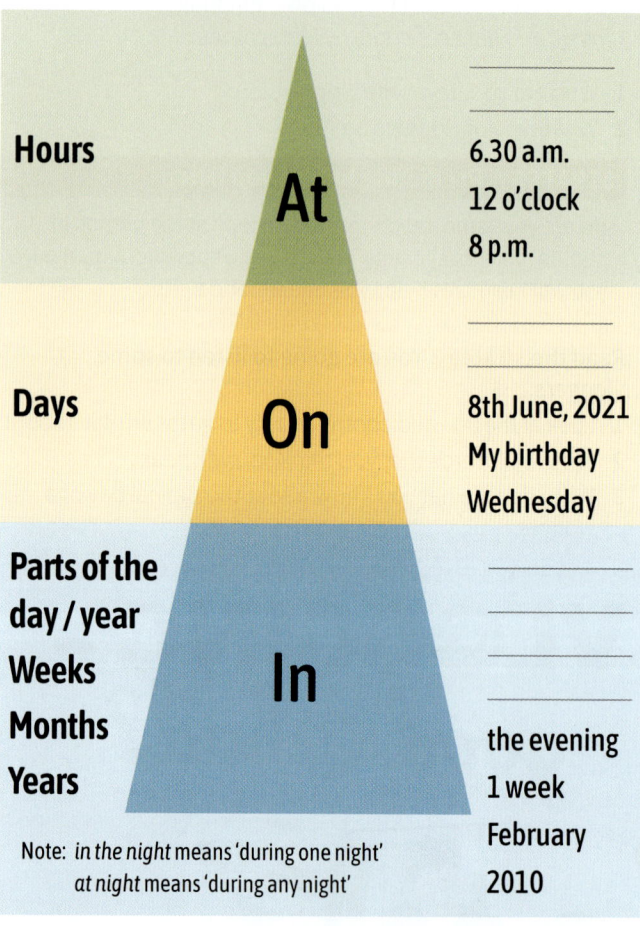

Hours — **At** — 6.30 a.m. / 12 o'clock / 8 p.m.

Days — **On** — 8th June, 2021 / My birthday / Wednesday

Parts of the day / year / Weeks / Months / Years — **In** — the evening / 1 week / February / 2010

Note: *in the night* means 'during one night'
at night means 'during any night'

6 🔊 1.08 Complete the sentences with prepositions of time. Then listen and check.
1 The music school party is ___ the 14th of October.
2 I go home ___ half past five.
3 ___ Sunday evenings, you make a list of the things you need to do ___ the week.
4 I have extra classes ___ Tuesdays.
5 Write down all the things you do ___ the morning.
6 I have a hot shower ___ night.
7 You can study and relax ___ school days.

7 Write two true sentences about you for each preposition of time.

> I do my homework in the afternoon.

8 **THINK & SHARE** Work in pairs. Read your answers in Ex 1 and the tips in Ex 3 again. Decide how many hours to spend on your daily routines. Discuss how you can improve your day / week.

9 Write a plan for your week.

10 Share your plans as a class.

11 Answer the questions.
- Are you happy with how you manage your time?
- Do you think it's useful to manage your time? Why? / Why not?

Unit 1

Talk about hobbies.   **1.5 VOCABULARY**

Free-time activities

1 💬 Work in pairs. What do you do when you are bored? Do you have any hobbies?

12 cheap, fun hobby ideas!

Lots of people watch TV or look at their phone in their free time. Stop! Here are twelve things you can do instead.

- Get fit for free in your local park. Go for a walk, go for a run or ride a bike with friends.
- Take photos of the things you love with a camera or phone.
- Read a comic or book, or listen to audiobooks.
- Make a cake with an internet recipe and eat it with your friends.
- Listen to music on your mobile phone – you can even do it when you have a shower.
- Get some pencils and paper and draw a picture.
- Play a board game, e.g. chess, with your family.
- Tidy your room. It isn't fun, but you can sell your old things and make some money!
- Watch video tutorials and learn a language or how to design a website.

get fit – do exercise

2 Read the article. Are any of the hobbies on your list?

3 Match the highlighted words to the photos.

4 **VOCABULARY** Find the highlighted words in the article and check their meaning.
Name …
1 two activities that include art and technology.
2 a fun group activity that is a competition.
3 three activities that are types of exercise.
4 an activity you do on your own with a book.
5 an activity you do with your favourite bands.
6 an activity you do with things in your bedroom.
7 an activity where you cook something at home.
8 an activity you do in an English or Japanese class.
9 an activity you do on paper in an art class.

5 Write the free-time activities from the text in the diagram. Can you add any more?

Indoors   Outdoors

6 💬 Work in pairs. Choose three free-time activities in Ex 1. Draw a picture of each activity in one minute. Can your partner guess which one it is?

7 🔊 **1.09** Listen to three people talking. Match each person to hobbies or sports that they do from Ex 3.
1 _____
2 _____
3 _____

8 Complete the sentences.
1 We study grammar when we _____ a language.
2 Aunt Geeta _____ for a run in the morning to get fit.
3 My friends _____ a bike to school, but I take the bus.
4 Darius _____ his room on Sunday mornings.
5 I _____ to music at night on my headphones.
6 My brother and I _____ comics at night before bed.
7 On Saturdays, I _____ for a walk in my local park.
8 Mum _____ lots of photos of me and my sister.

9 Number the hobbies in Ex 1 in order of preference for you (1 = favourite).

10 💬 **THINK & SHARE** Work in pairs. Tell each other what your top-five activities are. Say where and when you do them and why you like them.

VOCABULARY BOOSTER Unit 1   13

1.6 GRAMMAR
Use the present simple negative and *yes/no* questions to talk about free time.

Present simple: negative and *yes/no* questions

1 Work in pairs. Match the words below to the icons in the table.

active   creative   practical

2 Think of three free-time activities for each category.

3 Read the quiz. Are any activities from your list in it?

What your free-time activities say about

1 Do you spend much time at home on Sundays?
A Yes, I do. I often read in my room.
B Yes, sometimes, when I watch TV.
C No, I don't! I go out with my friends instead.

2 Does your room look tidy at the weekend?
A No, it doesn't. There are books everywhere.
B Yes, it does. I tidy it all the time.
C I don't know. I don't spend much time in there.

3 Do you like sport and exercise?
A Sport doesn't interest me much. I draw instead.
B It's OK. I go to the gym to get fit.
C Yes, I love it! I go for a run every day.

4 Do you listen to music?
A Yes, I do. I play a musical instrument too.
B Sometimes. I don't do it every day.
C I listen to it while I exercise or play video games.

5 You've got an hour of free time. Do you …
A take some interesting photos?
B learn how to do something new?
C ride a bike with your best friend?

4 Read the quiz again. Answer the questions for you. Make a note of your answers.

5 Read the grammar rules. Complete the examples. Use the quiz to help you.

Present simple: negative
We form the present simple negative with *don't* and *doesn't* and the infinitive without *to*.
I / you / we / they ¹_____ spend much time at home.
He / she / it ²_____ like it.

GRAMMAR BOOSTER P133

6 Make these sentences negative.
1 Bako and I like rock music.
2 I design websites in my free time.
3 Lucas plays the piano.
4 My cousins go to school with me.
5 You study Spanish.
6 My teacher tidies the classroom every day.

7 Complete the grammar rules. Use the quiz to help you.

Present simple: *yes/no* questions
▶ Grammar animation
We form present simple *yes/no* questions with *do* or *does* and the infinitive without *to*.
¹_____ I / you / we / they listen to music?
Yes, I ²_____. / No, I ³_____.
⁴_____ he / she / it like sport?
Yes, she ⁵_____. / No, she ⁶_____.

GRAMMAR BOOSTER P133

8 Order the words to make questions and answers.
1 they / music / listen to / do / ?   don't / no, / they
2 Amir / does / homework / do / ?   he / does / yes,
3 your room / tidy / you / do / ?   do / I / yes,
4 take / do / the bus / you and Jo / ?   we / yes, / do
5 Ana / does / French / speak / ?   doesn't / no, / she

9 💬 Work in pairs. Student A: turn to page 150. Student B: turn to page 151. Ask questions in the present simple to complete your table.

10 🔊 **1.12** Listen to the quiz answers. Complete the text.

More As: You are a very creative person. You ¹_____ many practical activities. ²____ your parents ____ you to tidy your room all the time? Remember: practical things ³_____ to be boring. Why not design a website for your art or music?

More Bs: You are practical and active, but you ⁴_____ many creative activities. For example, you don't ⁵_____ because you think you can't draw. Do ⁶_____ to make something beautiful? Why not make an amazing cake?

More Cs: You are very active, and you ⁷_____ to do many creative or practical things. Do these activities need to be indoors? No, ⁸_____! Why not go for a long walk outdoors with friends and take lots of interesting photos!

11 🔊 **1.12** Listen again. Do you agree with your result?

12 💬 Work in groups. Ask questions and find somebody who …
- rides a bike to school.
- tidies their room on Saturdays.
- plays board games at the weekend.
- speaks two languages.
- has breakfast before 7.30 a.m.
- goes for a run every day.
- makes meals at home.
- goes shopping after school.

13 💬 **THINK & SHARE** What are the most / least common activities? Are there any popular activities which are not on the list?

14 Unit 1

Identify the main ideas in an article about teenage stress.

1.7 READING

Teenage stress

1 Read the definitions of the words *stressed* and *stress*. Which is the noun and which is the adjective?

> **stressed** /strest/ so worried and tired that you can't relax
> **stress** /stres/ worry caused by the problems in your life

2 💬 Work in pairs. Look at the bar chart and answer the questions.
1 Why are many teenagers stressed?
2 Which age group is more stressed?
3 Why do you think this is?

Teenage stress by age
Do your free-time activities and homework make you stressed?

✓ Yes, they do. / Stress is a big problem for us.
- 13–15 years **62%**
- 16–17 years **71%**

✗ No, they don't. / We don't feel very stressed.
- 13–15 years **38%**
- 16–17 years **29%**

3 Take a class vote on the question in the bar chart in Ex 2. Compare your results with the bar chart.

4 Read the online debate quickly. Do you think Louise is a teenager or a parent? What about Max? Why?

> **STRATEGY** Identifying main ideas
> To understand the main ideas in a text, find the content words. These are usually the nouns, verbs and adjectives, and they carry the important information.

5 Read the strategy. Read headings A–F. Underline the key words.
A Teenagers need to have free time.
B Stress teaches teenagers how to manage their time.
C Teenagers and adults want different things.
D Too much free time is bad for teenagers.
E Stress is unhealthy for teenagers.
F Stress prepares teenagers for their future.

6 Read the text again. Match headings A–F to paragraphs 1–6.

7 🔊 1.13 Read the text again. Answer the questions with short answers. When the answer is *no*, give the right answer.
1 Do high school students get a lot of homework?
2 Do all students go home when lessons finish?
3 Do teenagers play video games at after-school clubs?
4 Does Max think busy students work badly?
5 Does Max think teenagers watch TV because they are bored?
6 Do teenagers and adults want the same things?

8 💬 **THINK & SHARE** Work in pairs. Do you agree or disagree with the opinions? Why do you say that?

Some people say that today's teenagers do too many after-school activities. Do you agree?

Louise: No, I don't.

1 ___
It's good to be busy. Stress is a normal part of life, especially at work, so students need to understand this at high school.

2 ___
Many high school students do about four hours of homework per subject a week, and they also go to after-school clubs or language classes. Busy students learn to plan their schoolwork, and then they have time for their favourite activities. They understand that it isn't possible to do everything!

3 ___
I think that teens who have lots of free time do more unhealthy things, for example, they spend hours on their phones or play video games. Instead, at after-school clubs, teens can learn practical skills, like website design or how to make meals. And team sports are very good for students – they get fit and learn to work together.

Max: Yes, I do.

4 ___
Doing things all at the same time isn't good for us. When I'm stressed, I don't work well. Some of my classmates do their homework very quickly because they have lots of activities in the afternoon, but they don't always get good results.

5 ___
After a long day at school, we need some time to relax and do nothing. We just want to go home and watch TV or listen to music on our phones because we're very tired and we need a break! People with more free time are also more creative and do things like draw or make videos.

6 ___
My friends and I want to do more activities after school, but we also need to do all our homework and make our teachers happy. And we're stressed because we want to do fun things in the afternoons, like ride our bikes outdoors, read comics or play board games, but our parents tell us that we haven't got time because of our schoolwork …

1.8 SPEAKING Use consonant–vowel linking to talk about likes and dislikes.

Likes and dislikes

1 Work in pairs. Look at the timetable of after-school clubs. When and where can you …
  1 play chess?
  2 make cakes?
  3 do exercise?
  4 draw?
  5 do your homework?

2 🔊 **1.14** Listen to the conversation between two classmates. Tick (✓) the activities in the timetable they talk about. Which one do they choose to do together?

3 Look at the **Phrasebook**. Match the verbs below to the emojis.

| can't stand   don't like   enjoy   hate   like   love |

PHRASEBOOK Talking about likes and dislikes
😍 _____
🙂 _____ _____
😠 _____
😡 _____ _____

Agreeing
I love football. → Me too./So do I.
I don't like singing. → Me neither./Neither do I.
I can't stand reading. → Me neither./Neither can I.

Disagreeing
I love cooking. → Really? I don't.
I don't like drawing. → Really, I do!
I can't stand orchestra. → Really? I love it!

4 Complete the dialogues with the words below.

| don't   do (x2)   hate   like   neither   Really   So |

1
A I love cooking.
B _____ do I! Do you _____ making cakes?
A Yes, I _____. I love it! But I really don't like tidying the kitchen at the end.
B Me _____! It's boring.

2
A I like drawing comics.
B Really? I _____. I don't enjoy school art classes.
A Neither _____ I. And I don't like science.
B _____? I do. Do you _____ maths too?
A No, I don't. It's great.

5 💬 🔊 **1.15** Listen and check. Then practise in pairs.

STRATEGY Consonant–vowel linking
When a word finishes with a consonant sound, and the next word starts with a vowel sound, they sometimes sound like one word.
It's‿a‿fun game.

6 Read the **strategy**. Then look at the sentences. Circle the linking.
  1 I love it.
  2 She plays football twice a week.
  3 They don't like apples or bananas.
  4 What else can we do?
  5 I like music but I can't stand art.
  6 I think it's awesome.

7 🔊 **1.16** Listen, check and repeat.

8 💬 **THINK & SHARE** Write your own opinions on the activities below. Use the **Phrasebook** to help you.

| getting up early   drawing   tidying my room
doing homework   playing board games   going for a run
reading books   comics   sport   video games |

9 💬 Work in pairs. Ask each other about the activities in Ex 8. Give your opinions, and then agree or disagree politely.

  Do you like getting up early?

  No, I don't. I hate getting up early.

  Really? I don't. I love it. I love mornings.

10 **REFLECT** Work in pairs. Answer the questions.
  1 Can you ask questions about what you like and dislike using phrases in the Phrasebook?
  2 Can you use consonant–vowel linking in your sentences?
  3 Can you find one activity that you both like doing?

16 Unit 1

1.9 WRITING

Use pronouns, adverbs and conjunctions in a personal profile.

A personal profile

1 Read the personal profiles from the vloggers' websites. Do you like any of the same things as they do?

All about me
I'm Jan. I'm seventeen and I'm Polish. I haven't got any brothers or sisters. I go to Grantchester Boys' College in the UK. It's a boarding school, so I live there. This is my new student vlog!

My life
I love living with other students and I've got lots of new friends. Here, you choose three or four subjects for A levels. My subjects are history, computer science and art. It's difficult to study in English, but I love it!

My interests
After school, I have chess classes and I learn Mandarin Chinese. In the evenings, I relax with my friends. We watch TV together or we play games on the Xbox. I'm happy so I don't want to go home, but my family misses me!

All about me
Hello, my name's Labani. I'm fourteen and I've got three little brothers. Lots of people like our family vlog, *Homeschool is Cool!* In fact, 20,000 people watch us.

My life
I get up early and have a big breakfast. I don't go to school – I learn at home. I really like maths, so it is the first subject I study. Then I watch videos about technology or engineering on the internet. I enjoy them because they are very interesting. I don't feel stressed because I plan my own timetable.

My interests
Every day, I help make meals. My mum loves tidying the house, but I hate it. My brothers like riding their bikes, but I enjoy listening to music and taking care of horses instead.

2 Read the profiles again. How many paragraphs have they got? Which topics do they talk about? Tick (✓) the boxes.

	Jan	Labani
Number of paragraphs		
Type of vlog		
Type of school		
Family		
Daily activities		
Likes / dislikes		
School subjects		

STRATEGY Using pronouns or adverbs to avoid repetition
When you write, you can use pronouns (*he*, *me*, *her*, etc.) or adverbs (*there*) instead of repeating the subject or object in a sentence.

3 Read the **strategy**. Then underline all the examples you can find in the profiles.

4 What do these pronouns in the profiles replace?
1 … I live **there**.
2 … I love **it**!
3 … **we** play games on the Xbox.
4 … 20,000 people watch **us**.
5 I enjoy **them** because **they** are interesting.

5 Replace the words in **bold** with the pronouns or adverbs below.

| he | his | it | them | there | us | we |

1 I enjoy learning English – **English** is a very important language.
2 My friend Leon likes reading books and **Leon** has got lots of **books**. **Leon's** favourite book is *The Lord of the Rings*.
3 My sister and I hate taking the bus to school – **my sister and I** like riding our bikes **to school** instead. It helps **my sister and I** stay fit.

6 Read the **Language focus**. Find examples in the profiles.

LANGUAGE FOCUS Conjunctions: *and*, *but*, *or*
You can use conjunctions to link two ideas in a sentence. Use …
1 *and* to link similar ideas.
 I have chess classes and I learn Mandarin Chinese.
2 *but* to contrast ideas.
 My mum loves tidying the house, but I hate it.
3 *or* to link negative ideas.
 I haven't got any brothers or sisters.
4 *or* when there are two things to choose from.
 I watch videos about history or biology.

7 Complete the text with the correct conjunctions.
I enjoy making Japanese food, _____ I don't like eating sushi. I also love Italian food _____ my favourite meals are pizza _____ pasta. I don't enjoy watching football _____ going for a run, _____ I like going for walks on Sunday afternoons. At weekends, my friends and I ride our bikes _____ we stay at home and play board games instead.

8 Read the profile tips. Why are they important?
1 Don't give personal information (e.g. your address).
2 Only write true things about yourself.
3 Choose some interesting things to describe yourself.

9 Plan a personal profile for your website. Make notes about the topics in Ex 2 about you.

10 Choose your ideas in Ex 9 that you want to include for each paragraph.

11 Use your notes, the **strategy** and the **Language focus** to write your personal profile.

12 ✓ **CHECK YOUR WORK**
• Does your profile include three paragraphs?
• Does the heading match what you write about?
• Do you use pronouns and adverbs to avoid repetition?
• Are your spelling and grammar correct?

Unit 1 17

1.10 REVIEW

Grammar

1 Complete the sentences with the present simple form of the verbs below.

> do   go   not have   not like   not speak
> relax   study   teach

1 Erik _____ computer science at his school.
2 Students _____ to school from Monday to Friday.
3 My brother and I _____ in front of the TV.
4 You and your friends _____ playing chess.
5 Dad _____ lunch at work; he eats at home.
6 In Spain, people _____ German.
7 Asuka _____ her homework in the library.
8 Ms Mendes _____ geography at our school.

2 Complete the dialogue with the present simple form of the verbs in brackets and short answers.

Jo ¹_____ you _____ music? (like)
Lee Yes, ²_____ – I love it!
Jo Me too, but I can't play a musical instrument. ³_____ you _____ any instruments? (play)
Lee Yes, ⁴_____. I have guitar lessons. And my sister and I ⁵_____ music videos together. (make)
Jo Really? ⁶_____ she _____ guitar lessons too? (have)
Lee No, ⁷_____. She ⁸_____ instead. (sing)
Jo Wow! ⁹_____ your parents _____ your videos? (watch)
Lee No, ¹⁰_____. They hate vlogs!

Vocabulary

3 Match the sentences halves.
1 My friends and I listen
2 Twice a day, we brush
3 My sister and I don't take
4 My brother hates mornings, so he gets
5 After breakfast, Lisa gets
6 I wash my face or have
7 Every night, Jamal goes to
8 I'm not hungry, so I don't have

A bed at 10 p.m.
B up late at the weekend.
C our teeth.
D dressed in her bedroom.
E a shower before bed.
F the train to school; we walk instead.
G breakfast before I leave the house.
H to music on our phones.

4 Complete the free-time activities.
1 My family and I p_____ b_____ games together.
2 Do you l_____ to m_____? I do. Especially K-pop.
3 I'm good at art, and I d_____ p_____ of my friends.
4 I prefer to r_____ a c_____ instead of a book.
5 Many people l_____ a l_____ at school. We study German and French.
6 Cleo's active; she g_____ for a r_____ every day.
7 I m_____ c_____. My favourite ones are chocolate.

Cumulative review

5 Choose the correct answer to complete the text: A, B or C.

Hi! I'm Jada. I'm sixteen years old. I'm from Kansas, ¹___ I'm here in Tampere, Finland, for four months!! I've got an amazing host family with a girl called Mila. Finland and the USA are very different. From a young age, Finnish students go ²___ school on their own. They walk or ³___ their bikes. At nine years old, they also ⁴___ the bus to school. I ⁵___ up very early because school starts at 8.15 a.m. Finnish students aren't stressed like students in the US. They have ⁶___ at midday. It lasts ⁷___ hour and they also relax for fifteen minutes between classes. School ⁸___ at 2.45 p.m. US students go to after-school clubs and play sports, learn how to ⁹___ photos or design websites, but many Finnish students don't. Mila doesn't ¹⁰___ home after school – instead she visits her friends' homes or goes ¹¹___ a walk in town. ¹²___ she and her classmates do a lot of homework? No, they ¹³___! Mila only studies for 45 minutes a day! So, she ¹⁴___ got lots of free time to spend with friends and family. Mila also loves ¹⁵___ her room, but I don't. I ¹⁶___ stand it because it's boring.

> **host** – a person who has people staying at their house

1 A so   B but   C or
2 A –   B to   C to the
3 A ride   B read   C go
4 A have   B go   C take
5 A go   B get   C dressed
6 A breakfast   B lunch   C dinner
7 A an   B a   C –
8 A finish   B finishes   C finishes
9 A take   B make   C do
10 A goes   B go   C go to
11 A on   B to   C for
12 A Does   B Have   C Do
13 A don't   B doesn't   C haven't
14 A have   B has   C is
15 A tidy   B tidying   C to tidying
16 A don't   B 'm not   C can't

💬 Think & share

6 Answer the questions.
1 What's your favourite time of day? Why?
2 Does your daily routine change at the weekend? How?
3 What are your favourite free-time activities? Why?
4 Which school subjects do you like / don't you like?

18 Review

1.11 EXAM SKILLS

Reading

EXAM STRATEGY

When you complete a text with missing sentences, read the text carefully before and after each gap. Choose a sentence to complete the gap. Then read the text again to check your choice makes sense. Remember, you don't have to understand every word. Focus on getting a general idea of what the text is about.

1 Read the strategy above. Then read the short text below. Try each of the sentences A–C in the gap. Which one makes the most sense?

> My sister loves films. ___ Then she writes about them on her blog.

A She has hundreds of followers.
B She doesn't like teenage topics such as sport or fashion.
C She often goes to the cinema or watches films on TV.

2 There are six missing sentences in this article. Choose from sentences (A–F) the one which fills each gap (1–6).

Teenage bloggers

Every day, hundreds of people write blogs on the internet. Today, many of these bloggers are teenagers who write for young people. These bloggers are often very popular. **1**___ The bloggers write interesting articles about teenage topics. Popular subjects are music, sport, fashion and beauty. **2**___ The great thing is, shops love teenage bloggers and often send them free products. They want the bloggers to write about these products on their blog.

Jake Hardy is a teenage blogger. **3**___ Every day, he gets up early and goes for a run. He spends a lot of hours on his computer and thinks it's important to be fit. Jake always eats a healthy breakfast and then he goes to school. Jake likes school. His favourite subject is English because he loves writing. He doesn't do any clubs at school because he understands there's no time to do everything and he doesn't want to be stressed. **4**___ Then he works on his blog.

Jake is different from other bloggers because he doesn't write about typical teenage subjects. **5**___ He loves food and he writes about that. At weekends, he visits cafes and restaurants. At home, he makes interesting meals and puts the photos and the recipes on his blog. Chefs often invite Jake to their restaurants. **6**___ Jake wants to be a chef one day. He also wants to write a recipe book and have a TV show. Right now, thousands of people around the world read his blog. They love his food and they love Jake!

A He isn't interested in sport, music or fashion.
B They also write about language, art and film.
C They give him free meals and they sometimes give him cooking lessons.
D After school, Jake goes home and does his homework.
E They have thousands of readers every month.
F He is fifteen years old and is a typical teenager.

Speaking

EXAM STRATEGY

In an interview, do not give one-word answers. Always answer in full sentences and say as much as you can.

3 Read the strategy above. Then match questions 1–4 to answers A–D below.

1 Do you play a musical instrument?
2 Does your brother enjoy football?
3 Do you spend time outdoors at weekends?
4 Does your best friend like computer games?

A Yes, she does. She's in a gaming club at school and she loves going online and meeting new people.
B Yes, I do. I love music. I play the piano and the guitar. I also have violin lessons and I'm in the orchestra at school.
C Yes, I do. I like riding my bike. I also love taking photos in the park. I hate staying at home and I don't enjoy watching TV.
D No, he doesn't. He thinks it's boring. But he loves tennis. It's his favourite sport and he's in the tennis club at school.

4 Answer the questions about your life.
1 What sport do you do at school?
2 How often do you listen to music?
3 Does your brother / sister / friend speak a foreign language?
4 What do you usually do at the weekends?
5 Do you enjoy blogging or vlogging?

Exam skills 19

1 VISION 360° Another world

Learn about a biodome and create an information leaflet

Unit 1 360° hotspots ▲ ● ○ ■ ◆ ★

1 **THINK & SHARE** Work in pairs. Read the definition and discuss the questions.

> **biodome** /ˈbaɪə(ʊ)dəʊm/ (n) we use a biodome to create what it's like in a particular place in a different part of the world, e.g. a desert, a rainforest or another planet.

1 What things do you think you can find inside a biodome?
2 Are biodomes useful? Why? / Why not?
3 Is there a biodome in your country? What's inside it?

EXPLORE 360°
Access the interactive 360° content now!

2 Look around the photo. What can you see? Why are these people inside it?

3 ▲ Watch the video and choose the correct answers.
1 The HI-SEAS biodome is ___.
   A on Mars   B on Earth   C in the UK
2 It's the home of these people for eight ___.
   A days   B weeks   C months
3 They want to study what happens when people ___ together.
   A live and work   B do homework   C relax and play

4 **ALL HOTSPOTS** Explore the hotspots. Find one that tells you about …
1 exercise.   4 special clothes.
2 free time activities.   5 food.
3 everyday problems.

5 Go online and find the answers to the questions.
1 What colour is Mars?
2 Is it hot or cold on Mars?
3 Is Mars the third, fourth or fifth planet from the sun?

6 ● Watch the video. Are the sentences true (T) or false (F)?
1 When you're in space, you need to stay fit.
2 The people do exercise three days a week.
3 They don't do exercise outside.
4 They hate doing exercise on machines.

7 ● Watch the video and answer the questions.
1 Which meals do they have together?
2 What do they add to their food? Why?
3 What do they do on a special food day?
4 What is an example of something they eat on this day?

8 ■ Write a question to ask Jay. Work in pairs, exchange questions and write a reply from Jay.

20 Vision 360

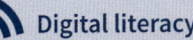 Digital literacy

9 Watch the video and answer the questions. Use short answers.
1 Do the people do lots of experiments outside?
2 Do they wear normal clothes outside?
3 Does it feel like they're on Mars?

10 Read the opinions. Is the biodome a good place for the people below to live and work? Why? / Why not? Discuss in pairs.

Nasser I don't like small spaces.

Elena Cooking is my favourite hobby.

Boris I prefer being outdoors.

Mo I enjoy working with different people.

Yasmin I'm good at solving problems.

Kiara I like spending time with my family.

11 **THINK & SHARE** Work in pairs. Discuss the questions.
1 Do you think the biodome is a good place to live? Think of two good and two bad things.
2 Are you a good person to be in the biodome? Why? / Why not?

CREATE ... an information leaflet

STEP 1

RESEARCH IT!
Go online and find a biodome in ...

Canada   Spain   the Netherlands   the UK

STEP 2
You are going to create an information leaflet about a biodome. Work in groups. Choose the one you want to write about and decide which information to include.

cost of tickets   name   opening times   place
reviews of visitors   size   things to do   things to see

STEP 3
Do research online to find information for your leaflet. Make notes.

STEP 4
Use your notes to write the different parts of your leaflet. Find photos online to use in it.

STEP 5
Share the leaflets with the class. Which ones give you lots of information? Which biodome do you want to visit? Why?

Vision 360   21

2 Healthy living

- **VOCABULARY** Staying fit, Food and drink
- **GRAMMAR** Adverbs of frequency, question words, There is / There are, some, any, a lot of, much and many
- **READING** Healthy eating habits
- **LISTENING** Daily routines
- **GLOBAL SKILLS** Food labels
- **SPEAKING** Ordering food and drink
- **WRITING** Completing a form
- **DOCUMENTARY** Soccer in Soweto

VOCABULARY BOOSTER P114–115
GRAMMAR BOOSTER P134–135

Crazy about sport

1 Look at the video stills and answer the questions.
 1 Do you think Callum likes running? Why / Why not?
 2 Do you like sports? What's your favourite one?

2 ▶ 🔊 **2.01** Write a list of all the sports you can think of. Watch or listen. Do you hear any of the sports on your list?

3 ▶ 🔊 **2.01** Watch or listen again. Are the sentences true (T) or false (F)?
 1 Callum and Zara both enjoy sports. ___
 2 He goes skateboarding once a week. ___
 3 Zara doesn't like playing sport. ___
 4 Callum plays team sports for his school. ___
 5 Zara can't stand winter sports. ___
 6 She does exercises in the gym every day. ___
 7 Her routine has got four different exercises. ___
 8 Callum tries Zara's new exercises. ___

4 **REAL ENGLISH** Choose the correct meaning for the words and phrases in **bold**.
 1 I'm **pretty** fit.
  A not
  B quite
 2 **I'm crazy about** sport!
  A hate
  B love
 3 But that's **just for fun**!
  A because I enjoy it
  B because I need to do it
 4 First, we need to **run on the spot**.
  A run fast
  B run in the same place
 5 Next, let's **work on** our legs.
  A rest
  B exercise
 6 **Nice one**, Zara.
  A well done
  B please

22 Unit 2

Talk about staying fit. **2.1 VOCABULARY**

5 **VOCABULARY** Match the words and phrases below to the definitions.

| athlete   dance class   diving   fit   football   gym
| skateboarding   snowboarding   surfing   swimming
| tennis   volleyball   windsurfing   workout

1 two water sports you can do indoors
2 a person who runs and plays sport
3 an activity with music and exercise
4 regular exercise helps you stay this way
5 two activities you do on a board in water
6 three sports you play with a ball
7 a routine with different types of exercises
8 two activities on a board with no water
9 a place you go to do exercise using machines, etc.

6 🔊 **2.02** Listen to six activities. Write the activities in Ex 5 that you hear. More than one answer may be correct. Listen again and check your answers.

1 _____
2 _____
3 _____
4 _____
5 _____
6 _____

7 💬 Work in pairs. Take turns to choose an activity from the photos. Your partner can ask you five *yes/no* questions about it. Can they guess what it is? Use the words below to help you.

| ball   board   in a team   indoors   music   on your own
| outdoors   water sport   winter sport

Is it a water sport?   No, it isn't.
Do you do it outdoors?   Yes, you do.
Do you play in a team?   Yes, you do.
Do you use a ball?   Yes, you do.
Is it football?   Yes, it is.

8 💬 **THINK & SHARE** Make a list of all the activities that you …

- do to stay fit.
- like or hate watching on TV.
- find easy.
- find difficult.
- do in P.E. class.
- do in the summer.
- do in the winter.

9 💬 Work in pairs. Share your ideas, compare them and ask your partner an extra question about them.

I go snowboarding in winter to stay fit.

Really? I don't. I don't like winter sports. Do you go snowboarding with your family?

No, I don't. I go with the local team.

VOCABULARY BOOSTER Unit 2   23

2.2 GRAMMAR Use adverbs of frequency to talk about sport and exercise.

Adverbs of frequency; question words

1 Do you remember the vlog about sports and exercise? Which activities do Callum and Zara love doing?

2 ◉ 2.05 Read the interview on a fitness vlog. Name three things Jade does as well as vlogging.

FITNESS VLOG > Interviews

Tony Today's guest fitness vlogger is my Indonesian friend, Jade. Hi Jade! Can I ask you some questions before your amazing workout?
Jade Ah, thanks, Tony! Of course you can.
Tony Now, you're very fit. How often do you do exercise?
Jade Well, I do workouts every day and I usually make three new videos a week. And I also play *sepak takraw* twice a week with my team.
Tony What's *sepak takraw*, Jade?
Jade It's an Asian sport. It's also called kick volleyball.
Tony Interesting! Where does your team play?
Jade We always play inside, as it's often very hot in Indonesia. We hardly ever play outside.
Tony And when do you go to the gym?
Jade Um, I never go to the gym, Tony. I prefer playing sport or exercising at home instead.
Tony OK. And whose vlogs do you like?
Jade Yours, of course! And I sometimes watch athletes' vlogs, to get new ideas for my videos.
Tony Nice one, Jade. Now it's time for your routine!

---

3 Complete the table with the highlighted adverbs of frequency in the interview.

| always | usually | ___ | ___ | ___ | ___ |

4 Complete the grammar rules with *before* and *after*.

Adverbs of frequency
We use adverbs of frequency to say how often we do something.
We usually put adverbs of frequency ¹_____ the verb.
I usually make three new fitness videos a week.
We put adverbs of frequency ²_____ the verb *be*.
It's always great to speak to you.
GRAMMAR BOOSTER P134

5 Add an adverb of frequency to the sentences so they are true for you.
 1 I go to the gym.
 2 P.E. lessons are fun for me.
 3 My best friend plays tennis.
 4 I am tired after a workout.
 5 My family and I go swimming.
 6 I am busy at the weekends.

6 💬 Work in groups. Guess the answers to the questions in Ex 5 for the people in your group.
 I think Otto never goes to the gym.
 No, I sometimes go to the gym at the weekends.

7 Read the grammar rules. Underline all the question words in the interview. Then complete the rule.

Question words
We use question words such as *what, who, which, how, what time, why* ¹_____, ²_____, ³_____ and ⁴_____ to ask a question.
We put them at the beginning of the sentence.
What do you do to stay fit?
GRAMMAR BOOSTER P134

8 Choose the correct alternative.
 1 '**What time** / **day** do you have P.E.?' 'On Friday.'
 2 '**How often** / **When** do you play football?' 'Once a week.'
 3 '**Where** / **How** do you go to school?' 'By bike.'
 4 '**Which** / **Whose** ball is that?' 'A tennis ball.'
 5 '**Who** / **Where**'s your P.E. teacher?' 'Ms Camara.'
 6 '**Why** / **When** do you go surfing?' 'Because it's fun.'

9 💬 In pairs, ask and answer both questions in Ex 8.
 What time do you have P.E.?   *At eleven o'clock.*
 What day do you have P.E.?   *On Friday.*

10 ◉ 2.06 Write questions. Then listen to the conversation between two friends and check.
 1 Which sports / you love doing?
 2 How often / you have P.E. lessons?
 3 What / you do in P.E. lessons?
 4 What / you and your family do to stay fit?
 5 Who / you do exercise with?
 6 When / you and your brother go to the gym?

11 ◉ 2.06 Now listen again and answer the questions.

12 **THINK & SHARE** Write questions about sport to ask a partner. Use the words and phrases below to help you.
 Are you crazy about sport?

 How often …?   Who … with?   Which …?
 Why …?   Where …?   When?

 dance classes   do workouts   enjoy P.E.
 exercise   go to the gym   play team sports
 skateboarding   stay fit   talk about sport
 watch football or tennis on TV   water sports

13 💬 Work in pairs. Interview each other, using your questions. Is your partner crazy about sport?
 How often do you go swimming?   *I go twice a week.*
 Who do you go with?   *I usually go with my sister.*

14 Write a short report about your partner.

24 Unit 2

Recognise common collocations in an interview about an athlete's schedule.

2.3 LISTENING

An athlete's schedule

STRATEGY Recognising common collocations

Collocations are two or more words that often go together. Examples of common verb + noun collocations are *do homework*, *go swimming* and *have breakfast*. When you listen, try to recognise collocations.

1 Work in pairs. Ask and answer the questions.
   1 Which sports competitions do you know?
   2 Who are the top sports stars and teams in your country?
   3 How often do you think they practise?
   4 How easy is it to play sports for your country?

2 **2.07** Listen to Part 1 of an interview with Raj. What does he talk about? Choose the correct answer: A, B or C.
   A How to stay fit in P.E. classes.
   B How to become a successful athlete.
   C How to be a good sports teacher.

3 **2.07** Read the questions carefully. Listen again and choose the correct answer: A, B or C.
   1 What does Raj do?
      A He teaches sport to teenagers.
      B He writes books about volleyball.
      C He's an Olympic athlete.
   2 What does the number 10,000 refer to?
      A The number of top athletes.
      B The money top athletes make.
      C The hours of practice top athletes need.
   3 At what age do many sports stars begin training?
      A Between four and five.
      B Between five and six.
      C Between 20 and 30.
   4 What do all top athletes do, according to Raj?
      A They manage their time well.
      B They have healthy eating habits.
      C They never stop trying.

4 **THINK & SHARE** Work in pairs. Ask and answer the questions.
   • What sports are you good at?
   • How often do you practise them?
   • Which do you think is more important: hard work, ability or a good teacher? Why?

5 **2.08** Read the strategy. Then complete the table with the phrases below to make collocations. Listen and check.

| a break   a shower   an orange   dinner   gymnastics |
| lunch   to bed   to the gym   workouts |

Do	Go	Have

6 **2.09** Listen to Part 2 of the interview about an Olympic athlete's daily schedule. Listen and complete their schedule.

Daily schedule

Wed 24	6.30 a.m.	gets up
Thurs 25	7 a.m.	goes _____
Fri 26	8.30 a.m.	does _____
	11.30 a.m.	has _____
Sat 27	2.30 p.m.	has _____
Sun 28	3 p.m.	does _____
Mon 29	5 p.m.	does gymnastics
	9.40 p.m.	has _____
Tues 30	10.15 p.m.	goes _____

7 **MEDIATION** You have a friend who loves sport and wants to become a top athlete. Think about both parts of the interview with Raj. Write down five pieces of advice for your friend.

8 Think of some questions to ask your partner about their daily routine. Look at the schedule to help you.

9 Work in pairs. Interview each other about your daily schedule. How do your lives compare with the top athletes?

Unit 2   25

2.4 GLOBAL SKILLS Talk about food labels.

Food labels

1 Look at the food label below. Answer the questions.
   1 What do red, orange and green mean on a real traffic light?
   2 How often do you read food labels?
   3 Do you think this food is healthy or unhealthy?

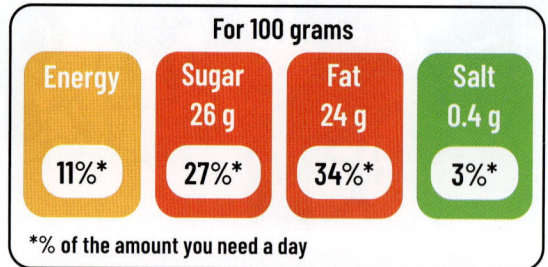

2 Read the information box and complete each gap with one word.

What's the traffic-light system?
The traffic-light system on food labels shows you the amount of _____, _____, _____, and _____ in food.
The _____ colours make it quick and easy for you to see how healthy the food is.
What do the colours mean?
_____ = it's high in something unhealthy, e.g. fat
_____ = it's medium, so it's OK for you
_____ = it's low in something unhealthy, e.g. sugar.

3 🔊 2.10 Listen to Lia talk to her friend, Alex. Where do they meet? Complete the missing information in the food label for the pizza below.

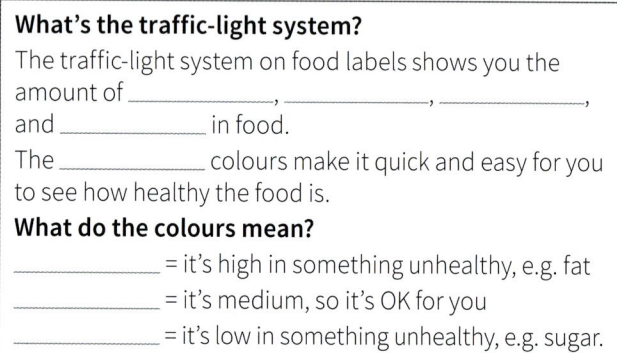

4 🔊 2.10 Complete the Phrasebook with the words below. Then listen again and check.

got   good   for   low   of   in

PHRASEBOOK Talking about food labels
It's ¹_____ for you.
It's bad ²_____ you.
What's it ³_____ in it?
Is it ⁴_____ in sugar?
It's high ⁵_____ salt.
It's got a lot ⁶_____ fat.

5 💬 Work in pairs. Discuss the four food labels below. Match them to the food and drink. Use the Phrasebook to help you.

breakfast cereal   cola   a hamburger   chocolate cake

I think this is … because it's low in …

Maybe, but it's also high in …

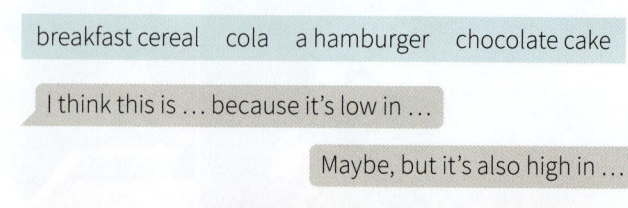

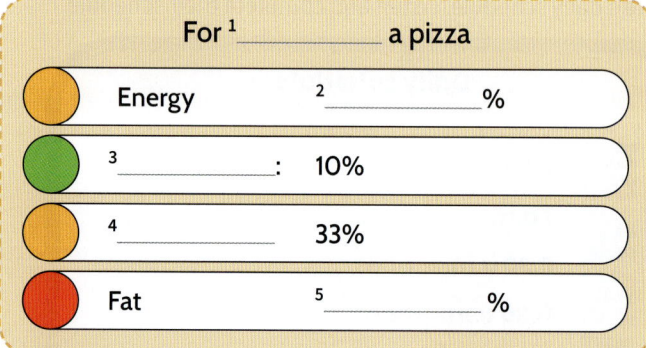

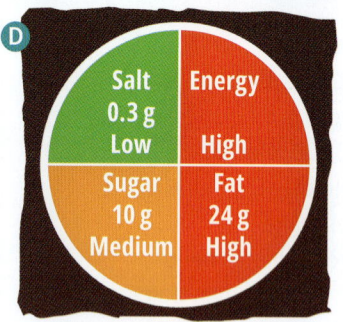

6 💬 **THINK & SHARE** Work in pairs. Ask and answer the questions.
   1 Are the food labels the same in your country?
   2 If not, how are they different?
   3 Do you find them easy to understand? Why? / Why not?

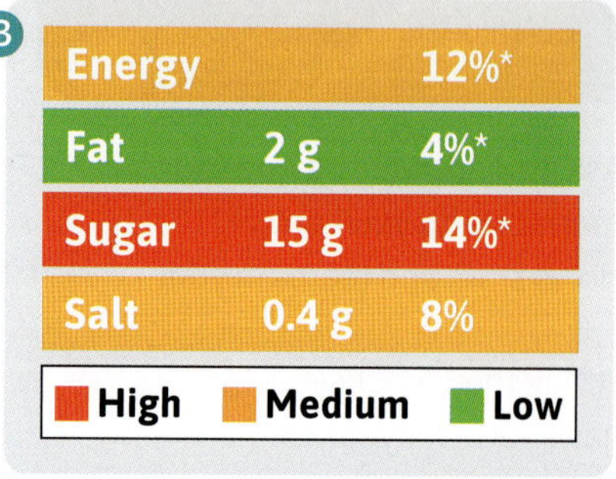

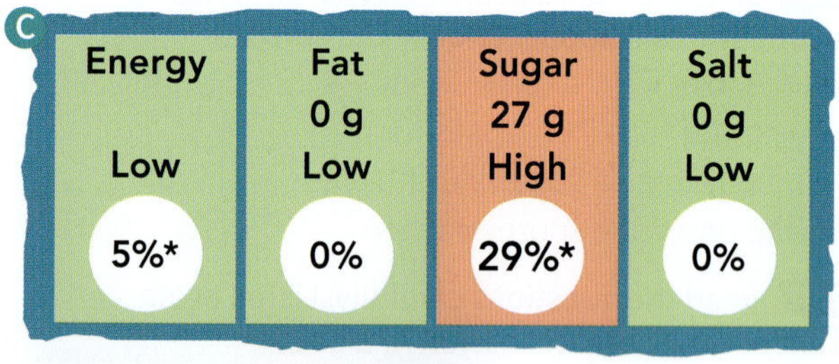

7 How important is it to check food labels?
   • How can traffic-light food labels help change people's food shopping habits?
   • Do you think they are useful?

26 Unit 2

Talk about food and drink. **2.5 VOCABULARY**

How to eat well

1 Work in pairs. Think of all the different foods you know. You have got two minutes.

2 Look at the Eatwell Plate. Read the article. Then answer the questions.
  1 Are any of the words from your list in Ex 1 on it?
  2 How many food groups are there on the plate?
  3 In a balanced diet, what do you only eat and drink a little of? Why?

How to eat well

The Eatwell Guide shows us the type of food we need every day for a balanced diet.

It's a great idea to eat many types of fruit and vegetables, for example, an apple, an orange, a banana, an avocado, strawberries, a tomato, some lettuce, broccoli or a carrot. You also need energy. Rice, bread, pasta and potatoes are all healthy options. We also need food to help us grow and stay healthy, for example, meat, chicken, fish, beans and eggs. Milk products like milk, cheese and yoghurt are good for you too, and water is always a healthy drink. But only have a little oil, chocolate, ice cream or cola a day, as these are all high in sugar and fat!

balanced diet – eating many different food groups
a little – a small quantity

3 VOCABULARY Match the highlighted words in the article to the pictures.

A _____   J _____   S _____
B _____   K _____   T _____
C _____   L _____   U _____
D _____   M _____ V _____
E _____   N _____   W _____
F _____   O _____   X _____
G _____   P _____   Y _____
H _____   Q _____   Z _____
I _____   R _____

4 Work in pairs. Think of a food word in Ex 3. Use three words or phrases to describe it. Can your partner guess what it is?

Milk product, breakfast, white.   Yoghurt.

5 Complete the sentences with words from Ex 3.
  1 _____ are orange and _____ and _____ are green – they are all vegetables!
  2 _____ and _____ come from milk.
  3 Spaghetti is a type of _____.
  4 'Would you like some meat?' 'No, thanks. I don't eat meat, _____ or _____.'
  5 We've got cola, orange juice, and _____ juice.
  6 _____ and _____ are red and they are both fruits.

6 Find all the countable and uncountable food words in the article. Complete the table.

Countable	Uncountable

7 Complete the sentences with *a* / *an* or – (no article).
  1 I've got _____ orange in my bag.
  2 She usually has _____ bread for lunch.
  3 Can I have _____ tomato, please?
  4 I love _____ rice and lettuce.
  5 Mum has _____ egg for breakfast.
  6 We often eat _____ meat at dinner.

8 PRONUNCIATION 2.11 The sounds /ɪ/ and /iː/ sound similar but are different. Listen and repeat.

/ɪ/	/iː/
fish	please

9 2.12 Look at the words below. Are the letters in **bold** pronounced /ɪ/ or /iː/? Add the words to the table in Ex 8. Then listen, check and repeat.

b**ea**ns   ch**ee**se   ch**i**cken   dr**i**nk
l**e**ttuce   m**ea**t   m**i**lk   **i**ce cr**ea**m

10 Draw your own Eatwell Plate. Add the food that you usually eat in the correct category.

11 THINK & SHARE Work in pairs. Ask and answer questions about your partner's plate. Do you both eat well? What's healthy and what isn't?

VOCABULARY BOOSTER Unit 2

2.6 GRAMMAR

Use *there is / there are*, *some*, *any*, *a lot of*, *much* and *many* to talk about food.

There is / there are, some, any, a lot of, much and many

1 Can you name any of the food in the photos? Is it countable or uncountable?

A  B  C

2 Read the text. Which countries are the meals in the photos from? What other countries does the text mention?

MEALS FROM AROUND THE WORLD

 In China, at a family meal, there are usually plates with noodles (pasta) with egg, chicken and fish on the table.

 How much meat is there in Indian cooking? There isn't much, because many Indians are vegetarians; up to 40% of them don't eat any meat.

 In Brazil's national dish *feijoada*, there's meat and beans, with some rice or potatoes, but there aren't many vegetables, and there isn't any lettuce.

 Are there any bento boxes in your school? These Japanese lunch boxes have a main meal in them and some side dishes too, e.g. some carrots and an apple.

 Is there a pizzeria near you? There aren't many Italians who eat pizza for lunch – they prefer it for dinner. At lunch, they eat pasta, meat and potatoes. Or they have some cheese and tomatoes in summer.

3 Read the examples from the text and complete the grammar rules. Use the text to help you.

There is / there are

Singular
Affirmative: ¹_____ often a lot of food on the table.
Negative: ²_____ any lettuce.
Questions: ³_____ a pizzeria near you?
Yes, there is. / No, there isn't.

Plural
Affirmative: ⁴_____ usually plates on the tables.
Negative: ⁵_____ many vegetables.
Questions: ⁶_____ any bento boxes?
Yes, there are. / No, there aren't.

GRAMMAR BOOSTER P135

4 Look at photos A–C in Ex 1. Complete the sentences with *there is / there are*.
A 1 _____ some tomatoes.
  2 _____ some cheese.
B 3 _____ some meat.
  4 _____ some noodles.
C 5 _____ some rice.
  6 _____ some beans.

5 Complete the grammar rules with *some* and *any*. Find other examples in the text. Are the nouns countable or uncountable?

some and any

▶ Grammar animation

We use *some* and *any* with plural countable nouns and uncountable nouns.
We use ¹_____ in affirmative sentences.
In summer, they have some cheese and tomato
We use ²_____ in negative sentences and questions.
Up to 40% of them don't eat any meat.

GRAMMAR BOOSTER P135

6 Complete the sentences with *some* or *any*.
1 We don't eat _____ fish.
2 I often have _____ rice for dinner.
3 Do we need _____ apples?
4 We haven't got _____ eggs at home.
5 Have you got _____ milk for my tea?
6 I've got _____ bread and cheese for lunch.

7 Complete the grammar rules with *countable* or *uncountable*.

A lot of, much and many

▶ Grammar animation

We use *a lot of* in affirmative sentences.
There's a lot of meat. There are a lot of vegetables.
We use *much* and *many* in negative sentences.
We use *much* with _____ nouns.
There isn't much meat. How much milk is there?
We use *many* with _____ nouns.
There aren't many vegetables. How many tomatoes are there?

GRAMMAR BOOSTER P135

8 Choose the correct alternative.

How ¹**much / many** rice do Indonesians eat? Lots! For them, it isn't a meal if there isn't ²**some / any** rice in it. They often have ³**some / any** fish or chicken with it too, but they don't eat ⁴**much / many** red meat. In Jamaica, they often have ⁵**some / any** green bananas with ⁶**some / any** rice or bread, but they don't eat ⁷**much / many** potatoes. ⁸**Much / A lot of** Jamaicans eat fish for breakfast too.

9 💬 Work in pairs. Student A look at the bento box on page 150. Student B look at the bento box on page 151. Ask and answer questions about them.

10 💬 **THINK & SHARE** Design your perfect bento box. What is in it? Share your ideas with a partner.

28 Unit 2

2.7 READING

Use general knowledge to predict the content of an article about food.

Healthy eating habits

1 **THINK & SHARE** Work in pairs. How many examples can you think of for each type of food below? Share your ideas as a class.

| fast food | fats | fruit | milk products | sweets | vegetables |

STRATEGY Using general knowledge to predict content

Before you read a text, look at the title and images or any extra information and answer these questions:
1 What can I see in the photo?
2 What do I know about this topic?
3 What do I think the main ideas are?

2 Read the strategy. Look at the photo and the title of the article. Then answer questions 1–3 in the strategy.

3 Work in pairs. Look at questions 1–4 in the article. Discuss possible answers to the questions.

4 🔊 2.15 Now read the article. Which of your answers in Ex 3 were correct?

5 Read the article again. Choose the correct answer: A, B or C.
1 Teenagers need to choose the right things to …
   A eat and drink.   B listen to.   C do in their spare time.
2 The Eatwell Guide says you can … eat foods that are high in fat and sugar.
   A never   B sometimes   C often
3 Which of these foods is often full of sugar?
   A nuts   B yoghurt   C juice
4 It's a good idea to drink … glasses a day if you do exercise.
   A 6   B 8   C more than 8
5 Which of these facts about fats is true?
   A They're never healthy.   B They give energy.
   C They have vitamins.
6 Which of these does NOT help you study well?
   A dark chocolate   B nuts   C avocados

6 Work in groups. Ask and answer the questions. Use *How much … ?* and *How many … ?*

How healthy are your habits?
- fresh fruit / eat a day?
- glasses of water / drink a day?
- sugar / have at breakfast?
- sugar / eat every day?
- vegetables / eat a day?
- fast food / eat a week?
- time / spend in front of a screen every day?
- hours / sleep a night?

How much fresh fruit do you eat a day?

7 Work in pairs. Ask and answer the questions.
1 Have you got healthy habits? Why / Why not?
2 Is there anything you won't eat or drink?
3 What's your favourite food / drink?

Healthy eating habits for active teenagers

Many lifestyle changes happen when you're a teenager. You can start making your own choices. You can choose your own clothes, the music you listen to, and how you spend your time. It's also important to make the right choices about what you eat and drink. Healthy eating can help you feel fit, be happy and do well at school. But how? We answer your questions.

¹ Can I eat chocolate and cake?

Yes, you can. You can still have all your favourite foods and drinks – cola, chocolate, cake and crisps. But these are all high in fat and sugar. Don't eat a lot of these things. You need a balanced diet. Use the Eatwell Guide to help you.

² I'm always tired at school. Can food help?

Yes, it can. Start the day right and have breakfast. A healthy breakfast gives you the energy you need for school. Cereal and fruit juice are quick and easy, but are high in sugar. Try and eat some eggs or nuts with these. They help your body use the sugar slowly.

³ How much water do I need to drink a day?

There aren't any rules, but try and have six to eight glasses a day. Water and low-fat milk are good options. This quantity increases if you play sports or do workouts. Don't drink a lot of fruit juice. Remember, juice is high in sugar. One small glass a day is OK.

⁴ Is there any fat which is good for you?

Yes, some fats give you energy and help your body get important vitamins. There are healthy fats in nuts, eggs, olive oil, fish and avocados. Fish, avocados and dark chocolate can help you think. But don't eat a lot of fast food – it's got a lot of unhealthy fats.

Unit 2   29

2.8 SPEAKING Order food and drink.

Ordering food and drink

1 Work in pairs. Look at the photo. Where are they? What can you see?

2 🔊 **2.16** Listen to the dialogue. Complete the waiter's notes with the food and drink they order.

Menu
apple juice	chicken curry
water	all-day breakfast
tomato soup	apple cake
avocado salad	fruit salad

	Starter	Main	Dessert	Drinks
Girl				
Boy				

3 🔊 **2.16** Read the Phrasebook. Who says what? Write *customer* (C) or *waiter* (W). Then listen again and check.

PHRASEBOOK Ordering food and drink
___ Can we have a table for (two), please?
___ Can we have the menu, please?
___ Are you ready to order?
___ I'd like the (soup) to start, please.
___ And for your main course?
___ Can I have the (chicken), please?
___ And for you, sir?
___ I'd like the (salad) followed by a (curry), please.
___ Would you like anything to drink?
___ The same for me, please.

4 Work in groups of three. Practise the dialogue.

5 🔊 **2.17** Listen to the second part of the dialogue. Who pays for the meal?

6 🔊 **2.17** Complete the Phrasebook. Listen again and check your answers. Who says what?

PHRASEBOOK Paying for your meal
Would you like _____ tea or coffee?
No, thanks. I _____ want anything else.
Can we have the bill, _____?
How _____ is it?
_____ £25. I'd like to pay for this.

7 Work in small groups. Prepare a role-play in a restaurant. Use the Phrasebook and prompts below to help you.
• Ask for a table and a menu.
• Order your food.
• Ask for the bill.

🏃 MOVE IT! gym café

Starters
• Chicken salad
• Cheese and tomato salad

Main courses
• Low-fat hamburgers (meat or veg) with lettuce, avocado and tomatoes
• Fish with carrots, beans and rice or potatoes

Desserts
• Low-sugar fruit cake
• Ice cream

Drinks
• Water
• Orange juice
• Apple juice
• Green tea

Price: £15 for two courses and drinks

8 Choose your roles and practise your dialogue. Then act them out to the class without reading them.

STRATEGY Rating your performance
When you finish a speaking activity, think about your performance. Use the traffic-light system to rate your performance: good 🟢, OK 🟠 or not good 🔴. Give reasons – think about your use of grammar, vocabulary, pronunciation and your interaction with your partner(s).

9 **REFLECT** Read the strategy. Then in your groups rate your performances for the role-play.

Use capital letters and abbreviations to complete a form.

2.9 WRITING

Completing a form

1. 💬 Look at the form. What is it for? What personal details does it ask for?

2. Read the form again. Answer the questions.
   1. Whose form is it?
   2. What is his date of birth?
   3. Where does he live?
   4. How often does he want to use the gym?

   STRATEGY Using capital letters
   We use capital letters …
   1. at the start of a sentence.
   2. for names and titles.
   3. for days of the week.
   4. for months of the year.
   5. in some postcodes.
   6. for some abbreviations.

3. Read the strategy. Find all the capital letters in the form. Match each one to uses 1–6 in the strategy.

4. Read the customer survey on the other side of the form. Match the questions to the answers.
   A. How many hours of exercise do you do a week?
   B. Please give details about the type / frequency of exercise.
   C. Please give details about your average daily diet.
   D. How long do you exercise for per workout?
   E. How many times a week do you go to the gym?
   F. What physical activities do you enjoy doing?

5. **THINK & SHARE** Read the survey again. How fit and active is Vijay? Is his diet healthy and balanced? Why? / Why not?

6. 💬 Work in pairs. Ask and answer the questions in Ex 4 about you.

   LANGUAGE FOCUS Abbreviations
   In forms, we often abbreviate words and instructions to save space. We do this by making words shorter or by using only the first letters of words, e.g. *Please turn over = PTO*.

7. Read the Language focus. Find all the abbreviations in the forms. Match them to their full form.
   1. minutes _____
   2. day, month, year _____
   3. mobile phone _____
   4. Road _____
   5. date of birth _____
   6. United Kingdom _____
   7. September _____
   8. hours _____
   9. male _____
   10. female _____

8. Imagine you need to fill in the customer survey form for your local gym. Turn to page 149. Complete the form in 60–80 words.

9. ✓ **CHECK YOUR WORK**
   - Are all of the parts of your form filled in?
   - Did you answer all the questions correctly?
   - Are there capital letters in the right places?
   - Are there any abbreviations in it?

MOVE IT!
FITNESS AND SPORTS CENTRE

Gym membership form – personal details
Please fill in all parts of this form.

Gender: (M)/ F
Surname: Gupta
First name: Vijay
DOB (DD/MM/YYYY): 22/04/2005
Address: 4 Crown Rd, Windsor, UK
Postcode: SL7 5NO
Email: vgupta@mail.com
Tel: Mob. +44 075 6852149
Job: Student
When would you like to use the gym?
Sept–June. On Friday p.m., Saturday and Sunday

PTO

MOVE IT!
FITNESS AND SPORTS CENTRE

Please fill in our survey and help us improve our services!

1 ___
tennis, football, swimming, gym, snowboarding

2 ___
three times

3 ___
45 mins

4 ___
about 8 hrs

5 ___
I go skateboarding every day, I play football twice a week and I go swimming on Monday evenings.

6 ___
I usually have a yoghurt and some milk for breakfast. For lunch, I often have a hamburger or some pizza. In the afternoon, I have an apple or an orange. We often eat fish or chicken with vegetables for dinner. I don't drink much water – I prefer cola.

Unit 2 31

2.10 REVIEW

Grammar

1 Choose the correct answer: A, B or C.
   1 There … a gym at my school.
      A are   B aren't   C is
   2 In the mornings, I … tired.
      A often am   B have often   C am often
   3 How … cola do you drink?
      A many   B much   C often
   4 We haven't got … carrots – only one or two.
      A many   B some   C any
   5 I … meat because I'm a vegetarian.
      A never eat   B eat never   C don't never eat
   6 We usually have … pasta for lunch.
      A a   B some   C any
   7 Are there … of players in your team?
      A many   B a lot   C much
   8 … do you go to school with?
      A Where   B Who   C What time

2 Complete the questions.
   1 Where _____ your grandparents _____?
     They live in the centre of Warsaw.
   2 What _____ you _____?
     We get up at half past seven.
   3 How _____ you _____ to the gym?
     I go there once a week.
   4 Why _____ Dad _____ every day?
     He goes for a run to stay fit.
   5 _____ exercise classes today?
     No, there aren't. Try again tomorrow.
   6 How _____ milk _____?
     There isn't any. We need to buy some today.

Vocabulary

3 Complete the definitions with the correct words.
   1 These are two green vegetables.
     l __ __ __ __ __ __ and b __ __ __ __ __ __ __ __
   2 You drink lots of this when it's hot.
     w __ __ __ __
   3 You make chips with these.
     p __ __ __ __ __ __ __ __
   4 A sandwich has got two pieces of this.
     b __ __ __ __ __
   5 Pizzas usually have this on them.
     t __ __ __ __ __ __ sauce and c __ __ __ __ __ __
   6 People sometimes have one or two of these for breakfast.
     e __ __ __ __
   7 People in India eat a lot of this.
     r __ __ __ __
   8 These are sweet, red summer fruits.
     s __ __ __ __ __ __ __ __ __ __ __
   9 A green fruit.
     a __ __ __ __ __ __
   10 This milk product can be natural or with fruit.
     y __ __ __ __ __ __

4 The **bold** words are in the incorrect sentences. Move them into the correct sentences.
   1 In winter, we go **skateboarding** in the mountains.
   2 Students often play ball sports like **diving** and **windsurfing** in P.E. class.
   3 I enjoy going **surfing** in the street with my friends.
   4 I have Latin American **snowboarding** classes twice a week. My favourite is salsa.
   5 Popular water sports in Australia include **workout**, **dance** and **tennis**.
   6 I'm very tired after a long **volleyball** in the gym.

Cumulative review

5 Complete the dialogue with one word in each gap.

Luis I want to get fit and healthy, but I don't know how. Alba, how ¹_____ exercise do you do?
Alba Um, I ²_____ workouts three times a week.
Luis Really? I don't enjoy workouts. ³_____ gym do you go to?
Alba I go to the one near our school. It's great. And I often ⁴_____ football too. Do you want to try playing for my team?
Luis No, thanks! I ⁵_____ play football in my free time – I can't stand it!
Alba Oh really? Well, ⁶_____ are many other types of exercise you can try too. There ⁷_____ an amazing new pool near the centre of town. Do you like ⁸_____ swimming? It's really good for you.
Luis Actually, ⁹_____, I do! I love it! Nice one, Alba!
Alba But remember, being healthy isn't just about doing lots of exercise. You also need a balanced diet. What type of food ¹⁰_____ you and your family eat?
Luis Um, we usually have ¹¹_____ chicken or meat, potatoes and vegetables for dinner, but we don't have ¹²_____ fish because we all hate it.
Alba Well, that sounds pretty healthy to me. And how ¹³_____ sugar do you eat?
Luis Oh, we don't eat ¹⁴_____ sweets or cakes – we only have them once a week. But we all love chocolate.
Alba ¹⁵_____ much chocolate do you eat?
Luis Well, I usually have some chocolate ¹⁶_____ a day – once in the morning and just before I go to bed.
Alba Oh, Luis!

💬 Think & share

6 Answer the questions.
   1 Which sports are good for teenagers? Why?
   2 How often do you exercise? What do you do?
   3 What do you usually have for lunch on school days?
   4 What types of food do you think are healthy or unhealthy? Why?

32 Review

2.11 EXAM SKILLS

Listening

EXAM STRATEGY

When you do a multiple choice task with photos, read the questions and look at the photos carefully before you listen. Think about who is in the conversation and what the conversation is about.

1 Read the **strategy** above. Then read the questions and look at the photos in the exam task in Ex 2. Answer these questions.
  1 What is this conversation about?
  2 Which three sports do the people talk about?
  3 Where is the boy?
  4 Which three places do the people talk about?

2 🔊 **2.18** For each question, listen and choose the correct answer (A, B or C).
  1 What does Lucy's dad make for breakfast?
  A  B  C

  2 Which sport does the girl do now?
  A  B  C

  3 What can the boy eat for his main course?
  A  B  C

  4 Where does Max want to go now?
  A  B  C

Use of English

EXAM STRATEGY

When you complete a text with missing words, read the words around each gap carefully. Think about what type of word is missing, e.g. noun, verb, question word, article, preposition, adjective or adverb.

3 Read the **strategy** above. Then look at the exam task in Ex 4. Read the whole text quickly. Then read the first two sentences again and look carefully at the words around the first gap. Which type of word do you think is missing? Choose A, B or C.
  A adjective   B noun   C article

4 Read the text below and think of the word which best fits each gap. Use only one word in each gap.

Eating for healthy living

Fumiko lives in Japan. On today's blog, we ask her about her diet.

Do you have a healthy diet?

Yes, I do. In the morning, I usually eat ¹_____ omelette and a piece of fruit. It's important to eat a ²_____ of different types of fruit. I love apples, bananas and strawberries. I also like avocados and tomatoes. At lunchtime, I usually have fish and rice with ³_____ vegetables. My favourite vegetables are broccoli and beans. I also like lettuce and carrots. There ⁴_____ always vegetables in my house! In the evening, I eat fish again. I don't eat much meat because I don't like it, but I sometimes have chicken.

How ⁵_____ do you eat fast food and sweet desserts?

I hardly ⁶_____ eat fast food. I like chips, but I don't like pizza or hamburgers. ⁷_____ is a very good sushi restaurant near my house. I often eat there ⁸_____ my friends. I don't like ice cream, but I sometimes have a little chocolate. I like cake too.

Writing

EXAM STRATEGY

When you write a reply to a letter or an email, use your own words to respond to the information they ask for. This shows you understand the meaning.

5 Read the **strategy** above. Then read the email in the exam task in Ex 6. Match each word or phrase in **bold** with the word or phrase A–C that has a similar meaning.
  A prefer
  B fantastic
  C clubs or hobbies

6 Read this email from your English-speaking friend Joe and make notes. Write your email to Joe using all the notes.

> **FROM:** Joe
> **SUBJECT:** New sports club
>
> Hi,
> How many **activities** do you do at school? What are they?
>   *Explain*
> Do you want to do a new activity at the weekend?
>   *Great idea ... because ...*
> There's an exercise class at the gym and a tennis club at the park. Which do you want to do?
>   *Say which you like best and why*
> Write soon!
> Joe

Exam skills 33

3 Looking good

- **VOCABULARY** Clothes from around the world / Character types
- **GRAMMAR** Present continuous / Present simple and present continuous
- **READING** Perfect selfies
- **LISTENING** Costumes
- **GLOBAL SKILLS** Being safe online
- **SPEAKING** Describing photos
- **WRITING** An informal email
- **VISION 360** A living room

VOCABULARY BOOSTER P116–117
GRAMMAR BOOSTER P136–137

What's your style?

1 **THINK & SHARE** Look at the video stills and answer the questions.
   1 Are these Zara and Callum's usual clothes? Why do you think this?
   2 Do you know the name of any of these clothes? Do you like them? Why? / Why not?

2 ▶ 🔊 **3.01** Watch or listen. Number the countries in the order they talk about them.
   ___ Norway   ___ India
   ___ Peru   ___ Scotland
   ___ China

3 ▶ 🔊 **3.01** Watch or listen again. Choose the correct answer: A, B or C.
   1 Whose wedding is it?
      A their cousin's   B their aunt's   C their family friends'
   2 Which colours are in their family's kilt?
      A red and green   B red and black   C red and yellow
   3 When does Callum wear a kilt?
      A at home   B at school   C on special days
   4 Which colour is common at Chinese weddings?
      A gold   B pink   C red
   5 Which colour is NOT part of the Norwegian *bunad*?
      A white   B purple   C black
   6 In which country do people wear special hats?
      A Ghana   B India   C Peru

34 Unit 3

Talk about clothes from around the world.

3.1 VOCABULARY

4 REAL ENGLISH Match the **bold** words and phrases to the meanings.
1 **You see**, we're going to our aunt's wedding today.
2 **See you later**!
3 It's **gorgeous**!
4 **Oh no**!
5 It's a **lucky** colour.
6 **Sorry to interrupt.**

A when something bad happens
B understand
C say goodbye
D it makes good things happen
E when you need to say something while somebody else is speaking
F beautiful

5 VOCABULARY Look at the words below. Match them to the descriptions.

beautiful	big	black	colourful	cream
dark	dress	hat	jacket	jeans	long
pink	pretty	red	shirt	shoes	short
skirt	socks	tie	top	trousers	T-shirt

1 four colours
2 something you wear on your head
3 two things you wear on your feet
4 seven words you use to describe something, e.g. its colour or size
5 nine words for clothes you wear on your body

6 Work in pairs. Which words go together to make opposites?

| big | black | dark | long | pale | short | small | white |

| pale | dark |

7 Complete the description of British weddings with the words below. What do people wear at weddings in your country?

| colourful | dress | jacket | shirt | shoes |
| skirt | tie | top | trousers | T-shirt |

Traditional British wedding clothes

At British weddings, the couple usually wear special clothes.
Women have often got a long, cream or white ¹_____ or they sometimes wear a ²_____ and a long ³_____ instead. They usually hold some ⁴_____ flowers in their hands.
Men usually wear a white ⁵_____ and a ⁶_____ around their necks. They usually wear a suit, even in the summer: a dark blue ⁷_____ on their top half and some ⁸_____ which are the same colour. On their feet, they wear black or brown ⁹_____. They never wear jeans and a ¹⁰_____!

8 Work in pairs. Choose a photo. Describe the clothes. Where do you think they are from?

> He's got long, red trousers …

 A

 B

9 🔊 3.02 Listen to two students talk about their designs for a couple's costume. Which student's designs do you think are good or bad?

10 🔊 3.02 Listen again. Complete the table.

Person	Clothes
1 Man	a pale _____ shirt with a dark grey _____ and _____, dark blue _____
1 Woman	a beautiful, pale pink _____ and a _____ white _____
2 Woman	a short, _____ T-shirt, a long, dark pink _____ and a big, purple _____
2 Man	a pale yellow _____, short, _____ trousers, long, cream _____ and big, dark _____ shoes.

11 THINK & SHARE You are going to design a special wedding costume for a couple. It can be funny or beautiful. Make notes about the clothes you choose. Then take turns to describe your designs to your partner.

> What clothes has your couple got?

> He's got … and she's got …

VOCABULARY BOOSTER Unit 3 35

3.2 GRAMMAR Use the present continuous to talk about things happening now.

Present continuous

1 💬 Do you remember the vlog about special clothes? Which countries and clothes do Callum and Zara talk about in the vlog?

2 Read Yuko's blog post. What special day is it about? What is the national costume in Japan?

Yuko's blog
NEW POST 30 JAN 3 COMMENTS

My favourite photo

This is my favourite photo of my mum and me. We're in national costumes, but we aren't going to a wedding. Why are we wearing these clothes? Because it's traditional on *seijin-no-hi*!

Seijin-no-hi is on the second Monday in January. It's the coming of age day in Japan. It's a day when young people get dressed in national costumes for a big party with family and friends. Here, my mum and I are going for a walk in Kyoto before the party. We're wearing beautiful, long dresses called kimonos. Mine is very colourful, and my mum's wearing a cream kimono. I'm holding my phone, but I'm not taking a photo of us – I'm making a video. My dad isn't standing with us because he's taking this photo! Am I having a good time? Yes, I am! *Seijin-no-hi* is amazing!!!!

national costume – a country's traditional clothes for special events
coming of age – a time when a child becomes an adult

3 Read the grammar rules. Read the blog post again and complete the examples.

Present continuous
▶ Grammar animation

We use the present continuous to talk about things that are happening now or around now.

Affirmative
I ¹_____ my phone.
He ²_____ this photo!
We ³_____ long dresses called kimonos.

Negative
I ⁴_____ a photo of us.
My dad ⁵_____ with us.
We ⁶_____ to a wedding.

Questions
⁷_____ I _____ a good time? Yes, I am. / No, I'm not.
Why ⁸_____ we _____ these clothes?

Spelling rules: -ing verbs
Most verbs:
Verbs ending in a short vowel and consonant – double the consonant: run → running, chat → chatting
Verbs ending in e – drop the e: take → ⁹_____
Verbs ending in ie – change to y: tie → tying

GRAMMAR BOOSTER P136

4 Complete the chat with the present continuous form of the verbs below and short answers.

go   not do   not go   ride   study   walk   watch

< Aneta

Hi Aneta! ¹_____ you _____ TV now?

No, I ²_____. I ³_____ for a walk in the park.

Wow! ⁴_____ Kim _____ with you?

Yes, she ⁵_____. Cecilia's here too, but she ⁶_____ a bike.

Are Ken and Yoshi there too?

No. They ⁷_____ anything today. Why don't you visit them?

I can't. I ⁸_____ out today. I ⁹_____ for a test. 😞

5 **PRONUNCIATION** 🔊 3.05 We pronounce the letters *ng* as a single sound similar to *n* but different. Listen and repeat.
/ŋ/   lo**ng**, thi**ng**, bri**ng**ing
We're buyi**ng** some thi**ng**s.
I'm not si**ng**ing the wro**ng** so**ng**.
Are you thi**nk**ing about swi**mm**ing or playi**ng** tennis?

6 💬 Work in pairs. Look at the photos on page 149. Choose one of the people. Do not tell your partner. Then ask and answer *yes/no* questions to find out who it is.

7 🔊 3.06 Listen to Nick describing a family photo. Where is he from? What special day is it?

8 Write questions about Nick and his family. Use the present continuous.
1 Where / they / stand / ?
2 What / Nick / wear under his costume / ?
3 What / he / hold / ?
4 He / stand with his friends / ?
5 What / his mum / hold / ?
6 What / his sister / do / ?
7 Who / wear / a yellow shirt / ?
8 What / Nick's uncle / do / ?

9 🔊 3.06 Listen again. Write full answers for each question in Ex 8.

10 💬 Work in pairs. Describe …
• what you are wearing today.
• what a classmate is wearing today.
• your favourite family photo.

Today, I'm wearing a pink t-shirt, blue jeans …

36 Unit 3

Identify examples in a podcast about clothes.

3.3 LISTENING

Costumes

1. 💬 Work in pairs. Discuss the questions.
   1 Are there costume parties in your country?
   2 What do people usually wear to them?

2. 🔊 **3.07** Listen to Part 1 of a podcast. Choose the correct option to complete the sentences.
   1 Her book is about **clothes** / **the internet**.
   2 She thinks people **can** / **can't** wear anything they want to a party.

   STRATEGY Identifying examples

   When people want to explain things or give more information about something, they often use examples. Examples usually start with the phrases *for example*, *such as* and *like*. Identifying examples will help you to understand a text better.

3. Read the strategy. Then look at the examples Jane gives to Matt. What do you think the missing words are?
   1 … for example, in _____ and Canada at this time of year, lots of teenagers and adults are going to costume parties. Some of them are wearing things such as _____ …
   2 … there are many photos on the internet of US students in national costumes like _____ at their high school graduation.
   3 And famous people, for example _____, sometimes wear Indian clothes such as _____ in their videos.

4. 🔊 **3.08** Now listen to Part 2 of the podcast and check.

5. 🔊 **3.09** Look at the photos. Write a list of the clothes the people are wearing. Then listen to Part 3 of the podcast and check your answers. Does Matt agree with Jane?

6. 🔊 **3.09** Listen again. Choose the correct answer: A, B or C.
   1 In the first photo there …
     A are Spanish people.
     B are Japanese and Spanish people.
     C are Japanese people.
   2 The women are wearing special dresses for …
     A a costume party.
     B a wedding.
     C a dance practice.
   3 The Canadian girls in the kimonos are …
     A going to a school party.
     B studying Japanese history.
     C visiting a family in Tokyo.
   4 Jane says we need to think carefully before we …
     A eat food from other countries.
     B listen to music from other countries.
     C wear national costumes from other countries.

   hurt (somebody) – make (somebody) feel sad
   culture – a country's traditions, history, language, art and music

7. 💬 **THINK & SHARE** What do you think? Do you agree with Jane?

8. 💬 Work in pairs. Imagine one of you is from a different country. Make questions from the prompts then ask and answer.
   1 what / your country's / national costume ?
   2 when / people / wear it ?
   3 what clothes / you + your friends wear / go out ?
   4 which type / clothes / like and dislike ?

9. 💬 Work in pairs. Think of examples to complete each sentence. Use the phrases in the strategy.
   1 We're studying subjects … this year.
   2 My classmates are wearing clothes … today.
   3 I'm doing lots of hobbies … these days.
   4 My family and I usually eat food … for dinner.
   5 There are many countries … in Europe.
   6 Sports … are popular in our country.

   > We're studying subjects such as maths, history and geography this year.

Unit 3   37

3.4 GLOBAL SKILLS — Share information safely online.

Being safe online

1 **THINK & SHARE** Discuss the questions about your online habits.
   1 How often do you do these things online?
      • show other people your photos
      • tell others where you are and what you're doing
   2 Who can see your social media?

2 Read the advice on the web page. Match the sentence halves.

Stay safe online – think before you post!

1 Don't share your address on social media –
2 Don't put anything which makes you look bad on the internet –
3 Think about any personal information which your photos or videos are showing –
4 Don't post anything about another person without asking them first –
5 Decide exactly who can see your personal posts, photos and videos –

A delete any photos, videos or messages which you don't want your parents or teachers to see!
B you need to know that all the people in it are OK with this.
C it isn't safe to tell people where you live.
D this can stop people you don't know from downloading or using them.
E for example, your school uniform tells everybody where you go to school.

3 **VOCABULARY** Complete the sentences with the highlighted words in the web page. Change the form if necessary.
   1 Don't give any _____ about you, e.g. your phone number, to people you don't know.
   2 Only _____ photos with your family and good friends.
   3 Don't _____ any pictures, ideas or videos that can hurt other people.
   4 Don't show the things that you have at home on _____, e.g. Instagram.
   5 _____ any photos of you which you don't want others, e.g. a future boss, to find one day.
   6 Don't forget that other people can _____ your photos onto their computers and use them.

4 **THINK & SHARE** Work in pairs. Discuss the advice. Do you agree or disagree with it? Why? / Why not?

5 ◆ 3.10 Listen to two friends talking. What advice in Ex 3 can you give them?

6 ◆ 3.10 Listen again. Are the sentences true (T) or false (F)? Correct the false ones.
   1 Jake is posting his photo online.
   2 Jake asks Olly if he can share his photo.
   3 They're wearing jeans and a T-shirt.
   4 They want everybody to find their photo.
   5 Nobody can see Jake's photos.
   6 Other people can download his photos.
   7 Olly wants to tell people they aren't at home.
   8 Jake decides to delete his post.

7 Work in pairs. Look at the list. Decide the following: do you delete, wait to post or share these now? Why?
   • a photo of you in front of your house
   • a post that says you're at the cinema
   • a photo of your favourite sports team
   • a post with your birthday on it
   • a video of you with your pet
   • a photo of you on a two-week holiday
   • a funny video of your little sister
   • a post with your phone number on it

8 Work in pairs. Discuss how you use the internet and answer the questions.
   1 What social media are you and your friends using?
   2 What do people post and share online and why?
   3 What are you and your friends doing to stay safe?

38 Unit 3

Talk about character types. **3.5 VOCABULARY**

Describing character

1 💬 What adjectives do you know that can describe a person's character?

2 Read the text. Answer the questions.
   1 How many main character types are there?
   2 Do you think people usually have one main character type?
   3 Do you think you can change your character? Why / Why not?

What character type are you?

Some scientists believe there are four main character types in the world. Most people are a mix of all four, with one or two dominant types. A person's character doesn't usually change a lot over time. This doesn't mean it's impossible to change your character – but you need to work hard to do this!

clever   popular   quiet   kind   friendly   honest   serious   funny

3 Read the quiz. Choose the right answers for you.

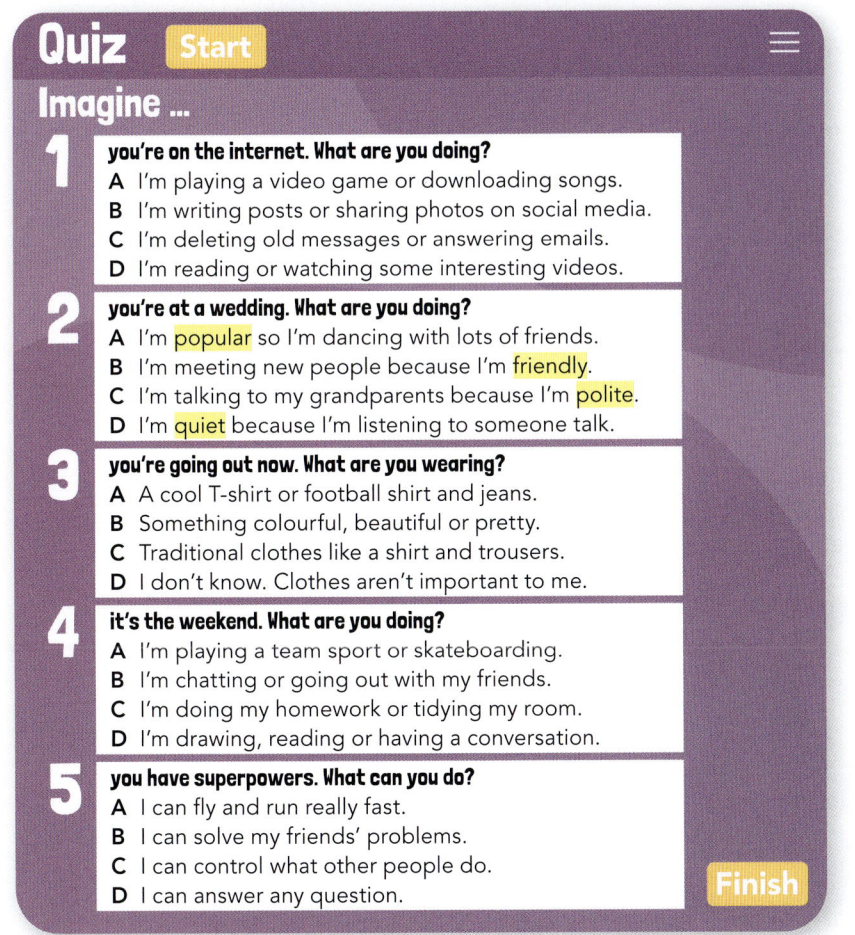

Quiz Start
Imagine ...

1 you're on the internet. What are you doing?
   A I'm playing a video game or downloading songs.
   B I'm writing posts or sharing photos on social media.
   C I'm deleting old messages or answering emails.
   D I'm reading or watching some interesting videos.

2 you're at a wedding. What are you doing?
   A I'm popular so I'm dancing with lots of friends.
   B I'm meeting new people because I'm friendly.
   C I'm talking to my grandparents because I'm polite.
   D I'm quiet because I'm listening to someone talk.

3 you're going out now. What are you wearing?
   A A cool T-shirt or football shirt and jeans.
   B Something colourful, beautiful or pretty.
   C Traditional clothes like a shirt and trousers.
   D I don't know. Clothes aren't important to me.

4 it's the weekend. What are you doing?
   A I'm playing a team sport or skateboarding.
   B I'm chatting or going out with my friends.
   C I'm doing my homework or tidying my room.
   D I'm drawing, reading or having a conversation.

5 you have superpowers. What can you do?
   A I can fly and run really fast.
   B I can solve my friends' problems.
   C I can control what other people do.
   D I can answer any question.

Finish

4 Read the score. Which letter matches your character type?

Score

More As: for energy! You're funny and brave and everybody knows who you are!

More Bs: for feelings! You're kind and patient with others so you're a very good friend.

More Cs: for good results! You're serious and honest, and you always follow the rules.

More Ds: for calm! You're clever and creative and you like learning new things.

5 Read the quiz score again. Answer the questions.
   Which character type ...
   1 likes doing the correct thing?
   _____
   2 loves getting lots of attention?
   _____
   3 enjoys studying how things work?
   _____
   4 loves spending time with others?
   _____

6 **VOCABULARY** Match the highlighted adjectives in the quiz and the score to the meanings.
   1 You don't mind waiting for others. _____
   2 You don't smile very often. _____
   3 You don't feel afraid often. _____
   4 You often say 'please' and 'thank you'. _____
   5 Many people like you. _____
   6 You like telling jokes. _____
   7 You treat other people well. _____
   8 You learn new things quickly. _____
   9 You say things that are true and correct. _____
   10 You don't speak very much. _____
   11 You like making new friends. _____

7 💬 **THINK & SHARE** Work in pairs. Tell each other your quiz results and your opinion about them. Then say which qualities you like or dislike in people and why.

8 💬 Use the sentences in Ex 6 to make questions for people in your class. When a classmate answers *yes* to one of the questions, ask them an extra question about it.

   Do you mind waiting for others?
   Yes, I do. I hate it.
   Why do you hate it?
   Because I think it's boring!

9 💬 **MEDIATION** Work in pairs. Imagine a friend of yours wants to know about the the main character types. Explain what they are.

10 💬 Ask family members and friends to answer the quiz questions. Make a note of their results. Compare your results with your classmates.

VOCABULARY BOOSTER Unit 3   39

3.6 GRAMMAR Use the present simple and present continuous.

Present simple and present continuous

1 Work in pairs. Look at the photos in the article. Choose one and ask and answer the questions.
   1 What's happening in the photo?
   2 What are the people wearing?
   3 What character do you think they have?

2 Read the article. Answer the questions.
   1 Which type is most like you? Why?
   2 What do profile photos say about people?

NewsFeed
News Trending Articles

What does your profile photo say about you?

A picture tells a thousand words. A recent study says that this is true for your profile photo on social media too. It seems your profile photo says a lot about your character.

This person is using a photo of a group of people. It's very colourful. The person is popular and hates staying at home on their own.

In this photo, we have a boy and an object. People who share photos with an object – such as a guitar or a cake – like learning new things. They're often creative.

This girl is covering her face with some flowers. This means she is kind but quiet.

Here the boy is wearing a suit and tie. He's patient and doesn't want to make mistakes.

He's smiling, but the photo is bad. He's kind, honest and friendly. Nice people can't take good photos.

3 Read the text again. Underline all the examples of the present simple. Circle examples of the present continuous.

4 Complete the grammar rules with *present simple* or *present continuous*.

Present simple and present continuous
▶ Grammar animation
We use the ¹_____
1 for something happening at this moment.
2 for something happening around this time.
We use the ²_____
3 for something that always, often or never happens.
4 for a fact that is always true.
5 with certain (stative) verbs that we don't usually use in the *-ing* form, e.g. *need*, *like*, *know*, etc.

GRAMMAR BOOSTER P137

5 Complete the sentences with the present simple or present continuous form of the verbs in brackets.
   1 My dad never _____ colourful ties. (wear)
   2 She _____ a jacket today. (not wear)
   3 Bill _____ today. He's on holiday. (not work)
   4 Jane _____ a good book at the moment. (read)
   5 My brother _____ to school on Wednesdays. (not go)
   6 I _____ the video now. (download)
   7 _____ you _____ maths this week? (study)
   8 How often _____ you _____ exercise? (do)

6 Find examples of stative verbs in the text. Can you add any more?

7 Complete the dialogue with the present simple or present continuous form of the verbs below.

| do draw know love not work study want work |

Jo Look at this profile pic. ¹_____ you _____ who this is?
Em Yeah, it's your cousin, James! What ²_____ he _____ in that photo? Is he holding a pencil?
Jo Yes, he is. I think he ³_____ a picture. He ⁴_____ art – it's his favourite hobby.
Em What ⁵_____ he _____ at the moment? He's a student, isn't he?
Jo Yes, he is – he ⁶_____ to become a doctor, and he ⁷_____ in a café as a waiter every evening.
Em Wow! He works very hard!
Jo Yes, he does … but he ⁸_____ as hard as I do!

8 Work in pairs. Take turns to describe people in your class. Use the present simple or continuous and the verbs below to help you. Can your partner guess who it is?

| do go hate have got like love
  sit speak think wear |

He's got a horse.

Is it Milan? He loves animals.

40 Unit 3

3.7 READING

Deal with unknown words in an article about appearance.

Perfect selfies

1 Work in pairs. Answer the questions.
 1 How often do you take photos of yourself?
 2 Look at the two photos in the article. How are they different from each other?

2 **VOCABULARY** Choose the correct alternative.
 1 Anna's got blond **eyes** / **hair**.
 2 The opposite of curly is **straight** / **wavy**.
 3 In summer, your **eye** / **skin** colour often changes.
 4 Dad's got green **face** / **eyes**, but mine are brown.
 5 My hair isn't very curly; it's **skin** / **wavy**.
 6 The front part of your head is your **face** / **skin**.

3 Work in pairs. Describe a) a person in your family, b) a friend, c) a famous person. Use the words in Ex 2 and the words below to help you.

| big | black | dark | long | nose | pale |
| red | short | small | wide | | |

My dad has got straight, black hair …

STRATEGY Dealing with unknown words

You don't need to know every word to understand a text. When you find an unknown word, decide if it is necessary for general understanding. If it is, keep reading and try to guess the meaning by looking at the context.

4 Read the strategy. Then with a partner discuss this question: what do you usually do when you see an unknown word? Why?

5 Read the first two paragraphs of the article. Underline any unknown words, but keep reading. Answer the questions.
 1 What is important for internet celebrities? Why?
 2 What can you do with technology on a phone?

6 Look at your underlined words. What do you think they mean?

7 🔊 3.13 Read the whole article. Underline any unknown words, but keep reading. Choose the best title for it.
 A Appearance isn't important to teenagers.
 B You can't believe everything you see.
 C Celebrity secrets for taking a great selfie.

8 Read the whole article again. Answer the questions.
 1 How much time do teenagers spend taking photos of themselves?
 2 Which parts of your face can you change with an app?
 3 What does Rankin think about people taking lots of selfies?
 4 What is Rankin's project called? What do you think the name means?
 5 What does he think many celebrities are doing?
 6 What's the difference between the two photos?

9 Look at your underlined words. Do they stop you from understanding? What do you think they mean?

10 Work in pairs. Ask and answer the questions.
 1 What do the people look like in Rankin's photos?
 2 How are the photos different from each other?
 3 Which one do you prefer?

11 **THINK & SHARE** Read these questions and make a note of your ideas. In pairs, discuss them.
 • Why are young people taking lots of photos now?
 • Do you agree with Rankin that photo apps are bad for teenagers? What makes you say this?

12 Write two or three sentences that summarise how you feel about the ideas in the text. Then share with the class and discuss your ideas.

Perfect selfies

Teenagers spend about 55 hours a year taking selfies to post on social media. Maybe they are copying famous celebrities. Social media stars, for example, often share photos of their faces – they think it is essential to look good because they want to get lots of 'likes'. In their photos, they always have perfect skin and make-up. But how do they manage to look so good?

Thanks to apps, you can modify yourself on a smartphone – in under two minutes, you can change your hairstyle. For example, short, straight, blond hair can become long and curly or wavy and blue! You can also delete things that you don't like, such as dark circles under your eyes.

What are these photo apps doing to us? According to Rankin, a British fashion photographer, this 'perfect selfie' culture is a serious problem. He thinks we are starting to compare ourselves to photos that aren't real. This often makes us unhappy with our appearance.

In his project, Selfie Harm, Rankin wants us to understand that many stars are deceiving us. He shows photos of fourteen people between thirteen and nineteen. The original photos are next to the edited pictures on the right. Interestingly, the teenagers all prefer their original photos!

3.8 SPEAKING   Describe photos of people.

Describing photos

1 🔊 **3.14** Listen to Liam describing one of the photos. Which one is he describing?

2 🔊 **3.14** Listen again. Tick (✓) the things Liam mentions.
1 the place
2 how old the people are
3 what they are doing
4 what they are wearing
5 their appearance
6 the number of people
7 their character
8 where they are in the photo
9 what he thinks they are saying

STRATEGY Brainstorming useful vocabulary

When you're preparing to describe a photo, think about the language you need. Try to brainstorm appropriate vocabulary for the topic that you need.

3 💬 Read the strategy. Work in groups. Write as many words in the mind map as you can think of.

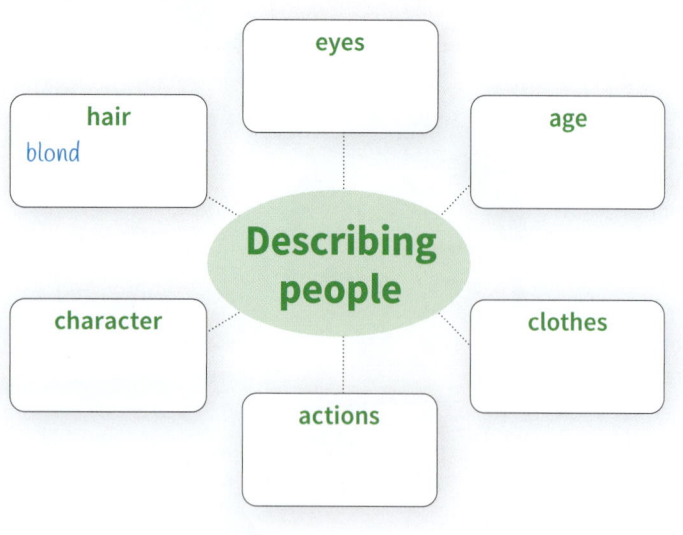

- eyes
- hair — blond
- age
- character
- clothes
- actions

Describing people

4 💬 As a class, share your words. Add any new ones from the other groups.

5 💬 Work in pairs. Describe people in your class. Use as many words as you can from your mind map.

> She's friendly and she's got long, curly red hair. She's wearing a dark green top and she's sitting …

6 Complete the **Phrasebook** with the words below.

background (x2)   got   left
looks   maybe   shows   think

PHRASEBOOK Describing photos

This photo ¹_____ a group of (five) people.
The girl in the foreground / ²_____ …
She's ³_____ (long, dark, curly) hair.
She ⁴_____ quiet and serious.
⁵_____ she's talking to her parents.
In the ⁶_____ there are two boys and a girl.
The boy in the middle / on the right / on the ⁷_____ …
I ⁸_____ they're friends / classmates / in a dance group.

7 🔊 **3.14** Listen, check and repeat.

8 💬 Work in pairs. Take turns to describe photo A. What do you think the people are saying? Use the **Phrasebook** to help you.

9 Student A: look at photo C. Student B: look at photo D. Make a list of all the language you need to describe it.

10 💬 Now describe your photo to your partner. Use your notes from Ex 9 and the **Phrasebook** to help you.

11 **REFLECT** Work in pairs. Answer the questions.
1 Was your description successful? Why? / Why not?
2 Which phrases from the Phrasebook did you use?

42   Unit 3

Write an informal email about yourself. **3.9 WRITING**

An informal email

1 Work in pairs. Read the definition. Ask and answer the questions.

penfriend (noun) a person you make friends with by writing emails or letters, often in another country

1 Have you got a penfriend?
2 How many emails do you send a week?
3 What do you write about?

STRATEGY Writing informal emails

When you write an email, start with a greeting, e.g. *Hello* (name). Use fixed phrases, e.g. *How are you?* Describe yourself, say what you are doing and ask lots of questions. End with *Love / Regards* (your name). Write *P.S.* at the end to add extra information.

2 Read the strategy and the email. Then answer the questions.
1 Who is it from?
2 Who is it for?
3 Does the writer follow all the advice in the strategy?

Dear Mirko,

Thanks for your email! It's great to hear from you!

How are you? I hope you're doing well. I'm tired because I'm studying hard for my exams right now … !

I'm seventeen, I'm from Johannesburg and I'm very happy you're my new penfriend! I'm brave and I love surfing. What do you like doing in your free time? What are you like?

Here's a photo of me and my family. We're sitting in a park. I'm wearing a T-shirt and jeans and I've got long, straight, hair and brown eyes. The girl on the left is my sister, Nora. She's got light brown hair and green eyes, so she doesn't look like me! My little brother, Billy, is on the right. He's got short, blond hair and big, blue eyes. He's popular, friendly and funny. My dad is in the background – he's wearing a cream shirt – and my mum is in the middle in a dark red top. What do you look like? Please send me a photo!

Write soon!
Regards,
Phoebe x

P.S. Do you think I look like my mum too?

3 Put the parts of the email in the correct order.
___ Describe your appearance
___ Describe your family
___ Ask how someone is
___ End the email
___ Greeting
___ Say what you are doing
___ Describe your interests
___ Describe your character

4 Read the email again. Answer the questions.
1 What's Phoebe doing now?
2 What does she like doing in her free time?
3 How does she describe her appearance?
4 Does Nora look like her sister?
5 How does she describe her brother's character?
6 What are her parents wearing?
7 Which family member does Phoebe look like?

5 Complete the fixed phrases with a word below. Then read the email again and check your answers.

dear   doing   for   hear   regards   write

Hi / [1]_____ / Hello Mirko,
Thanks [2]_____ your email / letter.
It's great to [3]_____ from you!
I hope you're [4]_____ well.
[5]_____ soon!
[6]_____, Phoebe

6 Read the Language focus. Which question asks about interests (I), appearance (A) or character (C)?

LANGUAGE FOCUS *like*

The word *like* has many different meanings and uses.
___ : What do you like doing? I love surfing.
      What do you like? Chocolate cake!
___ : What are you like? I'm popular and friendly.
___ : Who do you look like? My mother. We both have long, black hair.

7 Match the questions to the answers.
1 What do you look like?
2 Who do you look like in your family?
3 What do you like doing?
4 What are you like?
5 What's your mum like?

A I'm polite and serious.
B I love taking photos and making videos.
C She's quiet and clever.
D I've got long, blond hair and grey eyes.
E I look like my dad.

8 Work in pairs. Ask and answer the questions in Ex 7 about you.

What do you look like?   I've got …

9 Imagine you have a new penfriend. Think of a photo of you which you like. Make a note of all the things you can see in it. Use the list in Ex 3 to help you.

10 Now write an email introducing yourself. Refer to your notes and say …
• what you are doing now.
• what you look like / what you're like.
• what you like / what you like doing.

11 ✓ **CHECK YOUR WORK**
• Does your email have a greeting and an ending?
• Do you mention the main points?
• Is your use of *like* correct?
• Is your use of the present simple / continuous correct?

Unit 3   43

3.10 REVIEW

Grammar

1 Complete the dialogue with the present continuous form of the verbs below.

> dance   go   not be   not have   not wear
> share   stand   talk   wear

A   I **¹**_____ some photos online now. Do you want to see them?
B   Yes, please! What **²**_____ you _____ in the first photo? Those clothes are really unusual.
A   We **³**_____ to a wedding in that photo. We **⁴**_____ our normal clothes – we're dressed in our national costume.
B   Ah, I see. And what about that photo at the wedding? **⁵**_____ you _____ to your friends?
A   No, I **⁶**_____. I **⁷**_____ with my cousins.
B   Why **⁸**_____ that boy _____ in the corner on his own? He doesn't look very happy.
A   Oh, that's Malik. He **⁹**_____ much fun because he can't stand big groups of people.
B   Oh dear.

2 Complete the sentences with the present simple or continuous form of the verbs in brackets.
1   Liza _____ at all her old photos right now. (look)
2   I'm sorry, but I _____ you. (not believe)
3   Pria _____ very happy. Is she OK? (not look)
4   Carlos really _____ doing online quizzes. (love)
5   My classmates _____ right now; they _____. (not work / talk)
6   Wait! We _____ to come with you. (want)
7   My brother _____ black hair and blue eyes. (have)
8   I _____ a shower. Can you answer the phone? (have)

Vocabulary

3 Complete the sentences with the correct words.
1   My bedroom looks white, but it's actually c___ ___ ___ ___.
2   Don't forget your j___ ___ ___ ___ ___. It's cold outside.
3   Dad always wears a shirt and t___ ___ to work.
4   I can't walk in these s___ ___ ___ ___. They're very small!
5   I love your dress. You look p___ ___ ___ ___ ___ in it.
6   When the sun's hot, it's a good idea to wear a h___ ___ on your head.
7   A Scottish kilt looks like a s___ ___ ___ ___, but it isn't.
8   My favourite t___ ___ ___ is this dark green T-shirt.

4 Complete the sentences with the character adjectives below.

> brave   clever   honest   kind   patient   polite   quiet

1   You're so _____ – you never forget to say 'sorry', 'please' and 'thank you'.
2   I believe everything he tells me because he's always _____ with me.
3   My sister is doing very well at high school because she works hard and she's _____ too.
4   I don't like speaking in front of a lot of people, but it's important to be _____ and do it anyway.
5   Raul doesn't talk much – he's a very _____ boy.
6   Our English teacher is very _____ – she doesn't mind waiting for us to answer her questions.
7   _____ people are nice to others and like helping.

Cumulative review

5 Choose the correct alternative.

> **Who are the people in Gen Z?**
> Generation Z, or Gen Z, describes the young people born between 1997 and 2010. Gen Z is very special because it's the first generation of people that **¹aren't knowing / don't know** what life is like without the internet or social media.
> What **²do / are** the people in Gen Z like? Many people say that they're quite **³funny / serious** because they care a lot about the problems in the world and try to make it a better place. They also **⁴understand / are understanding** a lot about computers and technology and **⁵like / are liking** trying new things from different cultures.
> What **⁶are / do** they like doing? As they love meeting up with other young people, they're usually **⁷friendly / funny**. But studies show that they **⁸don't always go out / aren't always going out** in their free time. In fact, they often prefer staying at home. People from Gen Z often **⁹play / are playing** video games in their free time and they really **¹⁰enjoy / are enjoying** watching TV or films too.
> And what **¹¹is / does** Gen Z look like? Today, many teenagers **¹²want / are wanting** to wear fashion from the early 2000s, for example, a long **¹³socks / shirt** with baggy jeans. And instead of light colours, like **¹⁴dark / pale** blue, people in Gen Z prefer strong colours like red or black. And they **¹⁵aren't wearing / don't wear** long, beautiful dresses or suits at the moment – instead, they prefer active clothes like short trousers and **¹⁶ties / T-shirts**.

Think & share

6 Read the quote. Then answer the questions.

> ❝ **Beauty begins the moment you decide to be yourself.** ❞
> *Coco Chanel*

1   What is your idea of a beautiful person?
2   Do you and your friends dress like each other or do you each have your own style?
3   What do teenagers in your country look like at the moment?
4   What do you think Gen Z is really like?

3.11 EXAM SKILLS

Reading

EXAM STRATEGY

When you do a true / false task, read the statements carefully and underline the key information in each one. Then read the text and find any matching information.

1 Read the strategy above. Then look at the exam task in Ex 2. Underline the most important words in each statement. Then find the matching information in the text. There is an example to help you.

2 Read the posts about teenagers and clothes. For each statement 1–6, write true (T) or false (F).

DISCUSSION BOARD

I have a job in a café on Saturdays so I have some money, but I don't want to spend it all on clothes. I don't like walking around the shops for hours either. I like to buy books and listen to music. My friends think I'm a very serious person! Some of my friends wear different clothes every day. They're always taking selfies and posting them online. The problem is that social media stars share photos and videos of themselves every day. They always wear different clothes and have perfect make-up. My friends want to do the same. But these celebrities don't pay for their clothes. Shops send them new designs. This means that their followers are spending a lot of money, but social media stars are not. It's not right!

Talia

I like clothes, but I don't buy many. I often go to town with my friends at the weekend, but I also enjoy having lunch with them or going to the cinema. At the moment, I'm doing a project on fast fashion at school. Fast fashion is when people buy cheap clothes and only wear them a few times. Then they buy some more. I think fast fashion is terrible because it is bad for the world around us. My sister Lia is very creative. She designs clothes, but she makes new clothes from old clothes. She's quite popular because she gives these clothes to her friends or to people in the family. She also sells them to other people on her website. Right now, she is making me a jacket. It's really cool.

Jack

1 <u>Talia works</u> at the <u>weekend</u>. ___
2 She enjoys buying clothes. ___
3 Celebrities don't buy their clothes. ___
4 Jack sometimes has lunch with friends at the weekend. ___
5 His project is about designer clothes. ___
6 Lia sells clothes to her friends. ___

Speaking

EXAM STRATEGY

When you describe a photo, try to say as much as you can. For example, you can speculate or make guesses about what the photo shows. There aren't any right or wrong answers.

3 Read the strategy above. Then complete the prompts with one of the words below. There is one word that you do not need.

| about | like | look | maybe | sure | think |

1 They look _____ seventeen.
2 They _____ like they're friends.
3 I _____ they're in a shopping centre.
4 It looks like London, but I'm not _____.
5 _____ they're celebrating.

4 Look at photos A and B below. Choose one of the photos and describe it. The following ideas may help you.
- the place
- the people
- what they are doing
- what they look like
- who they might be

Exam skills 45

3 VISION 360° Learn about technology and communication and create an idea for a video game
A living room

Unit 3 360° hotspots ▲ ★ ● ◆ ♥ ■

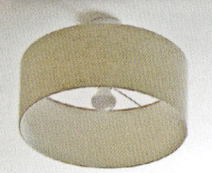

1 **THINK & SHARE** Work in pairs. Read the definitions. Think of ways to chill out. Which activities are sociable and which ones aren't? Make two lists.

chill out /tʃɪl aʊt/ **(v)** spend time relaxing
sociable /ˈsəʊʃəb(ə)l/ **(adj)** enjoying spending time with other people

EXPLORE 360°
Access the interactive 360° content now!

2 Look around the room. Who do you think the people are? What are they doing?

3 **ALL HOTSPOTS** Read or listen to the hotspots. Describe what's happening in each hotspot in one sentence.
▲ Tom's talking to his grandma on the phone.

4 ▲ Listen to the conversation. Answer the questions.
1 What does Tom always do on Saturdays?
2 Where are his brothers and sisters right now?
3 What is his sister Gabi doing?
4 What are the others doing?

5 ★ Read the messages. Do you send messages when you're watching a TV programme? Why? / Why not?

6 ● ■ Read or listen to the hotspots. Are the sentences true (T) or false (F)?
1 Five people are designing a game.
2 Isabel is looking for someone.
3 Oliver can't help her.
4 Alice knows where the key is.
5 The boy using his phone is doing something sociable.
6 He's discussing vlogs with friends.

7 ◆ Listen to the conversation. Answer the questions.
1 Is Katy living at home now? Why? / Why not?
2 Why is Bella feeling sad?
3 What are Katy's teachers like?
4 What are the other students like?
5 Does Katy like Jade? Why? / Why not?
6 What does Bella think of Katy's new top?

8 ♥ Read the online article. Work in pairs and discuss the questions.
1 What do people often like to do when they are with friends?
2 How important are these activities?
3 How often do you look at your phone when you're with friends?
4 Do you prefer to have real conversations or online ones? Give reasons.

46 Vision 360

Digital literacy

9 Work in pairs. Read the opinions about playing video games. Do you agree with them? Why? / Why not? Discuss and give reasons.

- It's a good way to relax.
- It isn't very sociable.
- It can make you clever.
- You can have fun.
- It's a good idea to stop playing after an hour.
- It can affect things like sleep and exercise.

10 **THINK & SHARE** Think about your answer to Ex 1 and what you have learned about technology and communication. Do you want to move any activities to a different list?

CREATE … an idea for a video game

STEP 1
RESEARCH IT!
Go online and find the answers to the questions.
1 What's a popular video game in your country / the world?
2 How many people can play it?
3 What do they do in it?

STEP 2
You are going to create an idea for a video game. Work in groups. Discuss the type of game and what you want the players to do in it. Choose some of the ideas below or think of your own ideas.

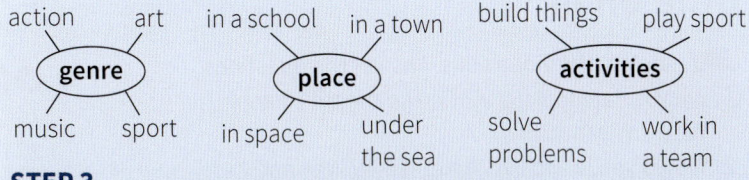

genre: action, art, music, sport
place: in a school, in a town, in space, under the sea
activities: build things, play sport, solve problems, work in a team

STEP 3
Do research online to find ideas and information for your game. Make notes.

STEP 4
Use your notes to describe your game. Find photos online to use in it.

STEP 5
Look at the video game ideas of other groups in your class. Say one thing you like about each game and decide which one you want to play.

Vision 360 47

4 Where we live

- **VOCABULARY**
  Houses and rooms
  Places and geographical features
- **GRAMMAR**
  Comparative adjectives
  Superlative adjectives
- **READING**
  Favourite countries
- **LISTENING**
  Unusual houses
- **GLOBAL SKILLS**
  Designing a better classroom
- **SPEAKING**
  Asking for and giving directions
- **WRITING**
  A description of a place
- **DOCUMENTARY**
  Fairytale house

VOCABULARY BOOSTER P118–119
GRAMMAR BOOSTER P138–139

Come on in

1 Look at the video stills. Answer the questions.
   1 What is Zara looking at? Do you think it's her house? Why? / Why not?
   2 Would you like to live there? Why? / Why not?

2 ▶ 4.01 Watch or listen. Answer the questions.
   1 What is Callum doing?
   2 Where is the flat?
   3 Is Callum enjoying his visit?

   carpet – cloth covering the floor in homes
   mansion – a very large house

3 ▶ 4.01 Watch or listen again. Complete the sentences.
   1 Zara can't visit the flat because she's got _____.
   2 Their cousin, James, is a _____.
   3 Zara _____ the carpet on the floor.
   4 The kitchen has got some _____ in it.
   5 The flat is only _____ minutes from the centre.
   6 The house has got _____ bedrooms.
   7 From one of the bedrooms, you can see the _____ outside.
   8 The kitchen is very _____.

48 Unit 4

Talk about houses and rooms.   **4.1 VOCABULARY**

4 **VOCABULARY** Label the photos with the words below.

> balcony bathroom bedroom cupboard
> dining room flat floor fridge hall
> kitchen living room oven sink sofa

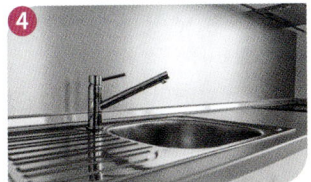

5 **VOCABULARY** Which of these adjectives can describe the photos in Ex 4?

> clean comfortable dirty huge large narrow small

6 Think about your house, your school, etc. Can you give examples for each of the adjectives in Ex 5?

7 **REAL ENGLISH** Match the words and phrases in **bold** to the meanings.
1 **Come on in** and let's take a look!
2 So, it's OK, I **guess**.
3 **I'm not a fan of** the colour.
4 … **not too bad**! It's small, but it's got everything you need.
5 **Hang on**, I'm sure I've got photos here.
6 **Check it out.**

A wait a moment
B please enter
C quite good
D think
E Look at this.
F I don't like

8 🔊 **4.02** Listen to a boy being interviewed about his new home. Answer the questions.
1 Does he live in a house or a flat?
2 What's his favourite room?
3 What colour is it?

9 🔊 **4.02** Listen again. Label the floor plan with the words below.

> balcony bathroom bedroom (x3) cupboard
> hall kitchen living room shower

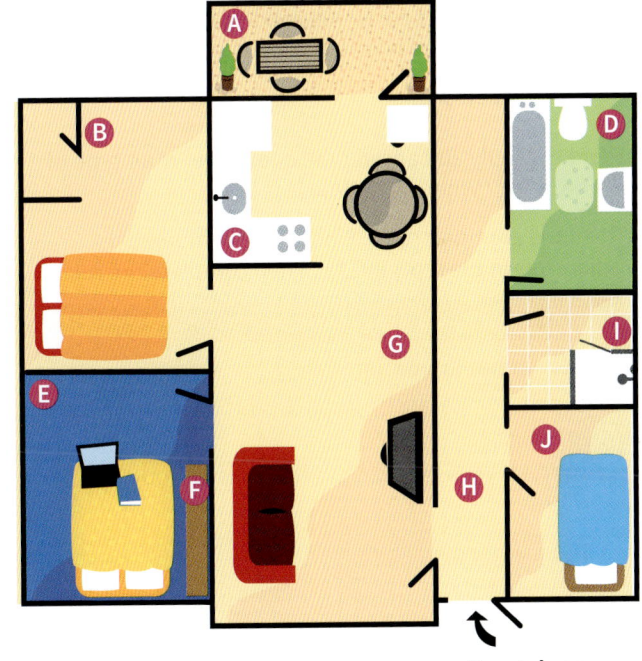

Front door

10 Draw a plan of your home. Label the rooms.

11 💬 Write some questions to ask your partner about their home or the house of their dreams. Then take turns to interview each other and take notes on the answers.

> Is it a flat or a house?
>
> What's the living room like?
>
> How many bathrooms are there?
>
> What's your favourite room and why?

12 💬 Tell your class about your partner's home.

VOCABULARY BOOSTER Unit 4   49

4.2 GRAMMAR — Use comparative adjectives to talk about places.

Comparative adjectives

1 💬 Work in pairs. Describe the photo from a reply to Zara's question 'What's the house of your dreams?'

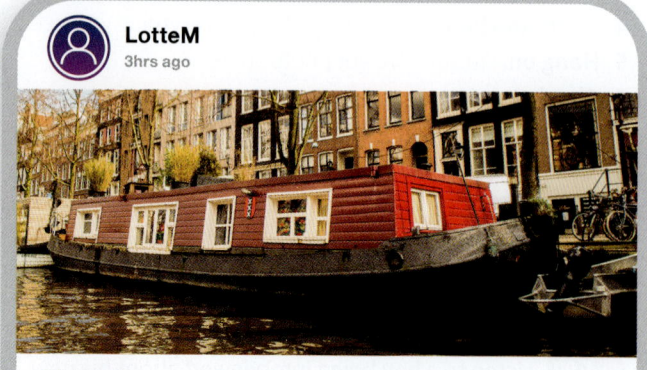

LotteM 3hrs ago

@LotteM
I & Z – My cousin Marta lives on this houseboat in Amsterdam – there are over 2,500 houseboats there! It's the house of her dreams! I think it is very small. My living room is bigger than Marta's home!!! 😂 Her home hasn't got any bedrooms – it's open-plan, but there is a small bathroom. The kitchen in my flat is larger than Marta's and hers is narrower too. Houseboats in the centre are more popular, but they're also more expensive than in other parts of the city. My cousin is living in a quieter area, but it's further from her work. Which is better: a flat or a houseboat? Marta thinks living on the water is more beautiful, but I don't agree. Houseboats are worse than flats because they're often older, dirtier and wetter.

open-plan – a space which hasn't got any walls in it

2 Read the reply and answer the questions. What type of home is this? Where is it? Whose is it?

3 Read the grammar rules. Find all the comparative adjectives in the reply in Ex 2. Then complete the rules.

Comparative adjectives
▶ Grammar animation
We use a comparative adjective and *than* to compare two things.
They're more expensive than houseboats in other parts of the city.

Short adjectives

old	1 _____	+ -er
big	2 _____	double consonant + -er
dirty	3 _____	-y > -ier
large	4 _____	+ -r

Long adjectives

popular	5 _____	*more* + adjective

Irregular

good	6 _____	
bad	7 _____	
far	8 _____	

GRAMMAR BOOSTER P138

50 Unit 4

4 Choose the correct alternative. Use the reply to help you.
1 Marta's home is **smaller** / **larger** than Lotte's.
2 Lotte's kitchen is **smaller** / **bigger** than Marta's.
3 It is **cheaper** / **more expensive** to live in the centre.
4 Marta's home is **nearer to** / **further from** her work.
5 Lotte thinks flats are **better** / **worse** than houseboats.
6 Lotte says many flats are **cleaner** / **dirtier** and **newer** / **older** than houseboats.

5 💬 Work in pairs. Complete the sentences in the quiz with a comparative form of the adjective in brackets and *than*.

Quiz: true or false?
1 The Eiffel Tower is _____ (tall) the Statue of Liberty.
2 Amsterdam is _____ (large) Berlin.
3 English winters are _____ (cold) Scottish winters.
4 Gold is _____ (expensive) silver.
5 A kilometre is _____ (long) a mile.
6 The temperature on Mercury is _____ (high) on Venus.

6 🔊 4.05 Do the quiz. Are the sentences true or false? Listen and check.

7 🔊 4.06 Listen to the podcast. How many houseboats are there in London? Which city has more: London or Amsterdam?

8 🔊 4.06 Complete the summary with the comparative form of the adjectives below. Then listen again and check.

early   expensive   friendly   good
high   hot   near   popular

In London, houseboats are ¹_____ than ever – many young people live in them. There is a ²_____ number in East London than anywhere else in England. Jake gets to work ³_____ because he lives ⁴_____ to the centre. Flats which are further away are ⁵_____ than Jake's bigger houseboat. People on houseboats are ⁶_____ than many other people in the city. Jake thinks that houseboats are ⁷_____ in the summer than the winter because the temperature is ⁸_____.

9 **PRONUNCIATION** 🔊 4.07 The schwa /ə/ is a common weak vowel sound in English. Pay attention to *-er* and *than* in connected speech. Listen and repeat the words.
1 /ə/ bigg**er**, furth**er**, clean**er**, happi**er**
2 /ə/ **A** flat is bett**er** th**a**n **a** houseboat.

10 🔊 4.08 Circle the schwa sounds in the sentence. Then listen and check.
The cupboard in her sister's flat is smaller than my mother's.

11 💬 **THINK & SHARE** Work in pairs. Compare your opinions about these pairs of things. Use the adjectives in brackets. Give reasons for your answers.
1 flats / houseboats (good / bad)
2 Amsterdam / Dubai (old / new)
3 My kitchen / my living room (important / unimportant)
4 bed / sofa (uncomfortable / comfortable)
5 bath / shower (good / bad)
6 science / languages (easy / difficult)

> I think houseboats are worse than flats because they're narrower.

Recognise prepositions of place in an interview about unusual houses.

4.3 LISTENING

Unusual houses

A B C D

1 **Work in pairs.** Look at the photos and the names below. Try to guess the names of the houses.

Crazy House   Glass House
Mirror House   Seashell House

shell – the hard part of an animal that lives in the sea
upside down – in a position where the top of something is where the bottom usually is

2 🔊 **4.09** Listen and check.

STRATEGY Recognising prepositions of place

To understand where things or people are in a text, you need to recognise prepositions of place, e.g. *in* and *on*.
There's a toilet *in* my bathroom.
There's a glass *on* the table.

3 Read the **strategy**. Label the diagram with the prepositions below.

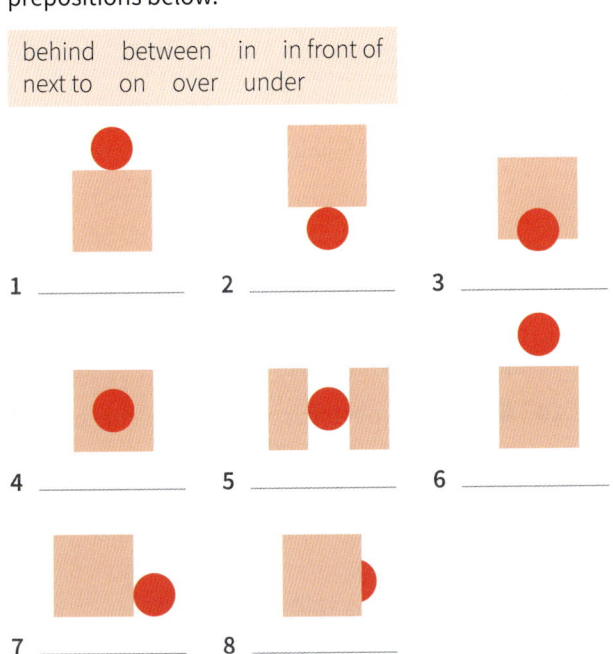

behind   between   in   in front of
next to   on   over   under

1 _____   2 _____   3 _____
4 _____   5 _____   6 _____
7 _____   8 _____

4 Which houses (A–D) in Ex 1 do the sentences describe?
  1 It's between other houses.
  2 There are mirrors on the outside.
  3 There's a roof under the house.
  4 There are mountains behind it.
  5 It isn't next to the sea: it's in the city.
  6 It disappears when it's in front of you.
  7 People live in it.
  8 The floor is over your head.

5 🔊 **4.09** Listen again and check.

6 💬 Work in pairs. Ask and answer questions about where things are in the photos.

> Where's the roof in the Crazy House?
>
> It's on the ground!

7 🔊 **4.10** Listen to an interview for a TV programme. Where are the people?

8 🔊 **4.10** Listen again. Are the sentences true (T) or false (F)?
  1 The name of the programme is 'Unusual Homes'. ____
  2 The presenter shows the man some photos. ____
  3 There are photos of a living room and a bedroom. ____
  4 The Crazy House is in Mexico City. ____
  5 The balcony has got some chairs under it. ____
  6 The man imagines the Seashell House is easier to clean. ____
  7 He likes the Seashell House more. ____
  8 He says the sofa next to the wall is beautiful. ____

9 💬 **THINK & SHARE** Work in pairs. Ask and answer the questions.
  • Which house do you prefer and why?
  • Which house is worse than the others? Why?
  • Choose two houses. Can you compare them with each other?
  • Do you know any other unusual houses? Where are they? What do they look like?

Unit 4   51

4.4 GLOBAL SKILLS — Identify problems and think of solutions.

Designing a better classroom

1. 💬 Work in pairs. Look at photos A–D. What rooms and furniture can you see? Which ones do you prefer? Compare them using the adjectives below.

   big   boring   clean   creative   dark   dirty   interesting
   light   modern   narrow   old   practical   serious   small

   A   B
   C   D

2. Read about the competition and answer the questions.
   1. How many hours are students at school?
   2. What does a 21st-century classroom look like?
   3. What is the competition about?
   4. How much money can you win?

   ★ Competitions ★

   Competition: design a better classroom

   Many students spend over 40 hours a week in school.
   A study shows that a 21st-century classroom can help you learn better. Tips for good classroom design:
   • Put group projects and art on the walls to make a classroom look more beautiful.
   • Use pictures, e.g. charts and maps, to make learning easier.
   • Put photos of amazing people in front of you.
   • Use natural light to feel more active.
   • Keep spaces tidier – leave 40% of the walls empty and put things in cupboards.
   • Make classrooms friendlier for wheelchairs by making space for them to move around.

   Can YOU design a better classroom?
   Send us your ideas and win £500 for your new classroom!
   More information on #redecorateyourschool.

   wheelchair – a chair with wheels for people who can't walk

3. 💬 Work in pairs. Discuss your own classroom. Use the questions below to help you.
   • How much work is there on your walls?
   • How many photos of people are there?
   • How much light is there?
   • How tidy is it?
   • How much space is there?

4. 🔊 4.11 Read these students' problems. Then listen to them discussing the problems. Number them in the order they talk about them.
   A Our classroom walls are all the same colour. ___
   B Some students need to relax more. ___
   C Wheelchair users can't enter the room. ___
   D Our classroom is old and dirty. ___
   E There isn't space to work in groups. ___

5. 🔊 4.11 Match solution 1–5 to problems A–E in Ex 4. Listen again and check your answers.
   1. Have lessons in rooms with wider doors, e.g. the hall. ___
   2. Move the desks so students can face each other. ___
   3. Paint the walls different colours. ___
   4. Tidy the room and show new work. ___
   5. Make a part of the classroom more comfortable. ___

6. Read the steps. Choose the correct alternative.

   Better Problem-solving skills

   Step 1: **Identify** / **Solve** what the problem is.
   Step 2: Think about possible solutions and **say** / **write** down your ideas.
   Step 3: **Consider** / **Solve** which of your ideas are better.
   Step 4: **Ask** / **Decide** together what the best solution is.

7. Read the Phrasebook. Which steps does it help with?

   PHRASEBOOK Problem-solving
   I find (groupwork) difficult.
   Why don't we … ?
   How about (choosing three colours)?
   I'm not so sure. Maybe … is a better idea?
   Good / Great idea!
   I agree! Let's (buy) …

8. 💬 Work in pairs. Think about your own classroom and follow these steps.
   1. Identify any problems.
   2. Think of solutions.
   3. Consider all your ideas.
   4. Decide on the best solution.

9. 💬 Work in groups. Compare your ideas. Then design your new classroom. Use the Phrasebook and the steps in Ex 6 to help you.

10. 💬 Share your ideas as a class. Decide on the top three problems and solutions.

11. 💬 **THINK & SHARE** Discuss the questions.
    1. Do you enjoy problem-solving in a team?
    2. Which parts do you find easier or more difficult?
    3. Are you happy with your final idea?
    4. Are there any other ideas that you like?

52 Unit 4

Talk about places and geographical features. **4.5 VOCABULARY**

Places in the world

1 💬 Work in pairs. Look at the photos. Which country do you think they are in? What words do you know to describe them?

2 Read the quiz and choose the correct answer: A or B.

3 🔊 **4.12** Listen and check.

4 **VOCABULARY** Complete the table with the highlighted places in the quiz. Can you add any other words?

Natural	Man-made

5 Find the highlighted opposites of the adjectives in the quiz.
   1 narrow   4 wet
   2 quiet   5 short
   3 modern   6 shallow

6 💬 Work in pairs. Take turns to compare two places in the quiz. Use the adjectives below in the comparative form.

   ancient busy deep dry
   famous modern narrow wide

   > I think the buildings in Tulum are more ancient than those in Acapulco.

7 Complete the text about Singapore with the words and phrases below.

   ancient buildings   busy streets   dry deserts
   high mountains   long rivers   modern architecture
   Ocean   thick forest

   Singapore is both a city and a country. It is on an island in the South China Sea, which is a part of the Pacific ¹_____. Its highest point is only 180 metres. There aren't any hills or ²_____. It's very hot, but it often rains – it hasn't got any ³_____. There aren't any ⁴_____ either – the main one is only 3.2 km long. And the capital isn't full of old squares with ⁵_____. So, why is Singapore so popular with tourists? Firstly, it's amazing for shopping. Areas like Chinatown are always full of people and have ⁶_____ and shops. The city centre is also famous for its ⁷_____ and many tall buildings. And just outside the city, in a big park with a lake, many tourists come to see the 'super' trees. But these enormous trees aren't in a ⁸_____. They are new, man-made structures which are 25 to 50 metres tall.

8 💬 Work in pairs. Ask and answer the questions.
   1 Which is better – life in a town or city, or life in the country? Why?
   2 How does Singapore compare with your home town?

9 💬 **THINK & SHARE** Think of two places in your country. Write five sentences to compare them with some of the places in the quiz. Then share your ideas with your partner.

🏠 > Travel > Competitions

How good is your geography? Take part in our competition to win a free holiday!

1 Which of these busy squares with tall buildings and wide streets has more visitors?

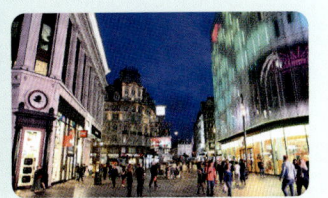

A Times Square   B Leicester Square

2 Which of these famous beaches is next to a deep ocean?

A Tulum   B Acapulco

3 Which of these seas is a very large, ancient lake?

A the Caspian Sea   B the North Sea

4 What is the island of Singapore more famous for?

A its modern architecture   B its thick forests

5 Which place has got a longer river going through it?

A the Brazilian rainforest   B a dry desert in Africa

VOCABULARY BOOSTER Unit 4 53

4.6 GRAMMAR Use superlative adjectives to talk about your local area.

Superlative adjectives

1 💬 Work in pairs. Where is the girl? Is the place natural or man-made?

Trending articles

Where can you take great selfies?
#Instagram Top 3

1 The Grand Canyon is the most famous national park in the USA. Maybe this is because it is one of the deepest canyons with some of the highest and most ancient rock structures. But it is also one of the most dangerous places in the world. Each year, people fall while trying to take a cool selfie.

2 In Valencia, there is a lot of amazing modern architecture. One of the best examples of this is L'Oceanogràfic. The biggest aquarium in Europe is just outside the city centre and it's near to some of the widest and longest beaches in Spain.

3 Santorini is one of the most popular islands in the Mediterranean Sea because its blue and white buildings look great in photos. But it isn't one of the emptiest. In fact, this is the worst Greek island to visit in August. In the busiest month, thousands of people fill Santorini's narrow streets and squares all trying to take the best selfies ever.

canyon – a deep valley with a river running through it

2 Read the text. Match sentences A–C to places 1–3.
  A This place has got a lot of visitors in the summer. ____
  B This place is popular, but it isn't very safe. ____
  C This place has got many new buildings in it. ____

3 Underline all the examples of the superlative form in the article. Then complete the table.

Superlative adjectives
▶ Grammar animation

Short adjective	Superlative	Rule
long	the longest	+ -est
big	1 _____	double consonant + -est
empty	2 _____	-y → -iest
wide	3 _____	+ -st
Long adjective	**Superlative**	**Rule**
famous	4 _____	the most + adjective
Irregular adjective	**Superlative**	
good	5 _____	
bad	6 _____	
far	the furthest / farthest	

GRAMMAR BOOSTER P139

4 Choose the correct alternative.
  1 Deserts are the **driest / wettest** places in the world.
  2 I love Central Park. It's the **best / worst** place.
  3 The most **modern / ancient** architecture in the world is the Egyptian pyramids.
  4 Asia is the **largest / smallest** continent.
  5 This is my **best / worst** selfie ever. I hate it.
  6 Mountains are the **safest / most dangerous** places.

5 Complete the quiz. Use the superlative form of the adjectives in brackets.
  1 What's _____ mountain in the world? (high)
  2 What's _____ river in Europe? (long)
  3 Which country is _____ from the UK? (far)
  4 Where's _____ canyon in the world? (deep)
  5 What's _____ city? (expensive)
  6 What's _____ country in the world? (small)
  7 Which is _____ tropical rainforest? (large)
  8 Where's _____ national park in the world? (big)

6 💬 Work in pairs. Ask and answer the quiz questions. Use the places below to help you.

China   Everest   Greenland   New Zealand
Singapore   the Amazon   the Volga   Vatican City

7 🔊 4.15 Listen and check.

8 💬 Work in pairs. Compare the places below using the adjectives given.
large: cities / squares / balconies
dry: deserts / rainforests / tropical islands
narrow: a river / a sea / an ocean
high: a beach / a hill / a mountain
busy: a city centre / a small town / the country

> Squares are larger than balconies, but cities are the largest.

9 **THINK & SHARE** Ask and answer questions about your local area. Use superlative adjectives.
  • good / place for a selfie
  • interesting / square / city centre
  • ancient and modern / building
  • expensive / place / town
  • bad / place to visit
  • near / lake or sea / your home

> Where's the best place for a selfie? Why?

10 Imagine that a foreign student is coming to visit your class. Complete the short message below. Tell them all about the most interesting things in your local area, according to you and your classmate(s).

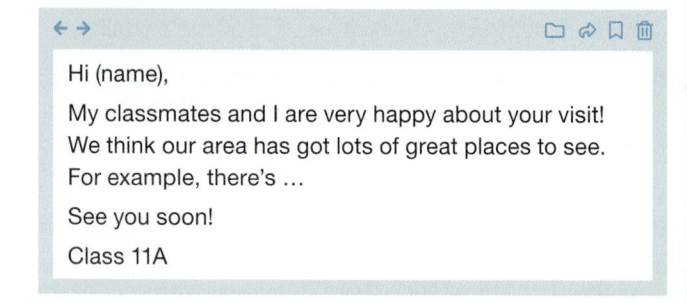

Hi (name),
My classmates and I are very happy about your visit! We think our area has got lots of great places to see. For example, there's …
See you soon!
Class 11A

54 Unit 4

Recognise different word forms in a factual text about countries.

4.7 READING

Favourite countries

1 How many countries can you name? You have got two minutes.

2 💬 Work in pairs. Read the introduction to the article and look at the photos. Try and think of some interesting facts about each country.

What a wonderful world!

What's your favourite country in the world? This is a very hard question to answer! But here are a few facts about some of the most interesting and wonderful places on Earth.

Peru has the second-largest area of rainforest after Brazil. The thick Amazon rainforest has the highest number of different birds on Earth. It also has the world's fastest river. Many other amazing animals, plants and insects live there too.
- The Andes have many very old and beautiful sites, like the city of Cusco. But the most popular place is Machu Picchu.
- Probably the strangest thing in Peru is its enormous desert drawings – the Nazca Lines. Nobody knows why these exist. Some people think they are alien art!

Hungary isn't near the sea, but it is popular for beach holidays because of Lake Balaton. This is the largest lake in Central Europe.
- There is no better place to feel well and healthy than in one of Hungary's many natural spas.
- It's also easy to see why Budapest is one of the most popular European cities. It has many old buildings and long bridges over the Danube. This fast, wide river runs through ten countries, from the Black Forest in Germany to the Black Sea in Romania. But it is not black!
- Hungarian is also one of the most unusual languages – it has got 44 letters. Many people say it is the hardest language in the world to learn!

Japan has got faster ways to travel and more modern cities than Europe, and people can find work easily there.
- Japan has also got very little crime. People can walk around with their backpacks open!
- Not only is Japanese food one of the healthiest, it also includes one of the strangest fruits. Japanese watermelons are square because they are easier to fit in fridges – and easier to cut!
- And because they eat healthily, Japanese people live longer than anyone else – some up to 117 years!

alien – a creature from another world
crime – an illegal act, e.g. stealing

3 🔊 4.16 Read the text. Check your answers in Ex 2.

STRATEGY Recognising different word forms

Try to identify the different forms of words that appear in a text. If you know one form, it can help you to understand the meaning of other forms. We form different words from some adjectives, e.g. from the adjective *quick*: *quicker* (comparative), *the quickest* (superlative) and *quickly* (adverb).

4 Read the strategy. Then complete the table. Use the text to help you.

Adjective	Comparative	Superlative	Adverb
_____	_____	_____	fast
_____	_____	the easiest	_____
good	_____	_____	_____
_____	healthier	_____	_____

5 Read the text again. Write the name of the countries.
1 _____ is the best place to go to for a hot water bath.
2 It is very easy and safe to travel in _____.
3 Many languages are easier than the one from _____.
4 One of the easiest places in the world to find many different living creatures is _____.
5 _____ has the healthiest and oldest people in it.
6 One of the most famous rivers is in _____, but it isn't the world's fastest.
7 _____ has a river that flows faster than any others.
8 In _____, you can eat very well and healthily.
9 _____ is a good place to see unusual and ancient architecture.

6 💬 Work in pairs. Ask and answer the questions.
- Which of these countries is most interesting to you?
- What is the most unusual fact in these texts? Why?
- What's your favourite country in the world? Why?

7 Choose the correct alternative.
The Japanese are very [1]**healthy** / **healthiest** people because they eat the [2]**higher** / **highest** amount of fish. In the USA, fast food is [3]**more** / **most** popular, but it is [4]**bad** / **worse** for your health. Only 20% of the US population is young, so most people are [5]**oldest** / **older**. Many people in the USA live [6]**well** / **good** because it is [7]**easiest** / **easier** to find work in US cities, but some of them aren't very [8]**safe** / **safely**.

8 **MEDIATION** Imagine you have won a travel competition and the prize is a holiday to Peru, Hungary or Japan. Write to your friend, telling them which one you will choose and say why. Use two or three ideas from the text.

9 Write a list of all the things that you think make your country interesting. Think about the things below.

famous places   food   language
nature   unusual facts

10 **THINK & SHARE** Work in small groups. Share and compare your ideas.

Unit 4 55

4.8 SPEAKING Ask for and give directions.

Asking for and giving directions

1 💬 Work in pairs. Look at the floor plan of the school. Answer the questions.
1. How many classrooms are there?
2. What other rooms are there?
3. How does it compare to your school?

2 💬 Work in pairs. Ask and answer where the places are.

Classroom 1   Hall   Teacher's room   Canteen   Library

> Where's Classroom 1?

>> It's on the ground floor, next to Classroom 2, opposite the stairs.

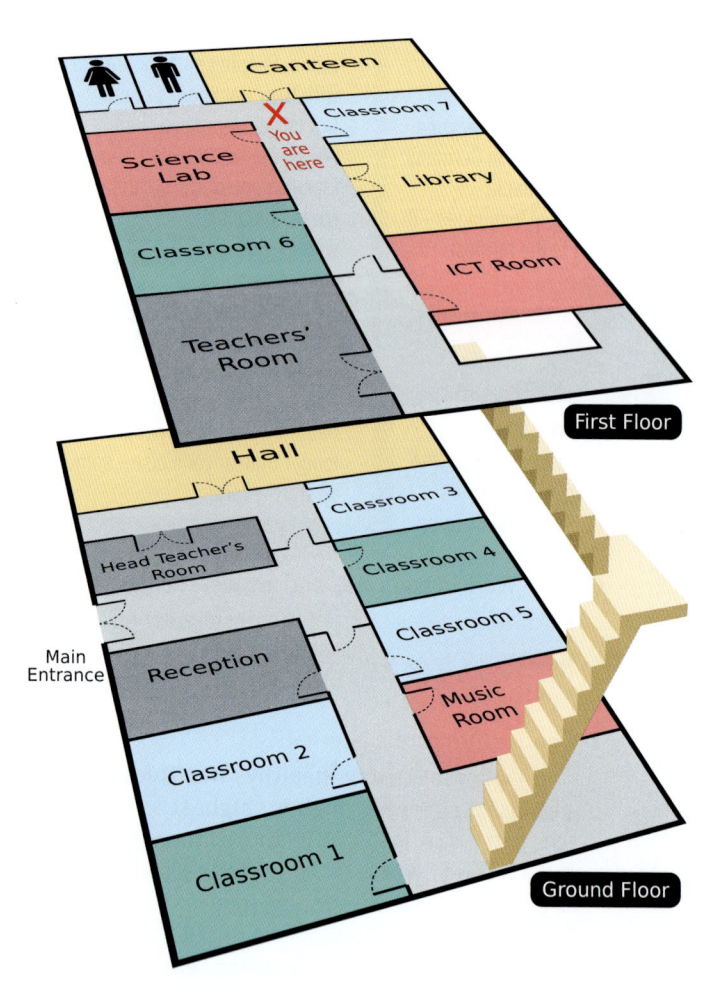

3 🔊 **4.17** A new student is outside the canteen. Listen to the dialogue. Follow the directions on the map. Where does she want to go?

> Can you tell me where to go?   Sure…

4 🔊 **4.17** Complete the Phrasebook with the words below. There are two words you don't need. Then listen again and check.

along   down   for   left   on   past   right   through   up

PHRASEBOOK Directions
Asking for directions
Excuse me, I'm looking ¹_____ (the hall).
Giving directions

Go ² _____ the corridor.   Go ³ _____ the library.

Go ⁴ _____ the stairs.   Turn ⁵ _____ .

Go ⁶ _____ the doors.   It's ⁷ _____ the right.

STRATEGY Asking for clarification
If you don't understand or don't hear something that somebody says, you can ask that person to speak more slowly, repeat it or clarify using these phrases:
Could you speak more slowly, please?
Sorry, could you repeat that, please?

5 🔊 **4.18** Read the strategy. Then listen to two dialogues. Where does each person want to go?

6 💬 Work in pairs. Take turns to ask for and give directions to the places below. Use the strategy and the Phrasebook to help you.

Girls' toilet   Library   Music room
Science lab   Canteen   Classroom 7

> Excuse me, where's the Girls' toilet?   Turn left …

7 **REFLECT** Work in pairs. Answer the questions.
1. Can you ask for and give directions successfully? Why / Why not?
2. Which phrases in the Phrasebook can you use?
3. Can you ask for help when you don't understand?

56 Unit 4

Make your descriptions more interesting.   **4.9 WRITING**

A description of a place

1 Look at the two photos. Answer the questions.
 1 Where do you think they are?
 2 What buildings can you see?
 3 Which things are natural and which are man-made?
 4 Which place would you prefer to visit? Why?

2 Read the articles. Answer the questions.
 1 Which places do they describe?
 2 What's the competition?

3 💬 Work in pairs. Which of the places in the article do you prefer? Why?

4 💬 Work in pairs. Think of three ways in which these places are similar to and different from your local area.

> **STRATEGY**   Making your descriptions more interesting
>
> When you write a description of a place, it's important to make it interesting for the reader. To make it interesting, try and …
> - give the description an interesting title.
> - ask the reader questions.
> - use a variety of adjectives.
> - give your opinion of the place.

5 Read the strategy. Then complete the table with examples from the article.

Interesting title	Questions	Adjectives	Opinion

6 You want to write an article for the competition. Think of one of your favourite places. Write a list of …
 - buildings / places / things to see there.
 - adjectives to describe them.
 - reasons why you think it's the best place.

7 Write your article in 80–100 words. Use your notes and the strategy to help you.

8 ✓ **CHECK YOUR WORK**
 - Has your article got an interesting title?
 - Do you ask any questions?
 - Are the comparative and superlative adjectives spelled correctly?
 - Do you give your opinion at the end?

AROUND THE WORLD

destinations > your articles

The City of Gold!
Sasha, 17

Do you know where Dubai is? It's a city in the United Arab Emirates.

Dubai is most famous for its modern architecture, such as the Palm Jumeirah, its shopping centres and the amazingly tall building, Burj Khalifa. How much taller is it than the Eiffel Tower? At over 800 metres, it is three times bigger!

Dubai also has some of the most expensive hotels in the world, e.g. the underwater hotel or the Burj Al Arab, which has gold walls, and is the only seven-star hotel.

But the thing I like best about Dubai are its many beaches and islands, and the beautiful deserts near Dubai are some of the easiest in the world to visit.

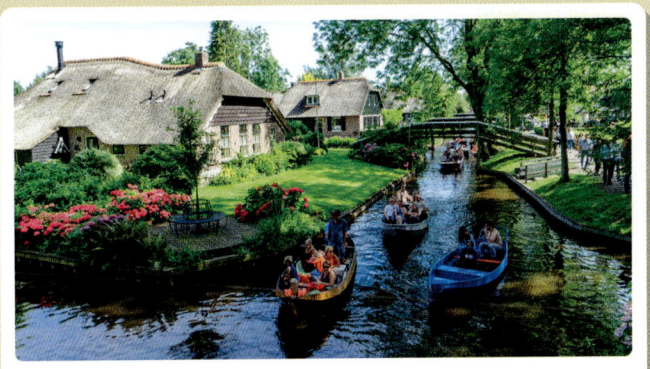

Dutch Venice
Amir, 16

The quietest place in Europe is a small village in the Netherlands called Giethoorn.

Why is it so quiet? Because there aren't any cars in it. Instead of wide streets, there are green parks, thick forests, narrow rivers and clean lakes.

Over 2,600 people live in Giethoorn's beautiful, old houses, and most people travel around by boat, or they ride a bike or walk over its 150 little bridges.

Giethoorn is most popular and busiest in the summer, but it isn't the best time of year to visit. When is it better? I prefer spring or autumn. That's when the people are friendlier, the temperatures are more comfortable and it's much emptier.

📢 **Competition!** Our online magazine is looking for articles by teenagers about their favourite places or buildings. The best article wins £100!

Unit 4   57

4.10 REVIEW

Grammar

1 Write sentences, changing the adjectives to comparatives.
1. Dad / two years old / Mum
2. In our country, spring / hot / autumn
3. Gold / always / expensive / silver
4. Mountains / large / hills
5. Your school bag / heavy / mine
6. I think flats / good / houses
7. We / far / from Lima / London
8. In my opinion, books / bad / comics

2 Complete the second sentence so that it has the same meaning as the first. Use the superlative and the adjectives below.

| bad | big | busy | good | high | interesting | new | wide |

1. All other rivers are narrower than the Amazon.
   The Amazon _____ river in the world.
2. I find all subjects boring compared to maths.
   Maths _____ subject in my opinion.
3. The other flats around here are older than ours.
   Our flats _____ in the area.
4. No other mountain is taller than Everest.
   Everest _____ mountain in the world.
5. Of all the days, I hate Monday the most.
   For me, Monday _____ day of the week.
6. The other rooms are all smaller than my kitchen.
   The kitchen _____ room in the house.
7. My favourite place is my home town.
   My home town _____ place in the world for me.
8. Most people go to see our famous, old buildings.
   The areas with old buildings _____ parts of town.

Vocabulary

3 Complete the words.
1. People usually relax and watch TV in here: l_____
2. This adjective describes a sofa or bed: c_____
3. This is the opposite of clean: d_____
4. This keeps milk and yoghurt cold: f_____
5. People eat meals in this part of the house: d_____
6. A space inside the entrance or front door of a building: h_____
7. You usually brush your teeth in front of this: s_____
8. You keep things like plates or shoes in this: c_____

4 Are the sentences true (T) or false (F)? Correct the false sentences with one word only.
1. The pyramids of Giza are famous examples of modern architecture.
2. Beaches are areas of land next to the forest.
3. A lake is a large area of fresh water.
4. An ocean is smaller than a sea.
5. Big cities usually have wider streets than towns.
6. There are many tall trees, and it is often wet in a river.
7. Rainforests receive less than 25 cm of rain a year.
8. You often find important squares in capital cities.

Cumulative review

5 Complete the email with the correct form of the words below.

balcony	bathroom	beach	beautiful	cheap
dry	friendly	happy (x2)	island	large	low
near	tall	thick	toilet	unusual

Hi Diego,
I love studying Spanish here in Mexico City! I'm living with a girl from the USA called Gloria. She's very nice to me; in fact, she's one of the ¹_____ people I know! Our flat is much ²_____ to the centre than my old flat in London.
In the evenings, we love sitting on our ³_____ watching the busy streets below us. The biggest problem with our home is it's got the narrowest ⁴_____ in the world!! Every time I have a shower, water goes on the ⁵_____ and floor too.
Anyway, I'm learning so much about Mexico. It has some of the ⁶_____ deserts in the world and the ⁷_____ rainforests. And with nearly 122 million Mexicans, it's the world's ⁸_____ Spanish-speaking country.
Mexico City is a ⁹_____ place to live than London, so I'm not spending a lot of money. But the ¹⁰_____ thing about the capital is, it's going down fast! Mexico City moves 90 cm ¹¹_____ every year because it sits on an ancient Aztec city on an ¹²_____ in the middle of a dry lake. Mexico's got lots of very old sites, like the ¹³_____ pyramid in the world at 55 metres: the Great Pyramid of Cholula. Chichen Itza is also very pretty … I think it's ¹⁴_____ of the new seven wonders of the world.
Mexicans are amazingly positive. A recent study shows they're ¹⁵_____ than any other nationality, except the Costa Ricans. They're ¹⁶_____ people in the world!
This week, Gloria and I are going diving on Cozumel – an island in the Caribbean Sea. We're going to an amazing ¹⁷_____ with white sand and palm trees on it. I can't wait!
Write soon,
Love
Angie xxx

💬 Think & share

6 Speak or write. Read the quote. Then answer the questions.

❝ There's no place like home. ❞
Dorothy, from the film The Wizard of Oz *(1939)*

1. Do you think that homes are special places? Why do you think that?
2. What has your perfect home got in it? Why?
3. Which do you prefer: the town or the country? Why?
4. What are the best places to visit near your home? Why do you say that?

4.11 EXAM SKILLS

Listening

EXAM STRATEGY

When you do a matching task, read the statements carefully before you listen. Think of different ways to say the ideas in the statements. Speakers usually use different words and phrases and give more details.

1 Read the strategy above. Then match statements 1–3 below with sentences A–C.
  1 This person explains why they hate living here.
  2 This person says how often they come to this place.
  3 This person talks about the things they like.
  A The garden is beautiful and it's very quiet here.
  B I visit about six times a year because I love it here.
  C It's terrible because it's noisy and very small.

2 ◆ 4.19 You will hear five people talking about homes. For speakers 1–5, choose from the list (A–F) what each speaker says. Use the letters only once. There is one extra letter that you do not need to use.
Which person
  A explains that they visit this house a few times a year? ___
  B says their home is noisy in the summer? ___
  C describes their future dream house? ___
  D compares their new home to the old one? ___
  E talks about someone else's house? ___
  F explains why they dislike where they live? ___

Use of English

EXAM STRATEGY

When you do a multiple-choice task, don't worry if you can't complete all the gaps the first time you read. Complete the gaps that you know. Then read the text again. When the other gaps are complete it is usually easier.

3 Read the strategy above. Then look at the short text below. Read it quickly and complete the gaps you know. Then read again more carefully to complete the task.

> I'm looking ¹___ a very unusual building. It's the ²___ house in the city. The walls and the roof ³___ glass. You can see the people inside. It's a very ⁴___ place.

  1 A on   B at   C with
  2 A tall   B taller   C tallest
  3 A is   B are   C of
  4 A strange   B stranger C strangest

4 Read the text below and choose the correct answer (A, B or C) for each gap.

Keret House

There are many examples of modern architecture in Europe and many examples of strange-looking houses. Some of them have got strange shapes. Some of them are bigger or smaller ¹___ normal houses. I'm a fan ²___ Keret House, which is in Warsaw in Poland. Warsaw is the ³___ city in Poland. It is also the capital. There are many things to see and do in Warsaw. Keret House is famous because it is ⁴___ than any other house in the world. So how narrow is Keret House? The narrowest part of the building is 92 cm and the ⁵___ part of the building is 152 cm. The house has three floors. There is one bedroom, a bathroom, a kitchen and a living room. The walls are white. In the bedroom, there is a bed in ⁶___ of the window and a small desk. So can people live in it? I don't think people live there now, but tourists can visit. You can find it near Chłodna Street and 74 Żelazna Street. It stands ⁷___ two other buildings. When people look ⁸___ it, they often don't find it because it is so thin!

  1 A from   B than   C as
  2 A of   B for   C to
  3 A large   B larger   C largest
  4 A narrow   B narrower   C narrowest
  5 A wide   B wider   C widest
  6 A front   B opposite   C behind
  7 A on   B next   C between
  8 A at   B for   C on

Writing

EXAM STRATEGY

When you write an article, use different adjectives to make your writing more interesting to readers.

5 Read the strategy above. Then match the adjectives with the categories. Add some more adjectives to the lists.

> amazing   beautiful   friendly   gold   kind   large
> modern   narrow   orange   patient   pink   serious
> silver   strange   tall   wide

size _____
colour _____
personality _____
other _____

6 You see an advert in an online magazine for English language students. Write an article for the magazine.

My dream home

We want you to write an article about your dream home. Where in the world is your home? What does it look like? Why is it more interesting than other homes?

Exam skills 59

5 Time out

- **VOCABULARY** Entertainment Film and TV
- **GRAMMAR** Past simple: regular verbs Past simple: the verb *be* and *can*
- **READING** Street art
- **LISTENING** The life of Frida Kahlo
- **GLOBAL SKILLS** Researching and evaluating information
- **SPEAKING** Telling a personal story
- **WRITING** A diary entry
- **VISION 360** Hanbury Street, London

VOCABULARY BOOSTER P120–121
GRAMMAR BOOSTER P140–141

I'm into art

1 💬 Look at the video stills. Answer the questions.
   1 What is happening in the photos?
   2 Where do you think these festivals are? Give reasons for your answers.

2 ▶ 🔊 **5.01** Watch or listen. Answer the questions.
   1 When is the most famous Edinburgh festival?
   2 Which country is the Holi festival from?

3 ▶ 🔊 **5.01** Read the sentences. Watch or listen again. Complete the sentences with one word in each gap.
   1 Every year, there are _____ festivals in Edinburgh.
   2 _____ million people visit Edinburgh each summer.
   3 The Fringe is the world's _____ arts festival.
   4 You can listen to _____ from around the world.
   5 Last year, Callum watched about _____ shows.
   6 Zara really likes the school subject _____.
   7 Holi is also called the Festival of _____.
   8 People celebrate Holi in the _____ too.

60 Unit 5

Talk about entertainment. **5.1 VOCABULARY**

4 **REAL ENGLISH** Match the **bold** phrases to their meaning.
1 There are street concerts **all over the place**.
2 You can hear **all kinds of** music.
3 **Don't miss it**!
4 **I'm into** art.
5 **Big mistake**!

A in different areas
B a bad idea
C you really need to see this
D many different types
E I really like

5 **VOCABULARY** Work in pairs. Read the words and phrases below. Write them in the correct part of the mind map. Some can go into more than one category. Can you add any more words?

concert   crowded streets   cultural events   drums
exhibition   festival   hip-hop   incredible artists
painting   rock   screens   show   street theatre

Art

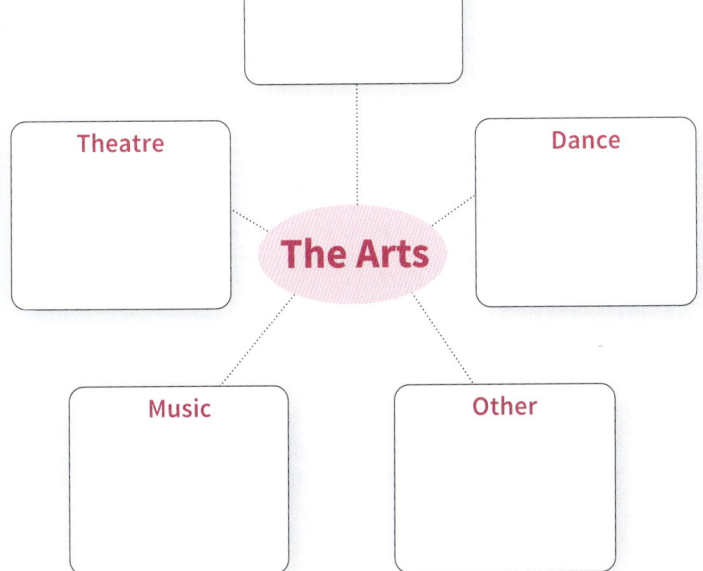

Theatre

Dance

The Arts

Music

Other

6 Work in pairs. Ask and answer the questions.
1 Which of the arts in Ex 5 do you like most?
2 Can you think of an example for each type?
3 What words can you use to describe them?

7 Complete the text with the words below.

artists   concerts   crowded   events
exhibitions   festival   incredible   shows

The BIGGEST PARTY in the world

One of the best cultural ¹_____ in Spain is the April Fair of Seville. This Spanish ²_____ takes place every year and lasts one week. It includes music, dancing, art ³_____, great food and national costumes. Seville is famous for its flamenco and there are lots of dance ⁴_____ around the city. There are also music ⁵_____ with famous ⁶_____. They come from all over Andalusia to play there. The festival is also popular with tourists, so the streets are very ⁷_____. Don't miss the ⁸_____ horse shows – they're the best in the world!

8 Work in pairs. Discuss the questions.
1 What can you see and do at Seville's festival?
2 Which of the events are you into? Why?
3 What is the most similar festival in your country?

9 **5.02** Listen to friends discussing an event. What does Amy like? Does Adam want to go?

10 **5.02** Listen again. Complete the fact file for the event.

Fact File
Festival name:
When?
Where?
Who can go?
What happens?

11 Work in pairs. You each have information about a different cultural event. Ask your partner about their event and complete the fact file. Student A: turn to page 150. Student B: turn to page 151.

12 **THINK & SHARE** Which of the festivals in this lesson seems most interesting to you? Why?

13 Work in groups. Imagine your town wants to start a new festival. Invent an event and design a poster for it to display in class.

VOCABULARY BOOSTER Unit 5 61

5.2 GRAMMAR — Use the past simple to talk about past events.

Past simple: regular verbs

1 Do you remember the video about arts festivals? What cultural events did they talk about?

2 Read the blog posts about people's favourite arts festivals. Answer the questions.
   1 What are the festivals' names?
   2 Where are they?
   3 What happens in each one?

Festival chat

The Colours of Ostrava, Nina Novak, 17

My friends and I are into music, so we decided to go to a big music festival in Ostrava in the Czech Republic last July. It's called the Colours of Ostrava. The events all happened in an old factory next to a big park. We watched all kinds of concerts, like rock, hip-hop and jazz, and listened to lots of cool bands. As it's an international festival, artists come from all over the world. One artist from Senegal played the drums really well. Everybody danced when the music started!! I also chatted to lots of friendly people. We enjoyed it so much! I don't want to miss it next year!!!

The Biennale, Franc B, 16

At middle school, two years ago, I studied art and I travelled to Italy with my art class. We visited Venice because we wanted to see the Biennale, a famous art exhibition. We looked at lots of interesting paintings and photos on big screens. We also walked around the old city. Venice is incredible, but it's also very crowded! When I arrived back home, I showed my amazing photos to my friends and family, and they really liked them.

3 Read the grammar rule. Then complete the spelling rules and find an example in the text for each one.

Past simple: regular verbs
▶ Grammar animation

Affirmative
We use the past simple to talk about completed actions in the past. The form is the same for all subjects.

A With most regular verbs, we add -ed to the infinitive of the verb without to, e.g. 1_____.

B For verbs that end in -e, add 2_____, e.g. 3_____.

C For verbs that end in a consonant + y, change -y to 4_____, e.g. 5_____.

D For verbs that end in a vowel + consonant, double the final consonant and add 6_____, e.g. 7_____.

GRAMMAR BOOSTER P140

4 🔊 5.05 **PRONUNCIATION** There are three ways to pronounce -ed. Listen and repeat the sounds.

/d/	/t/	/ɪd/
happened	walked	started

5 🔊 5.06 Complete the table with the regular verbs below. Listen and check.

arrived   enjoyed   decided   liked   looked
travelled   visited   wanted   watched

6 🔊 5.07 Complete the text with the past simple form of the verbs in brackets. Then listen and check.

Dubrovnik Summer Festival

Last year, my family and I 1_____ (travel) to Croatia on a summer holiday. We 2_____ (stay) in Dubrovnik because we 3_____ (want) to see a famous cultural event called the Dubrovnik Summer Festival. First, we 4_____ (walk) around the crowded, old city streets; then we 5_____ (visit) the arts festival. We 6_____ (watch) many incredible events, such as a great dance show by a traditional Croatian music and dance group. My sister 7_____ (love) the guitar concerts, but I 8_____ (prefer) the piano concerts. We both 9_____ (hate) the jazz orchestra! We 10_____ (plan) to see Shakespeare's *Hamlet*, but our holiday 11_____ (finish) before we could go. I really 12_____ (enjoy) my time in Croatia.

7 🔊 5.08 Listen to someone describing a holiday. Find out the name of the country he visited and the name of the festival.

8 🔊 5.08 Listen again and complete the sentences about the holiday.
   1 He travelled to …
   2 He visited it with his …
   3 His holiday happened in the month of …
   4 It lasted …
   5 During his holiday, he visited many beautiful …
   6 He liked the … best of all.

9 💬 **THINK & SHARE** Think about a cultural event you visited. Make notes about it. Then tell your partner about it. Use the prompts in Ex 9 and the time references below to help you.

a year ago   in 2020   last week

A year ago, I travelled to … I visited it with …

62   Unit 5

5.3 READING

Scan for information in an article about street art.

Street art

1 💬 Work in pairs. Look at the photos. What type of art is it? What can you see in the photos? Do you like it? Why? / Why not?

> **STRATEGY** Scanning for information
>
> When you need to find specific information in a text, e.g. a name, you do not need to understand every word. You can scan the text instead. To scan …
> - know what information you are looking for, e.g. numbers, dates, people or places.
> - move your eyes quickly up and down the page.
> - don't read a complete sentence until you find the answer or word you need.

2 Read the strategy. Then read the sentences below. What information do you think you are looking for?
1 Blek decided to go to the USA at _____ years old.
2 He completed his art studies in _____.
3 At first, Blek only painted pictures of _____.
4 People say _____ copied Blek's art.
5 The film about street artists is called _____.
6 Blek's anniversary party happened in _____.

3 Scan the text and find the information to complete the sentences in Ex 2.

4 **VOCABULARY** Scan the text for the words below. Can you guess their meaning from the context?

| empty   homeless   wild

5 **THINK & SHARE** Work in pairs. Ask and answer the questions.
1 Why do you think graffiti artists paint at night?
2 Why do artists not use their real names?
3 Is it OK for one artist to copy another? Why? / Why not?

6 🔊 5.09 Read the text again more carefully. Are the sentences true (T) or false (F)?
1 Xavier is really called Blek. ___
2 Street art started in Paris. ___
3 Blek painted graffiti on walls in New York. ___
4 Blek used his graffiti to consider city problems. ___
5 Banksy and Blek sometimes painted the same subjects. ___
6 Blek isn't famous in other countries. ___

7 **THINK & SHARE** Work in pairs. Ask and answer the questions.
1 How much graffiti is there in your town or city?
2 Where is it? What does it look like? Do you like it?
3 Do you think graffiti is a real art form? Why? / Why not?
4 In your opinion, which subjects are best for street art? Why do you think that?

A street artist called le Rat

Blek le Rat introduced people all over the world to a new and exciting type of street art. Many artists still copy his style today.

Blek le Rat's real name is Xavier Prou. He travelled to New York in 1972, at the age of 21, when graffiti first started to appear on buildings. Blek watched as young people painted incredible graffiti on walls around the city. He wanted to do the same thing in Paris, so he studied art at the Beaux-Arts school in Paris.

He finished art school in 1982 and decided to become a street artist. He walked around Paris looking for empty, old buildings. Some teenagers helped him paint hundreds of rats, the only wild animals in the city.

In the 2000s, Blek wanted people to think about serious problems. In Paris, many people lived on the streets, so Blek started painting homeless people all over the city. Everybody looked at his art, but nobody helped solve the problem.

Many compare Blek to the famous British graffiti artist Banksy. In the 2010 film *Graffiti Wars*, we learn that Banksy copied Blek's style and pictures. For example, he painted a man with a screen head and rats that looked like Blek's.

Blek says his street art is more popular abroad than in his home town of Paris. In 2011, he celebrated 30 years as a street artist in San Francisco, and today Blek has art exhibitions in cities all around the world.

5.4 GLOBAL SKILLS — Research and evaluate information.

Researching and evaluating information

1 Work in pairs. Ask and answer the questions.
   1 Where do you usually search for information?
   2 What type of information do you often search?
   3 Why do you need it?

2 ◆ 5.10 Listen to an expert talking about research. Answer the questions.
   1 What is her talk about?
   2 Which source does she talk about?
   3 What is her old blog about?

3 ◆ 5.10 Look at the chart. Complete it with the words below. Then listen again and check.

   answer   check   look   main   recent   understand   want

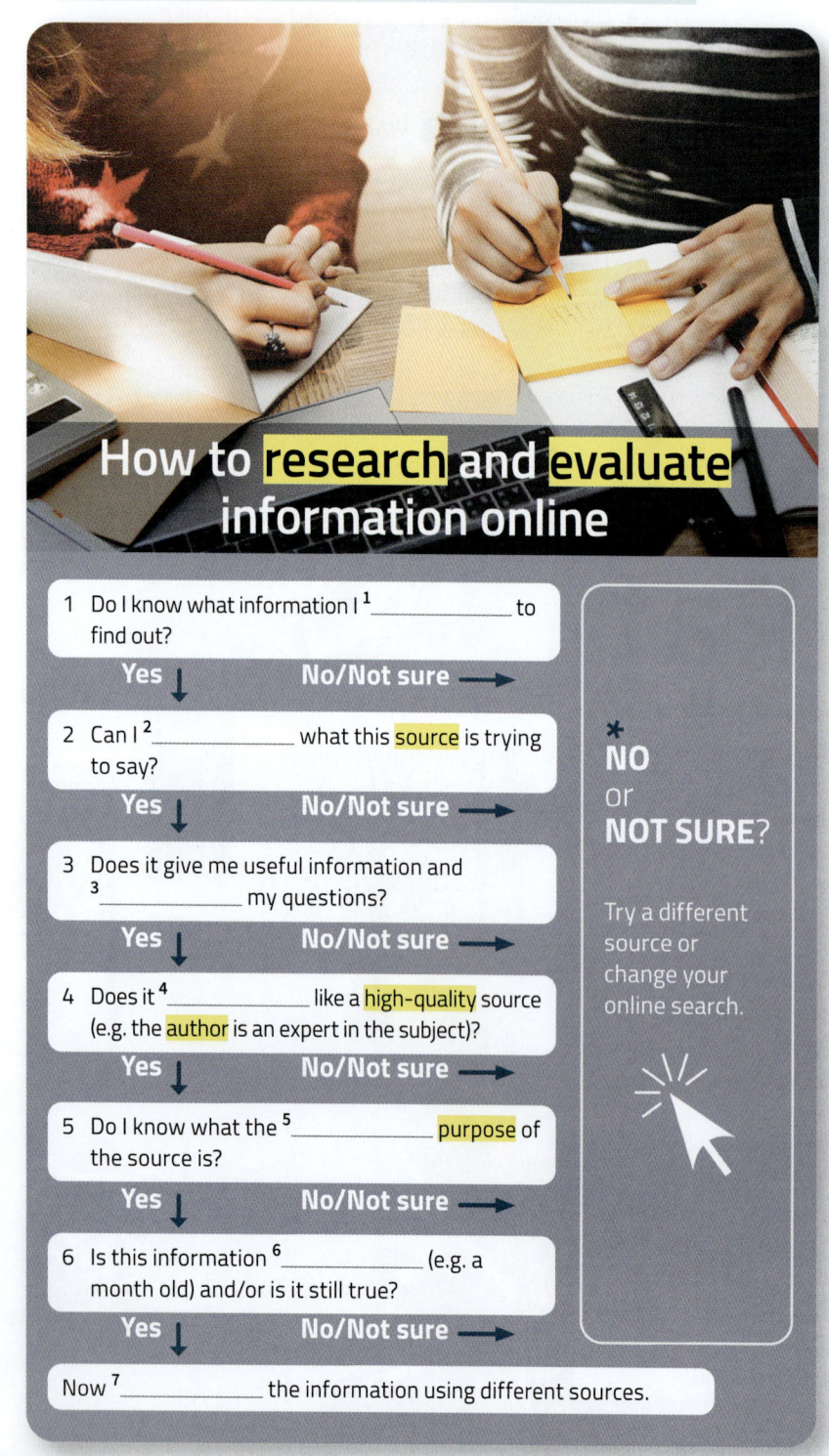

   How to research and evaluate information online

   1 Do I know what information I ¹_____ to find out?
      Yes ↓   No/Not sure →
   2 Can I ²_____ what this source is trying to say?
      Yes ↓   No/Not sure →
   3 Does it give me useful information and ³_____ my questions?
      Yes ↓   No/Not sure →
   4 Does it ⁴_____ like a high-quality source (e.g. the author is an expert in the subject)?
      Yes ↓   No/Not sure →
   5 Do I know what the ⁵_____ purpose of the source is?
      Yes ↓   No/Not sure →
   6 Is this information ⁶_____ (e.g. a month old) and/or is it still true?
      Yes ↓   No/Not sure →

   Now ⁷_____ the information using different sources.

   * NO or NOT SURE?
   Try a different source or change your online search.

4 **THINK & SHARE** Work in pairs. Ask and answer the questions.
   1 Which of the things in the chart do you do?
   2 What parts of research do you find most difficult?
   3 Do you read any sources that often contain opinions? What are they about?

5 **VOCABULARY** Match the highlighted words in the chart with the definitions.
   1 to form an opinion on a subject by thinking about it carefully
   2 something or someone that gives information
   3 to study a subject to discover new facts
   4 very good, serious
   5 a person who writes books or articles
   6 the reason why something exists

6 Complete the text with the words below.

   author   find out   high-quality   research   source

   At first, it is difficult to understand if an article contains ¹_____ information or if it is just a personal opinion of the ²_____. But like many skills, it becomes easier to ³_____ information with practice. It's important that you always evaluate any ⁴_____ you want to use carefully. Don't just read one – study many articles and try to ⁵_____ as much as you can about the subject. Then you can compare them with each other to check.

7 **THINK & SHARE** Choose a subject or event that you would like to research. Write down all the things you need to search for and three questions you want to answer.

8 Work in pairs. Discuss the questions.
   1 What would you like to research and why?
   2 What type of information do you want to find out?
   3 Which sources are you planning to use?
   4 Which websites are high-quality sources?

9 Now do your research in English. Use the chart to evaluate any sources. Then tell your class about your experience. Describe how you looked for the information and why you wanted to find out more.

10 Work in groups. Discuss the questions.
    1 What was the easiest and hardest part?
    2 Are you planning to do your research differently in the future? How?

64   Unit 5

5.5 VOCABULARY
Talk about film and TV.

Entertainment

1 💬 Work in pairs. Ask and answer the questions.
   1 What do one star and five stars mean on a review?
   2 How often do you read reviews before you watch a film or a new TV show?
   3 How often do you agree with them?

2 Read the reviews on the forum. Match the number of stars to the reviews.
   A 1   B 3   C 4.5

TV review

Today's most discussed reviews

★★★★★
High School Musical: The Musical: The Series
TV review by Carmen Jimenez

This TV series is about the same high school as the original Disney film. It's about talented teenagers who love singing and dancing! There are many brilliant songs and there are some excellent performances! I love it because it celebrates the arts at school, at a time when people think sport or science are more important. Don't miss it!

1 _____ out of 5 stars
by Pak, 12 November
I loved the films as a child, but this is also a wonderful show for teenagers! 😀

2 _____ out of 5 stars
by Seriousgirl, 12 November
It had terrible acting and boring characters. I hated all the romantic songs … I prefer listening to loud rock music anyway!

3 _____ out of 5 stars
by Angel, 12 November
I watched it last night. I liked the romantic ending, but the rest of it was just OK … Nothing special …

talented – with a special ability
performance – the act of performing a play

3 Read the reviews again. Answer the questions.
   1 Where does the film take place?
   2 What's it about?
   3 Why are science and sport mentioned?
   4 What type of songs or music does Seriousgirl like?
   5 Which part of the film does Angel prefer?

4 💬 Work in pairs. Ask and answer the questions.
   1 Which review do you believe the most? Why?
   2 Do you want to watch this show? Why? / Why not?

5 **VOCABULARY** Replace the words in **bold** with the highlighted phrases in the reviews. There is one phrase you do not need.
   1 I watched the **first movie**.
   2 I listened to **some very good singing** yesterday.
   3 My friend and I love the same **TV shows**.
   4 I read **people's opinions** before I watch a show.
   5 I enjoy listening to **the opposite of quiet music**.
   6 The street theatre is **not particularly good**.
   7 The film has a **final part about love**.
   8 There are **great singers, dancers and actors** in this musical.
   9 In that series, there are **people who aren't interesting**.
   10 Some shows have **very bad actors** in them.

6 Complete the table with the adjectives. Are there any words that don't fit? Can you add any more?

   amazing   boring   brilliant   excellent   loud
   nothing special   original   romantic   sad
   terrible   wonderful

Positive	
OK	
Negative	

7 💬 Work in pairs. Think of some TV series and films, characters, acting, performances and endings. Share your opinions about these using the words in Ex 6.

   I think … is a brilliant TV series.

   Really? I think the acting is nothing special.

8 **THINK & SHARE** Work in pairs. Think of a film, musical theatre show or TV series you watched recently. Tell your partner about it. Use the questions to help you.
   • What is it? What's it called?
   • What was the acting / music / ending like? Why?
   • What were the performances like? Why?
   • What were the characters / costumes like? Why?
   • How many stars out of five do you give it?

VOCABULARY BOOSTER Unit 5   65

5.6 GRAMMAR   Use the verb *be* and *can* to talk about the past.

Past simple: the verb *be* and *can*

1 **THINK & SHARE** Do you know any talented children? Are people born with special abilities or do they become talented through hard work?

2 Look at the photos. What are they doing? What can they do? Read the article and check your answers.

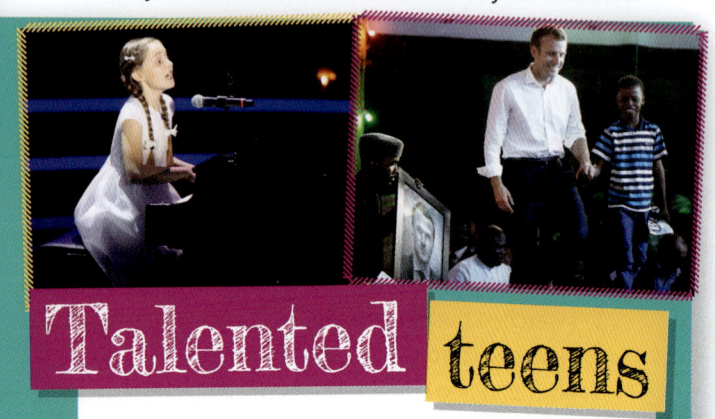

Talented teens

Alma Deutscher and Kareem Olamilekan weren't the same as other children. What were they like? What could they do?

Alma was born in 2005 in England. She could sing before she could talk. When she was three, she received a violin, and she couldn't stop playing. But the violin wasn't the only instrument that she loved. She could also play the piano and she started writing original music and performing when she was eight. 'Little Miss Mozart's' concerts received wonderful reviews.

Kareem was born in 2006 in Nigeria. Like Picasso, he could draw brilliant portraits when he was eight. His drawings weren't famous until the French president visited Nigeria in 2018 and Kareem created an excellent portrait of him. He couldn't believe how talented the eleven-year-old was!

3 Read the grammar rules. Underline all the examples of the past simple of *can* and *be* in the text. Then complete the grammar rules.

Past simple: the verb *be*

▶ Grammar animation

Affirmative
I / He / She / It + ¹_____ eight years old.
You / We / They + ²_____ good at drawing.
Negative
I / He / She / It + ³_____ very talented.
You / We / They + ⁴_____ famous.
Questions
⁵_____ I / he / she / it famous?
Yes, I / he / she / it ⁶_____. / No, I / he / she / it ⁷_____.
⁸_____ you / we / they good?
Yes, you / we / they ⁹_____. / No, you / we / they ¹⁰_____.

GRAMMAR BOOSTER P141

Past simple: *can*

The forms for *could* are the same for all persons.
Affirmative
He ¹¹_____ draw.
Negative
They ¹²_____ stop.
Questions
¹³_____ you swim?
Yes, I ¹⁴_____. / No, I ¹⁵_____.

GRAMMAR BOOSTER P141

4 Complete the sentences with the correct form of *be* or *can*.
1 He hated that painting, so his review _____ terrible.
2 You _____ quiet last night. Are you OK?
3 The songs _____ boring. I loved them!
4 When we _____ fourteen, we visited New York.
5 Liam _____ come with us last night – he was ill.
6 When I _____ a child, I _____ sing brilliantly.
7 I _____ hear you speak clearly because the music _____ loud at all.
8 My parents aren't Polish. They _____ born in China.

5 🔊 5.13 Complete the text with the correct form of *be* or *can*. Listen and check your answers.

Mini Monet

The newspapers ¹_____ interested in Kieron Williamson as a child, because he ²_____ paint like a master! In his first exhibition in 2008, aged six, the reviews ³_____ excellent. After that, his nickname ⁴_____ 'Mini Monet'. People ⁵_____ (not) stop buying his brilliant paintings! In three years, Kieron and his family ⁶_____ rich. They had £1.5 million! At the age of fourteen, he appeared in the TV show *The Making of a Master*. But his mum ⁷_____ (not) happy with his education; he ⁸_____ (not) go to school because he ⁹_____ too busy and famous.

6 Write questions.
1 What / Mozart do when he / four / ?
2 Mozart and his father / both / musical / ?
3 How old / Mozart when he first performed / ?
4 What / Picasso's first word / ?
5 Picasso / write before he / draw / ?
6 How old / he / when he started going to art school / ?
7 Picasso and Mozart / famous before they die / ?

7 🔊 5.14 Listen to the radio show. Answer the questions in Ex 6.

8 Work in pairs. Ask and answer the questions.
1 How old were you when you could first …
   • draw a face?
   • speak English?
   • swim?
   • sing a song?
   • play an instrument?
   • write your name?
   • ride a bike?
2 What could you do well as a child?

66 Unit 5

Understand the structure of an interview.

5.7 LISTENING

The life of Frida Kahlo

1 💬 Work in pairs. Look at the photo. What do you know about Frida Kahlo? How many artists can you name from …
   • your country?
   • other countries?

STRATEGY Understanding the structure of a listening text

When we listen to information, we sometimes need to follow instructions or put information in the correct order. Listen for words that are used to talk about ordering things, e.g. *First*, *then*, *next*, *after that*, *in the end*, etc. to help you understand better.

2 💬 Read the strategy. Then look at pictures of Frida Kahlo's important life events. Discuss what they are.

3 🔊 5.15 Listen to a radio show about Frida Kahlo. Look at the events below. Number them in the order that they happened.

'I paint my own reality.' – Frida Kahlo

A B C D E F G H I J

4 🔊 5.15 Listen again. Choose the correct answer: A, B or C.
  1 Joe learned about Frida Kahlo …
     A on TV.   B at an art show.   C at school.
  2 Frida couldn't paint until she was …
     A a small child.   B an old woman.   C a teenager.
  3 When she was young, Frida couldn't …
     A go to school.   B play any sports.
     C walk well.
  4 Frida's bus accident happened when she was …
     A 18 years old.   B 25 years old.   C 28 years old.
  5 The age difference between Frida and Diego was …
     A 20 years.   B 29 years.   C 30 years.
  6 In 1930, the couple moved to …
     A Mexico.   B the USA.   C France.
  7 In her lifetime, Frida created …
     A 47 paintings.   B 55 paintings.   C 143 paintings.

5 Match phrases 1–6 from the radio show to the definitions A–F.
  1 excellent self-portraits ___
  2 a brilliant exhibition ___
  3 original clothes ___
  4 a full-time artist ___
  5 a special talent ___
  6 separate lives ___

  A a natural ability
  B new and interesting things you wear
  C working all hours of the week
  D great paintings of the artist by the artist
  E a really good show
  F living in different places from each other

6 💬 **MEDIATION** Imagine that an English friend saw one of Frida Kahlo's paintings but does not know anything about her. Use the information in the listening and pictures in Ex 3 to tell your friend about the artist.
   • Describe how she was as a child.
   • Say how she started painting.
   • Describe how difficult her life was.
   • Say why you think she's interesting.

7 Draw a timeline for you (or a family member / friend).

8 💬 Work in pairs. Share your timelines and your life stories.

9 Write a short paragraph about a famous person.

10 💬 Read your paragraph to the class. Can they guess who the person is?

Unit 5   67

5.8 SPEAKING — Show interest and tell a personal story.

Telling a personal story

1 Work in pairs. Look at the photos. Answer the questions.
1 What type of story does each photo show?
2 What type of stories do you enjoy the most/the least? Why?

2 🔊 **5.16** Listen to Rick telling a personal story to Ava. Answer the questions.
1 Which photo in Ex 1 shows the musical Rick was in?
2 Which character was he?
3 Was his personal story funny, sad or romantic? Why?

STRATEGY Showing interest

During a conversation, we often use short phrases to show interest and react to what the other person is saying.
How amazing / wonderful / sad / terrible!
Oh no!
No way!
Poor you!
Lucky you!
Congratulations!
Wow!
Really?
Well done!

3 🔊 **5.16** Read the strategy. Listen again. Which of the phrases in the strategy do you hear?

4 Complete the table with the phrases in the strategy.

| Reacting to good news |
| Reacting to bad news |
| Showing surprise |

5 🔊 **5.17** Listen to the speakers. Repeat what they say and show interest using the phrases.

> I was hurt in an accident two weeks ago.

> You were hurt in an accident. Oh no!

6 🔊 **5.18** Complete the Phrasebook with the words below. Then listen, check and repeat.

ago   amazingly   happened   soon   was   wasn't

PHRASEBOOK Telling a personal story

The introduction
A few days / years / months ¹_____, I was (in middle school) …
The beginning
I was in a school theatre show … It ²_____ Beauty and the Beast …
The main events
First / Then / After that / As ³_____ as I (arrived) …
While I was there, something terrible / amazing ⁴_____.
The end
And, ⁵_____, … / It's funny now, but it ⁶_____ at the time.

7 Match the sentence halves.
1 Two years ago, I was in
2 After about two minutes, they asked
3 As soon as I arrived,
4 Wow, how
5 And, amazingly, all the
6 While I was there, I

A looked everywhere, but I couldn't find it!
B a really difficult situation.
C terrible!
D Belle looked at me strangely!
E me to go back and finish the ending of the story.
F students loved the new ending!

8 Think about something that happened to you or invent a story for one of the ideas below.
• a brilliant / romantic moment
• a wonderful / funny event
• a special / terrible day

Brainstorm your ideas, and then write them in the correct part of the mind map.

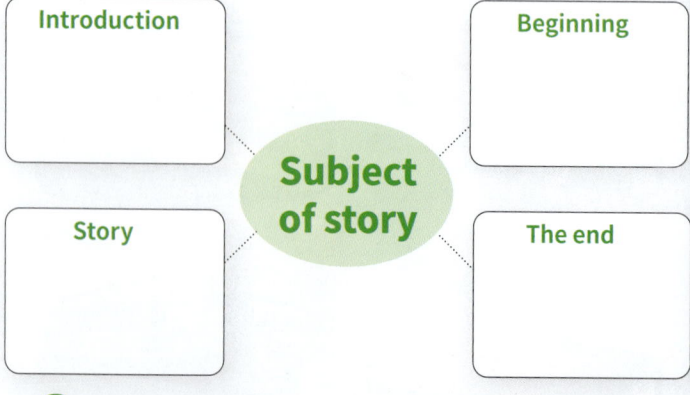

Introduction — Beginning — Story — The end — **Subject of story**

9 Work in pairs. Take turns to tell your story. Use the Phrasebook to help you. Use appropriate expressions from the strategy to show interest and react to your partner.

10 **REFLECT** Discuss in pairs.
1 Did your story have a clear structure?
2 Did you react using the phrases in the Phrasebook? Which ones did you use?

68 Unit 5

5.9 WRITING

Organise your writing.

A diary entry

1 Work in pairs. Look at the photo. Do you think the band are practising or performing? Why?

2 Read the diary entry. Answer the questions.
  1 How were her feelings before the event?
  2 How were her feelings after the event?
  3 Why were her lessons bad?
  4 Why wasn't she hungry?
  5 Where was the concert?
  6 Why was she worried?
  7 How many songs were there?
  8 How many people were at the concert?

Dear diary,
Wow! What a day!!! This is what happened …
First, school was really boring and I couldn't concentrate in class. I was really excited about my concert in the evening.
School finished. Then, I walked home quickly – I wanted to have dinner early. I was nervous and I couldn't eat much!
After dinner, I cycled to the theatre and practised with the band. Then, people started to arrive at the theatre. It was time for the concert to start. There were a lot of people in the audience. I was worried that I couldn't play well!
Then, Jodie introduced our first song. Everybody looked happy. After that, I started to relax.
We played fourteen songs. We sounded brilliant. I really enjoyed performing in front of 200 people!
Finally, our concert ended at 10 p.m. The organisers loved our performance. They offered us two more concert dates!
Lucky me! It was the most incredible day of my life!!!

> **STRATEGY** Organising your writing
> Before you start writing a diary entry or story, think about the events, and the order in which they happened. Then organise your ideas into different parts, e.g. the beginning, the main story and the ending.

3 Read the strategy. Separate the diary entry into the three parts of a story.

4 Number these events in the order they happened.
  ___ The band practised.
  ___ The concert started.
  ___ She wasn't very hungry.
  ___ The theatre asked them to play again.
  ___ She was at school.
  ___ She travelled to the theatre.

5 Read the Language focus. Underline the time sequencers in the diary.

> **LANGUAGE FOCUS** Time sequencers
> Use time sequencers (e.g. *first*, *then*, *next*) to show the order in which things happen.

6 Complete the table with the time sequencers below.

After that, …   Finally, …   First/Firstly, …
Lastly, …   Next, …   Then, …

  1 the beginning
  2 the middle
  3 the end

7 Number these events in the order they happened. Then, rewrite them using time sequencers.
  ___ I missed the bus to school.
  ___ I didn't have time to eat lunch.
  ___ I got up late.
  ___ I walked home.
  ___ I lost my bus ticket.
  ___ I was late for my first class.

8 Think of a memorable day you had. Make notes about why it was so special. Use the prompts to help you.
  • Write a list of the events.
  • Think about your feelings and opinions.
  • Organise your ideas into four parts:
    1 introduction   3 the main story
    2 the beginning   4 the ending

9 Write a diary entry about your day. Use your notes and the Language focus to help you.

10 ✓ CHECK YOUR WORK
  • Does your entry follow the story structure?
  • Do you use appropriate sequencing words?
  • Are the tenses of the verbs correct?
  • Are your spelling and grammar correct?

Unit 5   69

5.10 REVIEW

Grammar

1 Complete the sentences with the past simple form of the verbs below.

| chat | finish | love | paint | study | travel | visit | watch |

1 My brother and I _____ playing with each other as children.
2 I _____ German and French in middle school.
3 The arts festival _____ at 10.30 last night.
4 Yesterday, Finn and I _____ about our favourite show for two hours.
5 In 2001, my parents _____ around India.
6 Last night, Ola _____ a film about Frida Kahlo.
7 You _____ an amazing self-portrait in art class!
8 I _____ my grandparents last Sunday.

2 Complete the sentences using the past simple form of the verbs in brackets.

1 I _____ play the piano when I _____ nine years old. (can / be)
2 You _____ talk when you _____ a baby. (cannot / be)
3 _____ you a talented child? (be)
4 We _____ stressed when we _____ younger. (not be / be)
5 Luna's brother _____ draw faces as a child. (cannot)
6 _____ they dance when they _____ in middle school? (can / be)
7 Many people _____ happy in 2020 because they _____ go out. (not be / cannot)
8 _____ you speak English when you _____ ten? (can / be)

Vocabulary

3 Match the words below to the descriptions.

| art exhibitions | arts festivals | concerts | crowded |
| drums | incredible | screens | street theatre |

1 This is a musical instrument. _____
2 TVs or phones have got these. _____
3 People go to see bands play music at these. _____
4 There are cultural events here like shows, music and films. _____
5 Many people in a place make it become this. _____
6 People look at paintings, drawings and photos at these. _____
7 When people perform drama, music or dancing outside, it is called this. _____
8 This means very exciting or amazing. _____

4 The bold words are in the incorrect sentences. Move them into the correct sentences.

1 I always read online **terrible acting** before I go to see a film at the cinema.
2 Rock concerts aren't good for small children because the **nothing special** can hurt their ears.
3 There weren't any interesting people in that show – there were only **romantic ending**.
4 I love that band. They sing lots of **reviews**.
5 Yesterday, I watched the final part of a **loud music** about time travel. It was amazing!
6 That programme was OK – it's **TV series**.
7 Just before the film finishes, they fall in love. It's a really **boring characters**.
8 I didn't believe the characters were real because there was so much **brilliant songs**.

Cumulative review

5 Choose the correct alternative.

Augusta Savage, a US artist, [1]**were** / **was** born in Florida in 1892. She [2]**could** / **couldn't** make incredible animals with earth as a child. Sadly, her father [3]**was** / **wasn't** happy about her love of art. He was so angry about her talent, that she nearly [4]**started** / **stopped**. In 1915, her new high school [5]**could** / **couldn't** believe how talented she was, so they [6]**answered** / **asked** her to teach the other students.

At 29, Savage [7]**lived** / **moved** to New York City to study art. The teachers [8]**were** / **weren't** surprised about her original artwork, at a time when women artists weren't common. In 1923, Savage [9]**practised** / **wanted** to study on an important French arts programme, but [10]**could** / **couldn't** because of her skin colour. Savage tried changing this [11]**loud** / **terrible** rule, but she wasn't successful. So, she [12]**decided** / **was** to become an artist and created excellent sculptures of African-Americans.

In 1929, people loved her [13]**nothing special** / **wonderful** sculpture of a child. This helped her to become famous. Because of that, she [14]**studied** / **played** art in Paris and showed her work. Her art exhibition was a big success. Savage [15]**lived** / **visited** in Paris for a few years; then she [16]**started** / **returned** to the USA. In 1932, she opened the Savage Studio of Arts and Crafts, and then she [17]**decided** / **changed** the name to the Harlem Community Art Center. Her life story has a happy [18]**beginning** / **ending**; she produced many [19]**boring** / **brilliant** sculptures, and spent all her time teaching art and helping to fight for equal rights. She [20]**lived** / **died** in 1962.

sculpture – a work of art that is an object made from wood, stone, metal, clay, etc.
earth – the material plants grow in

💬 Think & share

6 Speak or write. Answer the questions.

1 Are there arts festivals in your country? Where?
2 What's your favourite art form? Why?
3 Describe the last show or film you watched.
4 Which artists do you know? Describe their life or work.

5.11 EXAM SKILLS

Reading

EXAM STRATEGY

When you have short texts with one multiple choice question each, read each text quickly and try to decide a) what the main idea is and b) the writer's reason for writing.

1 Read the strategy above. Then look at the exam task in Ex 2. Read the first text quickly and choose the main idea.
   A the type of art he prefers
   B what he likes to do in his free time
   C an art exhibition he wants to see again

2 Read the texts below. For each text, choose the correct answer (A, B, C or D).

Hey Ashu! I was at a Spanish art exhibition yesterday. It was brilliant, but there were so many paintings, I couldn't see them all. They had some great artists such as Picasso, but also some modern Spanish artists. The tickets aren't expensive so I'm thinking of going again. Do you want to come? I know you're studying art at university. What do you think? The exhibition is in the art gallery in town. Call me later. Darshna

1 Darshna wrote this message to …
   A tell Ashu about her favourite artists.
   B ask about Ashu's art course.
   C suggest going to an exhibition.
   D give her opinion on Spanish art.

Do you play music? Would you like to take part in a music festival? We're looking for new talent to perform at The Golden Disc Festival which takes place next month. You can perform any song or any type of music. Last year's winners were a local jazz band. They won a cash prize and are playing in different places around the country. Can you do that too?

2 This writer wants people to …
   A write a new song for a jazz band.
   B perform next month.
   C buy tickets for a festival.
   D play jazz at a festival.

This production of *Cats* is not brilliant. The acting was terrible and the singing was nothing special. I couldn't hear most of the words and I really think none of the performers were talented. There was one good thing … the theatre is wonderful. It's an old building in a great part of the city. Next time, I hope I see a better musical there.

3 What did the reviewer like about this musical?
   A the singing
   B the acting
   C the performers
   D the place

Hi Maria

Guess what? I'm performing in the school play next year. We're doing a performance of *Romeo and Juliet* with my theatre group and I'm Romeo. We had the auditions last week and I was very nervous. I never thought I could be in a Shakespeare play. I hope you can come and see me.

Bye!

Arthur

4 Arthur is writing this email …
   A to give some news.
   B to describe his theatre group.
   C to review a play.
   D to sell a ticket.

Today was the first day of our film festival. And what a fantastic day! Hundreds of people from all around the world were here. There were some amazing films from many different countries. The most popular today was the Spanish film called *La Casa*. It's a romantic film about two people in Madrid. The acting is brilliant. The story is incredible. Don't worry if you weren't at the festival today. You can also see this film on the final day. Remember, you can get tickets on our website. Students pay less.

5 What is the reason for the blog?
   A to advertise a festival
   B to review some films
   C to describe an actor
   D to talk about a film course

Speaking

EXAM STRATEGY

Learn phrases for making and responding to suggestions and for agreeing and disagreeing. This can help you when you take part in a discussion.

3 Read the strategy above. Complete the phrases with the words below. Can you think of other similar phrases?

   point   sure   think   Why

Making suggestions
1 _____ don't we … ?

Agreeing / Disagreeing
2 Yes. That's a good _____.
3 I'm not _____ about that.
4 I don't _____ that's a good idea.

4 You and your friends would like to go to a cultural event. Decide together where you want to go.
   A music festival
   B film festival
   C art exhibition

Exam skills 71

5 VISION 360°
Hanbury Street, London

Learn about life as a street artist and make a digital slideshow

Unit 5 360° hotspots

1 **THINK & SHARE** Work in pairs. What do you think life is like as a street artist? Think of good and bad things. Copy and complete the mind map with your own ideas.

good — street artist — bad

EXPLORE 360°
Access the interactive 360° content now!

2 Look around the photo. What are the people doing?

3 **ALL HOTSPOTS** Explore the hotspots. Find …
1. two people who talk about the life of a street artist.
2. something that gives you information about a bird.
3. something that gives you the history of a place.
4. something that advertises an event.
5. someone who is visiting the place.

4 Read the article. Answer the questions.
1. What is the East End?
2. Where did many people first come from in the area?
3. Why are there lots of art events there?
4. What are streets like Hanbury Street famous for?

5 Which events does the speaker mention? Do you want to go to any of them? Why? / Why not?

6 Go online and find answers to the questions.
1. When does Chinese New Year happen?
2. Why do people in London celebrate it?
3. What types of events can you enjoy there?

7 Read the post and choose the correct answer.
1. ROA is the name of a ___.
   A bird   B picture   C street artist
2. Bangladeshi people think ___ are important.
   A cranes   B storks   C all birds
3. ___ doesn't want to see pictures of street art on social media.
   A K_D   B Dingo   C artisart

8 Read Lucia's message and complete her review.

REVIEW
Name of tour:
Type of tour:
Days and times:
Tour leader:
Number of stars: ★ ★★★ ★★★★★

Submit

72 Vision 360

Digital literacy

9 🟩⭐ Listen. Are the sentences about street artists true (T) or false (F)?
1 They never know what they want to paint when they start.
2 Bad weather can be a positive thing.
3 There aren't enough places to paint.
4 A picture can take several hours to paint.
5 They don't want people to share photos of their work.
6 They sometimes get money for their work.

10 💬 **THINK & SHARE** Think about your answer to Ex 1 and what you learned about the life of a street artist. Can you add any other ideas to your mind map?

CREATE ... a digital slideshow

STEP 1

📡 **RESEARCH IT!**
Go online and find the answers to the questions.
1 Who is ROA?
2 What is special about his street art? In which cities can you find it?

STEP 2
You are going to create a digital slideshow about a street artist you like. Choose some of the ideas below to include.

age   name   nationality   types of picture they paint   how famous they are
how they started painting   where you can see their work   exhibitions

STEP 3
Do research online to find information and photos for your slideshow. Choose some of the adjectives below to describe the photos. Make notes.

amazing   boring   brilliant   excellent   original
romantic   sad   terrible   wonderful

STEP 4
Use your notes to write a short presentation for the slideshow.
… is a street artist from …   He / She usually paints pictures of …
He / She started doing street art when …   Here are some examples of his / her work: …

STEP 5
Present your slideshow to the class. Have a class vote on the best slideshow / street artist.

Vision 360   73

6 Digital detox

- **VOCABULARY**
  Technology
  Things you can't live without
- **GRAMMAR**
  Past simple affirmative: irregular verbs
  Past simple negative and questions: irregular verbs
- **READING**
  This man said goodbye to technology
- **LISTENING**
  Past events
- **GLOBAL SKILLS**
  Social media etiquette
- **SPEAKING**
  Shopping
- **WRITING**
  A product review
- **DOCUMENTARY**
  TV time travellers

VOCABULARY BOOSTER P122–123
GRAMMAR BOOSTER P142–143

Phone zombies

1 Work in pairs. Look at the video still. Answer the questions.
   1 What's Callum doing? Do you ever do this?
   2 Do you think people spend too much time using their phones? Why? / Why not?

2 ▶ 6.01 Watch or listen. Answer the questions.
   1 Who couldn't imagine life without their phones?
   2 How many days was Callum without the internet?
   3 Does he want to live without technology now?

3 ▶ 6.01 Watch or listen again. Match the days of the week to the events.
   1 Monday
   2 Tuesday
   3 Wednesday
   4 Thursday
   5 Friday
   6 Saturday

   A He enjoyed having conversations with his friends.
   B He first learned how much more time he had without his phone.
   C He missed his songs.
   D He wanted to use his phone, but it didn't work.
   E He needed to ask Zara for help, but he couldn't.
   F He saw many people on different devices.

74 Unit 6

Talk about technology. **6.1 VOCABULARY**

4 **REAL ENGLISH** Look at the **bold** words and phrases. Choose the correct alternative.
  1 Welcome to my **digital detox**.
    a period of time **with** / **without** any digital devices
  2 Teenagers are all **phone zombies**.
    They **look** / **don't look** at their phones as they walk around.
  3 I **couldn't wait to go online**.
    I **was** / **wasn't** excited about going on the internet.
  4 We don't **chat face to face** very often.
    have a **real** / **online** conversation
  5 I **felt** pretty **left out**.
    I felt like I was **included** / **excluded** from a group of people.
  6 **Nightmare**!
    a **wonderful** / **terrible** situation

5 **VOCABULARY** Match the words and phrases below to the definitions.

| battery   Bluetooth speaker   check your messages |
| digital devices   laptop   music library |
| post on group chats   scroll through |
| text (v)   turn off   turn on |

  1 a computer which you can carry around
  2 the thing which gives power to your phone
  3 send messages to more than two people
  4 technology, e.g. phones and tablets
  5 see if you have any new texts from friends
  6 you need to do this to a device before you can use it
  7 send a phone message to somebody
  8 spend time searching social media websites
  9 a digital device used for listening to music
  10 a place where you can keep digital songs
  11 you need to do this to a device after you finish using it

6 Write the vocabulary in the correct part of the mind map. Add any more words you can think of.

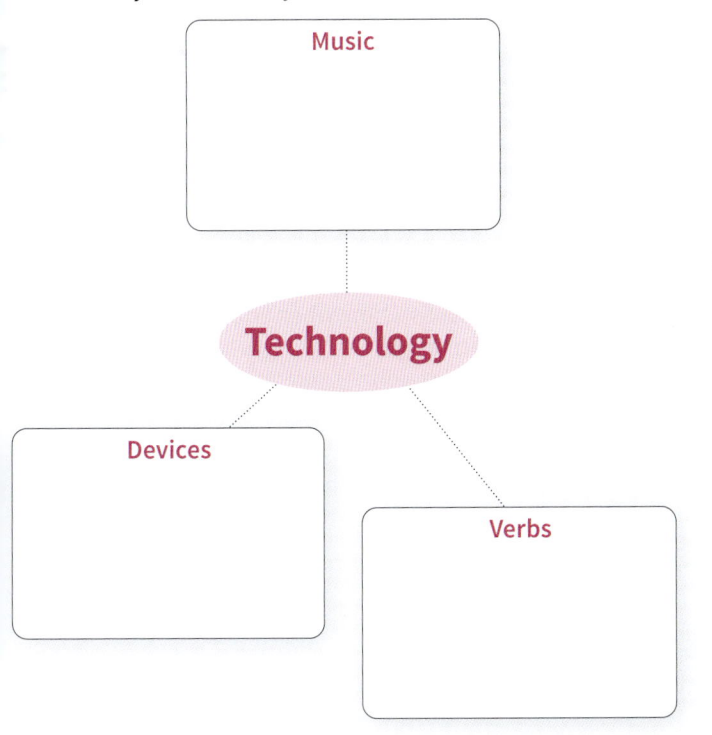

  - Music
  - Technology
    - Devices
    - Verbs

7 Complete the statements with phrases from Ex 5.
  1 Teenagers can't live without their _____.
  2 I usually _____ my phone as soon as I get up.
  3 While I have my breakfast, I _____ my messages.
  4 I _____ my social media, while I get dressed.
  5 I usually do my homework on my _____.
  6 My phone _____ dies after about ten hours.

8 Work in pairs. Are the statements in Ex 7 true for you?

9 Complete the questionnaire with the words below.

| battery   Bluetooth   digital   group chats |
| media   laptop   library   text |

Do you need a DIGITAL DETOX?

When was the last time you …
  1 worked on a _____ computer?
  2 talked to friends in your _____?
  3 scrolled through social _____?
  4 used your phone to _____ a friend?
  5 listened to songs in your music _____?
  6 used _____ speakers or headphones?
  7 charged your phone _____?
  8 wanted to buy a new _____ device?

10 Work in pairs. Ask and answer the questions in the questionnaire. Give extra information. Make a note of your partner's answers.

> When was the last time you looked at your phone?

> It was last night. I checked my messages.

11 **THINK & SHARE** Compare your answers. Do you need to take a break from technology? How do you feel about this?

12 Work in groups. Which is the best digital device in the world? Why? Think about which technology …
  • you use most often.
  • is most important in your everyday life.
  • you don't want to live without.

VOCABULARY BOOSTER Unit 6 75

6.2 GRAMMAR Use past simple irregular verbs to talk about past events.

Past simple affirmative: irregular verbs

1 Do you remember the vlog? What is a digital detox?

2 Read another person's report about their digital detox. How does it compare to Callum's experience?

Comments

My detox disaster!

So, after Callum told us all about his digital detox, I thought about doing it myself. I began my detox yesterday morning. At first, I found it easy not to scroll through my social media. But, then, after I had breakfast, my sister did something terrible … she brought me my phone and said 'There are some really interesting messages in our friends' group chat. Are you sure you don't want to read them?'

I really wanted to turn on my phone and check them, but I couldn't do it in front of her!!! After that, I became really stressed, so I went to my friend Harry's house after lunch (without my phone, of course). Then, when I got there, I saw there was a big football match on his laptop! My digital detox ended that moment. 😕 Please don't tell my sister!

Kaheem 🙂

3 Read the grammar rules. Find all the past simple forms in the text. Which are regular and which are irregular?

Past simple affirmative: irregular verbs

▶ Grammar animation

A Many verbs have irregular past simple forms. There aren't any rules, you just need to learn them.
 go – went
 have – had
 can – could

B Past simple verbs are the same for all persons, except for the verb *be* which has two forms (*was* and *were*).

GRAMMAR BOOSTER P142

4 💬 Work in pairs. Say the infinitive of the verbs that you found in the text. Use the irregular verbs list on page 142 to help you.

told — tell

thought — think

5 Complete the text with the past simple form of the verbs in brackets.

How do the experts feel about technology?

This is what experts in Apple, Google and Microsoft [1]_____ (say) about technology.

A few years ago, Bill Gates of Microsoft [2]_____ (become) worried when he [3]_____ (see) that one of his daughters couldn't stop playing video games. He also [4]_____ (find) that his children couldn't sleep after scrolling through social media. So, he [5]_____ (begin) a screen-free routine with no digital devices an hour before bedtime. His three children [6]_____ (get) their first mobile phone when they were fourteen years old (at a time when most ten-year-olds in the US had one).

Susan Wojcicki, CEO of YouTube has some rules about screen time for her children too. When she [7]_____ (be) young smart phones [8]_____ (not be) around – but TV was! She [9]_____ (can) watch some, but her parents also wanted her to do other things.

And Google's Sundar Pichai's family never goes online. Maybe because Sundar [10]_____ (do) very well at school without a phone, computer or TV at home.

6 💬 **THINK & SHARE** Work in pairs. Discuss the questions. Give reasons for your opinions.
 1 What's the best age to get your first mobile phone?
 2 When are the best times to turn off digital devices?
 3 How do you feel about 'no phones at mealtimes'?

7 Complete the sentences with the past simple form of the verbs in brackets.
 The last time I …
 1 _____ some good music online … (find)
 2 _____ about checking my messages … (think)
 3 _____ to school late was because I _____ on my phone … (get / be)
 4 _____ stressed after I _____ social media … (become / look at)
 5 _____ a friend something important in a text that I _____ them … (tell / send)
 6 _____ something interesting when I _____ on a group chat … (see / go)

8 💬 Work in pairs. Discuss a time when you did the activities in Ex 7. Give extra information.

> The last time I found some good music online was last Saturday. The song was …

9 🔊 6.04 Complete the table with the verbs below. Then listen, check and repeat.

brought   read   saw   said   sent   thought

/ɔː/	caught
/e/	went

76 Unit 6

Understand reason and result in an article about an unusual way of life.

6.3 READING

THIS MAN SAID GOODBYE TO TECHNOLOGY

No car, no TV, no internet, no mobile phone. Welcome to Mark Boyle's world. Mark is a writer and lives in Ireland. He doesn't use any modern technology.

It all started at university. He saw a film about Gandhi and wanted to live a simple life like Gandhi did. After university, he moved to Bristol and had a food business. Then, one day in 2008, he had a conversation about money with a friend. They agreed that money caused a lot of problems for people, society and the environment. Mark decided to start the 'Freeconomy Community' so people could share things for free. Later that year, Mark decided to live for a whole year without money. It lasted for three years. He wrote a book about his experience called *Moneyless Man: A Year of Freeconomic Living*, and now many people know him as 'Moneyless Mark'.

He realised that he enjoyed many things about modern life – televisions, phones, computers – but he still wasn't happy with life, so he moved back to Ireland and bought a small farm. He lived in a small, simple house and grew his own food.

Then, in 2019 he made his biggest change. He moved out of the house and into a small cabin and stopped using all modern technology. There isn't a shower or toilet because there's no running water. There isn't a TV or fridge because there's no electricity. And no mobile phone.

Friends were worried about how they could stay in touch. In the past, Mark phoned or texted them. Because he can't do that now, he writes letters to them or sees them face to face. Mark was also worried about his writing job. All his adult life he used computers to write books, articles or essays. Now, he can only use a pen and paper. It's slower because he can't quickly delete or change something, but he prefers it because it makes him more careful.

People often ask him if he finds life difficult without technology. He says that he's happier, calmer and sleeps better. His relationships with people are also better because he talks to people face to face and not on social media.

Mark made an extreme change to his life. But, perhaps there are lessons we can all learn from his way of life.

cabin – a small house usually made of wood
running water – a water system that brings water into a house or building

Goodbye to technology

1. Work in pairs. What can you see in the photo?

STRATEGY Understanding linking words: reasons and results

Some linking words, such as *because* and *so*, show why something happened or what the result is. We use *because* to show the reason. We use *so* to show the result. Recognising these words helps you understand reasons and results in a text.

2. Read the strategy. Then, match the sentence halves.
   1. I didn't go to the concert
   2. It was a holiday,
   3. I lost my house key,
   4. I arrived late for school
   5. I didn't like the film,
   6. I couldn't phone you

   A because my battery was dead.
   B because I was ill.
   C so I left.
   D so I didn't go to school.
   E because I got up late.
   F so I couldn't get in.

3. 🔊 6.05 Read the article about Mark Boyle. What did he do?

4. Read the article again. Answer the questions.
   1. How did the film about Gandhi change Mark's life?
      A He wanted to live the same way.
      B He wanted to move to a different city.
      C He wanted to meet Gandhi.
   2. Why did he start the 'Freeconomy Community'?
      A Because a friend told him to.
      B So people could help each other.
      C Because he needed a job.
   3. Why do people call him 'Moneyless Mark'?
      A Because he's poor.
      B Because he's a writer.
      C Because he lives without money.
   4. Why did he move back to Ireland?
      A So he could buy a farm.
      B Because he wanted to be happier.
      C So he could write more books.
   5. Why does he sometimes write letters to his friends?
      A Because they worry about him.
      B Because he doesn't have a phone.
      C Because he doesn't want to see them.
   6. Why are his relationships different now?
      A Because he has more friends.
      B Because he meets them in person.
      C Because he's calmer and happier.

5. **VOCABULARY** Match the highlighted words or phrases in the text with the definitions.
   1. the most recent scientific knowledge used to make things
   2. all the people who live in a particular area
   3. the natural world we live in
   4. living without modern machines, etc.

6. **THINK & SHARE** Make a list of the pros and cons of Mark's new way of life.

Living without technology	
Pros +	Cons –

7. Work in pairs. Share your ideas from Ex 6.

8. What do you think about Mark's life? What lessons can we learn?

9. **MEDIATION** Imagine a friend of yours is planning to live a simpler life. Write a letter telling them all about Mark's old and new life.

Unit 6 77

6.4 GLOBAL SKILLS — Be polite online.

Social media etiquette

1 **THINK & SHARE** Work in pairs. Look at the class group chat. Ask and answer the questions.
1 How often do you see messages like this online?
2 How do you feel when you read them?

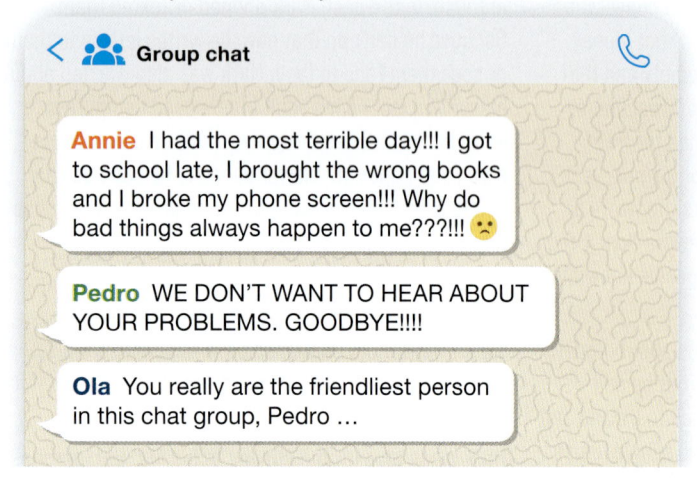

> **Group chat**
>
> **Annie** I had the most terrible day!!! I got to school late, I brought the wrong books and I broke my phone screen!!! Why do bad things always happen to me???!!! 😟
>
> **Pedro** WE DON'T WANT TO HEAR ABOUT YOUR PROBLEMS. GOODBYE!!!!
>
> **Ola** You really are the friendliest person in this chat group, Pedro …

2 Read the message from Rick, who looks after the group chat. What is he asking them to do? Why?

> **Group chat**
>
> in this chat group, Pedro …
>
> **Rick** Hey guys, please remember to THINK before you post. Is it: true, helpful, interesting, necessary and kind? Let's all try and help Annie feel a bit better! 🙂

3 🔊 6.06 Listen to two friends talking about the messages. Choose the correct alternative.
1 Jamie and Zoe **are** / **aren't** in the chat group.
2 Zoe thought Rick wanted to **start** / **stop** a fight.
3 Zoe thought that Annie's day **was** / **wasn't** bad.
4 Jamie **loved** / **hated** the way Pedro finished his post.
5 Jamie's grandmother taught him to be **kind** / **loud**.
6 They **could** / **couldn't** understand Ola's message.

4 Look at the phrases for discussing online behaviour. Complete them with the words below.

| bad | did | don't | good | thought | was | worst |

1 Was it a _____ / bad idea to post it?
2 _____ it necessary to (reply to her)?
3 I think he _____ it because he (wanted to be polite).
4 I _____ it wasn't (kind).
5 I _____ think it was necessary to (share her problems).
6 It's a good / _____ idea to (use all capital letters) online.
7 And the best / _____ thing about it was (the ending).

5 Work in pairs. Share your personal opinions about the messages. Use the phrases in Ex 4 to help you.

6 Read the online etiquette rules. Match the headings to the paragraphs.
A Don't forget to reply to people.
B Think about other people's feelings.
C Try to be positive online.
D Consider other people's opinions.
E Always be polite to others.

5 golden rules of online etiquette

Rule #1 ___
ALL CAPITAL LETTERS or lots of exclamation marks (!!!!!) can seem rude. People often use them to shout at others online. Also, watch out that your jokes don't hurt others; not everybody finds the same things funny.

Rule #2 ___
It's easy to forget that you are chatting to a real person online. Try to imagine receiving your message. How does it make you feel? If it isn't good, don't send it.

Rule #3 ___
We all see things differently, and we don't always agree. It's fine to disagree, but strong opinions often start arguments. Try to express your ideas in a friendly way.

Rule #4 ___
It isn't a good idea to post things when you're feeling very angry or sad because it can make you look negative. Why not talk about problems with a good friend instead?

Rule #5 ___
If somebody asks you a question or needs help online, it isn't polite to ignore them. Don't forget to answer their message or say that you received it.

shout – speak very loudly, often angrily
ignore – not reply or react

7 Work in pairs. Which rules are easier / more difficult to follow? Why?

8 **THINK & SHARE** Work in small groups. Follow the steps to create a poster about online behaviour.
Step 1: Use everybody's experiences to think of the rules people break most often.
Step 2: Decide what types of online behaviour you like / don't like.
Step 3: Add titles and pictures to add interest to your poster.

9 Share your ideas as a class. Whose poster was the most interesting?

10 Work in pairs. Discuss the questions.
- Do you know more about online etiquette now?
- Do you know why it is important?

Talk about things you can't live without.

6.5 VOCABULARY

Everyday items

1 Quickly read the article. Answer the questions.
1 What's the article about?
2 Whose things are they?
3 What's her favourite thing?

2 🔊 6.07 Read the article again. Match the items highlighted in the text to photos A–J.

3 Complete the text with items in Ex 2.

☰ My Blog

My new school is a long way from my home. It takes me nearly an hour to get to school by train. I often get up late, so I always have some ¹_____ in a small bag, a ²_____ for my hair, and a ³_____ - so I can check my appearance on the train! When I study French on the train, I use an online ⁴_____ to check new words. I always take a ⁵_____ for when I need a drink. To pay for things, I always use ⁶_____. I don't have any ⁷_____ in my wallet. My mum said I can get my first one next year. The one thing I can't live without is my phone. It does everything. I use it to read the news, talk to friends, and play games. My second favourite thing is probably my ⁸_____ – my phone is useless with a dead battery. And my third favourite thing is my ⁹_____ - it takes amazing photos - better than the ones I can take on my phone!

4 💬 Work in pairs. Think about how often and when you use the items in the photos. Compare your ideas.

5 Write an article about what's in your bag and what you can't live without. Why do you have the things? Use the texts in Ex 1 and 3 to help you.

What can't YOU live without?

This week, we ask people to share what's in their bag. What's important to them? What can't they live without?

This month we asked Alina from Oxford.

I've got my mobile phone. Doesn't everyone have one these days? I live in Oxford, but I work in London. I have a charger, so I can charge my phone on the train. I always have a book with me because I prefer reading on the train and not using my phone.

I'm learning Spanish at the moment. I use my dictionary to look up new words. I know there are good apps, but I prefer the dictionary. I have my wallet with my bank cards. I always carry some cash. You never know when you might need some. These days, I always take a water bottle with me. All those plastic bottles aren't good for the environment. I've also got a small bag with some make-up in it, a comb and a mirror.

Finally, the thing I can't live without – my digital camera. I love taking photos. There's a camera on my phone, but it's just not the same. I take my digital camera everywhere so I'm always ready to take that perfect photo.

VOCABULARY BOOSTER Unit 6   79

6.6 GRAMMAR Use the past simple to ask and answer about the past.

Past simple negative and questions: irregular verbs

1 **THINK & SHARE** Work in pairs. Discuss the questions.
   1 What were your parents like as teenagers?
   2 Were their teenage years better or worse than yours? Why? / Why not?

2 Look at the photos. What are they wearing? What are they doing? Which decade do you think it is?

3 Read the quiz. Choose the correct answers.

Generation X: teenagers in the 1990s!

1 What did they do when they got presents?
   A They posted 'thank you' letters.
   B They sent 'thank you' text messages.
   C They wrote 'thank you' posts on social media.

2 How did they work on a group language project?
   A They spoke about it on a group chat.
   B They had laptops and used online dictionaries.
   C They met in a library, did research there and wrote their ideas in an exercise book.

3 Did they read any news articles?
   A No, they didn't. They watched videos on their phones.
   B Yes, they did. They bought magazines and newspapers.
   C Yes, they did. They scrolled through social media posts.

4 How did they listen to their favourite bands?
   A They watched music videos on their phones.
   B They downloaded songs with a credit card.
   C They bought albums in shops. They didn't have a music library because these didn't exist!

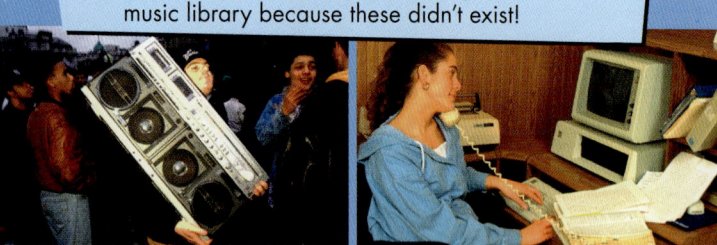

4 Find all the past simple negative and question forms in the quiz. Complete the grammar rules.

Past simple: irregular verbs

▶ Grammar animation

Negative and questions
A We form the past simple negative with subject + ¹_____ + the infinitive without *to*.
B We form past simple questions with ²_____ + subject + the infinitive without *to*.
C We form short answers with: *Yes*, + subject + ³_____. / *No*, + subject + ⁴_____.

GRAMMAR BOOSTER P143

5 Complete the second sentences with the past simple negative form of the verbs in **bold**.
   1 My parents **met** at work. They _____ at school.
   2 I **bought** a used laptop online. I _____ a new one.
   3 You **ate** pasta for lunch. You _____ pizza.
   4 Sal **wrote** a text message. She _____ an email.
   5 I **brought** my bank card. I _____ any cash.
   6 In 1995, people **had** CDs. They _____ smartphones.

6 Write three sentences in the past simple negative about people you know – two false and one true. Share them with your partner. Can they guess which one is true?

   My mum didn't live in this city when she was little.

   I think that's true.

7 Complete the questions with the past simple form of the verbs below.

   buy   go   listen   post   send   use

   1 _____ you _____ to the library after school yesterday?
   2 _____ you _____ anything in the shops at the weekend?
   3 _____ you _____ a thank you message after your last birthday?
   4 _____ you _____ on a group chat yesterday?
   5 _____ you _____ to an album last night?
   6 _____ you _____ a dictionary for your last English homework?

8 Work with a partner. Ask and answer the questions in Ex 7.

   Did you go to the library after school?

   No, I didn't. I went home instead.

9 Work with a partner. Ask and answer questions about last week. Find out more information.
   1 Where / you have / lunch / ?
   2 What / you bring with you to school / ?
   3 What / you read / ?
   4 Who / you send messages to / ?
   5 Where / go out / ?

   When did you scroll through social media last week?

   I looked at some friends' posts last weekend.

   What did you see?

   I found some interesting photos from five years ago.

80 Unit 6

Recognise specific information in a conversation about a past event.

6.7 LISTENING

Past events

1 👥 Work in pairs. Look at the dictionary definition below. Answer the questions.

time capsule (n) – a container filled with objects that people think are typical of the time they are living in; the capsule is then put in the ground, so that people in the future can find it and see how people lived then

1 What items do people put in time capsules?
2 Where do people put them and why?
3 What would you like to put in a time capsule?

2 👥 Work in pairs. Match photos 1–4 with descriptions A–D. Are any of these objects still popular today?
A games console   C video cassettes
B Rubik's cube   D music player

3 🔊 **6.10** Listen to the first part of a podcast. What did the family do for a year?

> **STRATEGY** Recognising specific information
> Sometimes you need to listen for specific information. Wh- questions can help you try to guess what type of details you need to hear, e.g. *When did he go?* means you probably need to listen for a date, a day, a time or a year.

4 Read the **strategy**. Look at the Wh- questions below. What type of information do you need to listen for?
1 Where was the family from?
2 When did their experiment start?
3 What were the mum and dad called?
4 How old were they when they decided to do it?
5 How many children did they have?
6 How old were the children?
7 Why were they worried about their children?
8 When were Blair and Morgan born?

5 🔊 **6.10** Listen again. Answer the questions in Ex 4.

6 👥 Work in pairs. Read the questions from the second part of the conversation. What do you think the answers are?
1 What technology did they have in the '80s?
2 Did they print the photos online?
3 Did visitors do the experiment too?
4 What part did the family find most difficult?
5 How did the experience go in the end?

7 🔊 **6.11** Listen to the second part of the conversation. Check your answers in Ex 6.

8 🔊 **6.11** Listen again. Correct the mistakes in the sentences.
1 In 1986, people read online maps and books.
2 They used the internet to find information.
3 *Spider-Man* was the most popular film in 1986.
4 The family took photos with digital cameras.
5 The parents couldn't use bank cards in the shops.
6 Guests could use their digital devices.
7 It was easy to communicate with others.
8 The parents thought the experience went badly.

9 💬 **THINK & SHARE** Work in pairs. Ask and answer the questions.
1 What do you think were the best / worst things about the experiment? Why?
2 Would you like to live for one year in 1986? Why? / Why not?
3 Is there a year in the past that you would like to live in? When? Why?

10 👥 Work in groups. Discuss these questions.
1 What was your life like when you were …
   • four years old?
   • eight years old?
   • eleven years old?
2 What are the differences and similarities?
3 Would you like to be younger again? Why? / Why not?

Unit 6   81

6.8 SPEAKING   Ask questions politely when shopping.

Shopping

1   Work in pairs. Ask and answer the questions.
    1 How often do you go shopping?
    2 What do you usually buy?
    3 What was the last thing you bought? When did you buy it? Which shop did you go to?

2 🔊 6.12 Read and listen to the dialogue. Which phone does the man buy? Why?

Assistant Hello. How can I help you?
Customer I'm looking for a new smartphone.
Assistant Well, the X8 is very popular, and so's the newer model, the X9. But it's more expensive.
Customer Has the X8 got a good camera?
Assistant Yes, it's excellent, but the one on the X9 is better.
Customer Ah, I see. How much is it?
Assistant The X9 costs £199.99 and the X8 is £50 cheaper.
Customer I'd like the X8, please.
Assistant How would you like to pay?
Customer Can I pay by card, please?
Assistant Sure. That's £149.99. Can you enter your PIN, please? Do you want a bag?
Customer No, thanks. I've got one.
Assistant There you are. Thank you very much.
Customer Thanks. Goodbye.

3 Look at the **Phrasebook**. Who says the phrases? Write *customer* (C) or *assistant* (A). Then complete the phrases with the words below.

| £20 bag cash change card |
| for help much |

PHRASEBOOK Shopping
How can I ¹_____ you?
I'm looking ²_____ (a tablet).
How ³_____ is it / are they?
It costs / They cost ⁴_____.
Can I pay by ⁵_____?
Can I pay in ⁶_____?
Here's your ⁷_____.
Do you want a ⁸_____?

4 Read the box. Answer the questions.

PHRASEBOOK How to talk about prices
50p = fifty p / fifty pence
£5.99 = five pounds ninety-nine / five ninety-nine
£250 = two hundred and fifty pounds

1 How much are the X8 and X9 in the dialogue?
2 How do you say the prices below?

| £0.10   £0.50   £1   £2.50   £10.99 |
| £12   £23.64   £798.99 |

5   Work in pairs. Take turns to ask for and give the price of these devices.

Special offers

£599.99 — 'HG9' laptop
£285 — 'FX1' digital camera
£173.99 — 'T6' tablet
£11.50 — 'S21' earphones
£44.05 — 'M34' Bluetooth speaker
£12.49 — 'Z4' phone case

> How much is the laptop?   It's £ …

STRATEGY Asking questions politely
When you ask questions, pay attention to the way your voice sounds (your intonation).
Polite intonation is important. Always sound friendly and interested when you ask people questions.

6 🔊 6.13 Read the strategy. Listen to the questions. Does each speaker sound polite / interested (P) or rude / uninterested (R)?

7   Work in pairs. Imagine you want to buy a new device (phone, tablet, etc.). Prepare a dialogue like the one in Ex 2. Use the **Phrasebook** to help you.

8   Practise your dialogue. Then act out your dialogue to the class.

9 **REFLECT** Work in pairs. Answer the questions.
    1 Was your conversation successful? Why? / Why not?
    2 Which phrases in the Phrasebook did you use?
    3 Did you use the correct intonation to sound polite?

82 Unit 6

6.9 WRITING

Write a product review.

A product review

1 **THINK & SHARE** Work in pairs. Ask and answer the questions.
   1 Do you research a product before you buy it?
   2 How often do you read customer reviews?
   3 Can you trust online reviews? Why? / Why not?

2 Read the product reviews for a laptop. How many stars do you think each reviewer gave?

Product reviews

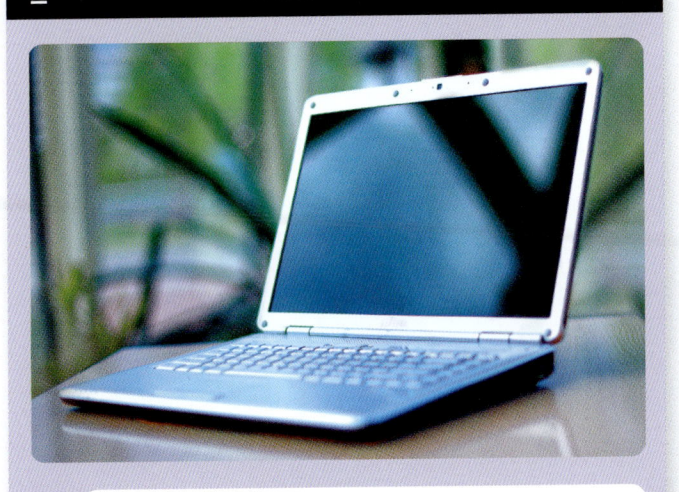

(stars: ___ / 5) Pavel
I did a lot of research before I bought this and read a lot of reviews. Then, I saw it was on sale cheaply online, [1]_____ I decided to buy it. I use it every day to do my homework or play games on it. It's cheaper than most other laptops. It isn't very fast, but it works perfectly for my needs.

(stars: ___ / 5) Kaarina
My old computer died last week, [2]_____ I needed a new one. I bought this online and it arrived very quickly. The best thing about it is the camera. The worst is the battery [3]_____ it doesn't last long. It works OK for my daily vlog.

(stars: ___ / 5) Bukayo
I bought this laptop [4]_____ I wanted to record some music. I chose it [5]_____ it was cheap. It was only £159. Unfortunately, I found out why it was cheap. The microphone isn't very good and the speakers are awful. It's also very slow. It's OK for home use, but sadly, it's terrible for making music on.

3 Complete the reviews with *so* or *because*.

4 Read the reviews again. Write a list of all the pros and cons of the laptop.

Pros	Cons

5 Work in pairs. Imagine you need to buy a new laptop. Is this a good laptop to buy for your needs? Why? / Why not?

STRATEGY Writing product reviews

A good product review usually says …
1 when and where the customer bought the product.
2 what they use it for and how it works.
3 some pros and cons of the product.
4 their personal opinions about it.
5 a rating of 1–5 out of 5.

6 Read the **strategy**. Find examples in the reviews that match numbers 1–5 in the strategy.

7 Work in pairs. Think of a product you bought recently. When and where did you buy it? What are some of its pros and cons?

LANGUAGE FOCUS Adverbs

Adverbs describe verbs and can appear in different places in a sentence. Most adverbs are made by adding *-ly* to adjectives, e.g. *careful – carefully, loud – loudly, slow – slowly*. Some adverbs have the same form as adjectives, e.g. *fast, late, early, hard*. The form of the adverb of the adjective *good* is *well*.

8 Read the **Language focus**. <u>Underline</u> all the adverbs in the reviews. What is their adjective form?

9 Read the review. Complete it with the adverb form of the adjectives below.

bad   fortunate   good   long   perfect   unfortunate

★★★★★

I bought this Bluetooth speaker online. [1]_____, I didn't receive it on time! I'm not sure why it took so [2]_____ to arrive! It was packed very [3]_____ too – the box was open. [4]_____, nothing was wrong with it. I'm very happy to say that it works [5]_____. In fact, I gave it five stars because it works [6]_____ with my smartphone! I love it!

10 Imagine you want to write a review about a digital device you bought. Choose a real product you bought (or invent one). Make notes about …
   • when and where you bought it.
   • some examples of when you used it.
   • what you think of it and why.
   • how many stars you give it out of five and why.

11 Write your review in 60–80 words. Use your notes, the **strategy** and the **Language focus** to help you.

12 **CHECK YOUR WORK**
   • Does your review cover the points in the strategy?
   • Do you use the correct tenses?
   • Does it include any adverbs?
   • Did you check it carefully for any mistakes?

Unit 6   83

6.10 REVIEW

Grammar

1 Complete the text with the past simple form of the verbs in brackets.

When his children were younger, billionaire Mark Cuban ¹_____ (find) that they only wanted to play on digital devices. He ²_____ (not like) this, so he created a system: they ³_____ (not have) any digital devices, but they could buy screen time when they ⁴_____ (do) different things. For example, each time his daughters ⁵_____ (read) a book, they ⁶_____ (get) two hours on a device. And his son ⁷_____ (have) time to play video games after he ⁸_____ (give) his dad the correct answer to maths questions. Cuban also ⁹_____ (see) what apps and games his children were on at all times. He ¹⁰_____ (can) turn off devices when he ¹¹_____ (think) they weren't good for them.

2 Complete the dialogue with the past simple form of the verbs below and short answers.

go have meet not pay not say
not stay send talk tell

Al   ¹_____ you _____ anyone in town last week?
Sue Yes, I ²_____. I met Masud. We went to a café for lunch.
Al   Which café ³_____ you _____ to?
Sue The new one in the square. It's got free Wi-Fi.
Al   Great! What ⁴_____ you and Masud _____ about?
Sue He ⁵_____ me a bit about his new job. But he was very quiet, actually. He ⁶_____ much.
Al   How strange! He isn't usually like that! What ⁷_____ you _____ for lunch?
Sue We ate burgers. Masud ⁸_____ long. In fact, he left after his meal, and he ⁹_____ for it! I did!
Al   No! How rude! ¹⁰_____ he _____ you a message to say sorry?
Sue No, he ¹¹_____. I texted him, asking how he was, and I'm still waiting for his answer.
Al   Oh dear!

Vocabulary

3 Match a word in A to a word in B to complete the sentences.

A Bluetooth group digital laptop
   music scroll turned (x2)

B camera computer chat library
   off on speakers through

1 You can work where you want to with a _____.
2 Ali _____ her phone because she needed to call me.
3 I sent a message, _____ my phone and went to bed.
4 You can take photos on a phone or a _____.
5 I often _____ photos on social media.
6 My friends and I have got a _____ so we can all talk to each other.
7 You keep songs and albums in a _____.
8 I can't play music on _____ in school.

4 Complete the sentences.
1 Use a d_____ to check words.
2 Agnes hates technology, so she only pays with c_____.
3 I've got some make-up and a m_____ in a small bag.
4 Ed uses a b_____ card to pay for things.
5 Dad uses a c_____ to tidy his hair.
6 I always carry a water b_____.

Cumulative review

5 Complete the story with the correct answers: A, B or C.

¹_____ Saturday, my mum asked me to go shopping. She put £100 in my ²_____ and texted me a shopping list. She ³_____ me to write it down too, because technology doesn't always work. I ⁴_____ to her advice. I ⁵_____ the house and took the bus into town. On the way, I found that my phone ⁶_____ was dead, so I went home again. When I got home, I saw that there ⁷_____ anybody in. I knew Mum was out because her bag wasn't there. I began looking for my phone ⁸_____, but I couldn't find it. My mum and I have got similar phones, so she probably ⁹_____ it. I wanted to call her on the house phone, but I didn't know the number. I always use my phone for that too! Then, I ¹⁰_____ the door open. It was my mum.
'¹¹_____ you find everything on the list?' she asked.
'No, I ¹²_____. My phone died, so I couldn't buy anything.'
'What ¹³_____ you about technology?' she laughed. Mum was right …

1	A Ago	B Next	C Last
2	A cash	B wallet	C tablet
3	A said	B spoke	C told
4	A didn't listened	B didn't listen	C not listened
5	A left	B went	C got
6	A screen	B battery	C camera
7	A didn't	B wasn't	C didn't be
8	A charger	B number	C screen
9	A taked	B did take	C took
10	A heared	B heard	C hear
11	A Do	B Have	C Did
12	A did	B didn't	C don't
13	A did I tell	B did you tell	C did tell

💬 Think & share

6 Answer the questions.
1 Is life easier with technology? Why? / Why not?
2 What are the three best digital devices? Why?
3 What do you never leave home without? Why?

6.11 EXAM SKILLS

Listening

EXAM STRATEGY

When you do a task with options for *True* or *False*, try to answer each question the first time you listen. If you can't answer, don't stop listening. Move on to the next question. You can try again the second time.

1 Read the strategy above. Then read the short extract from a listening text and look at the questions 1–4. Which of the questions did you answer the first time? Which questions did you need to read again?

> I'm Ellie. I like technology, but I can live without it. I usually check my messages after breakfast and scroll through social media, but then I turn off my phone. I don't look at it again until lunchtime. Last year, I did a digital detox. I found it easy.

1 Ellie really loves technology. ___
2 She checks her messages as soon as she wakes up. ___
3 She doesn't use her phone all day. ___
4 She did a digital detox this year. ___

2 🔊 **6.14** You will hear a radio presenter talking to a teenager, Rex, about technology. For each statement 1–8, write true (T) or false (F).
1 The radio presenter is talking about technology today. ___
2 She is asking students in the street about the topic. ___
3 Rex studies technology at a university in London. ___
4 Rex's parents think technology is a good thing. ___
5 He got a phone when he was eight. ___
6 He enjoyed school life, but he didn't work hard. ___
7 He often used his phone at meal times. ___
8 His family had one day each week without digital devices. ___

Use of English

EXAM STRATEGY

When you complete a text with missing words, cover the words before you read the text. Think of words that might fit in the gaps. Then look at the options and see if any of your ideas are there.

3 Read the strategy above. Then read the text below. Try to work out the missing words. Compare your ideas with a partner.

> Last year, the Benson family decided [1]___ give up modern life and move to the country. They said goodbye to technology and bought [2]___ old house with a huge garden. Now they don't [3]___ cash on food. They catch fish or grow vegetables.

4 Read the text below and choose the best word (A–J) that fits each gap 1–8. There are two extra words that you do not need.

Life at sea

Sami and Adel first [1]___ interested in travelling around the world when they read an article online about families living on boats. They had two children at the time and very busy jobs. As [2]___, they were both very stressed. They bought a boat and then they [3]___ their journey. The boat was small, but comfortable. The children had lots of books and [4]___ hard. They also [5]___ many amazing things and met lots of wonderful people. What about technology? [6]___ did they speak to their friends and family at home? It was more difficult to use the internet at sea than on land, but it was possible. They [7]___ also use their mobile phones. Today, the family are still at sea and their life is better, [8]___ they don't want to come home.

A started   F love
B asked   G a result
C studied   H so
D how   I became
E saw   J could

Writing

EXAM STRATEGY

When you write a formal letter, you need to use polite formal expressions. It's a good idea to learn some expressions that you can use.

5 Read the strategy above. Then complete the expressions with the words below.

| am   faithfully   forward   Madam   Ms / Mr / Mrs   Yours |

1 Dear Sir or ___
2 Dear ___ Harris
3 I ___ writing about …
4 I look ___ to hearing from you.
5 Yours ___
6 ___ sincerely

6 You bought a tablet online but it isn't working. Write a letter to the company that sold it and make a complaint. Use the ideas below to help.
• Say why you are writing.
• Explain what the problem is.
• Say what you'd like the shop to do about it.
• Ask for a quick reply.

Exam skills 85

7 A bright future

- **VOCABULARY** Life goals / Jobs
- **GRAMMAR** be going to / will
- **READING** Teens changing the world
- **LISTENING** New Year celebrations
- **GLOBAL SKILLS** My dreams
- **SPEAKING** Comparing and contrasting
- **WRITING** An informal invitation email
- **VISION 360** A visit to the museum

VOCABULARY BOOSTER P124–125
GRAMMAR BOOSTER P144–145

Go to drama school
Become an actor

Dream big

1 💬 Work in pairs. Look at the video still. Answer the questions.
  1 Does Callum have big dreams for the future? Why / Why not?
  2 What do you want to do when you're older?

2 ▶ 🔊 **7.01** Watch or listen. Which times of life are Zara and Callum comparing?

3 ▶ 🔊 **7.01** Watch or listen again. Are the sentences true (T) or false (F)?
  1 Children think that teenagers have a lot of fun.
  2 Zara spends all her time playing sport.
  3 She wants to continue studying when she leaves school.
  4 She wants to become a famous cook in the future.
  5 Callum started making videos when he was sixteen.
  6 Callum's first videos weren't very popular.
  7 He is quite famous now.
  8 Callum is having driving lessons.

86 Unit 7

Talk about your life goals. 7.1 VOCABULARY

4 **REAL ENGLISH** Choose the correct meaning of the **bold** phrases.
1. All **kids** dream about what they're going to be like.
   A adults
   B children and young people
2. It's good to **dream big**.
   A be realistic
   B want amazing things
3. My first video got 25 **likes**.
   A people who enjoyed it
   B people who hated it
4. I'm **not** famous **at all**!
   A quite
   B really not
5. I'm **not** going to get a driver **anytime soon**!
   A in a short time
   B in a long time
6. I think we're **living the dream**!
   A doing what we want to do
   B not being realistic

5 Work in pairs. Ask and answer the questions.
1. What do you think about Callum and Zara's dreams?
2. What do you think about their real life?
3. What do your parents / teachers think you do all day?
4. What do you really do all day?
5. What do you want to do one day?

6 Finish the sentences. Then work in pairs and compare your answers. How different is real life from your earlier dreams?
- When I was a child, I wanted to …
- I thought high school was …
- I thought teenagers were …

7 **VOCABULARY** Choose the correct word from the pair of given words to complete sentences a and b.
1. become / go
   a. I want to _____ to **university** next year.
   b. Do you need to study drama to _____ **an actor**?
2. manager / cook
   a. She wants **to become** a top _____ in a big company.
   b. You can **learn to** _____ meals online.
3. earn / share
   a. You can _____ **some money** from vlogging.
   b. Students often _____ **a house**.
4. drive / work
   a. Does she _____ **for** a bank?
   b. Did you **learn to** _____ a car at 17?
5. rich / famous
   a. When you **become** _____ everyone knows your name.
   b. Most YouTubers don't **become** _____ – they do it for fun, not money!
6. get / save
   a. Will you _____ **a degree** in business?
   b. You need to _____ **some money** for the future.

8 Write the words and phrases in Ex 7 in the correct part of the mind map. Then add any more words you can think of.

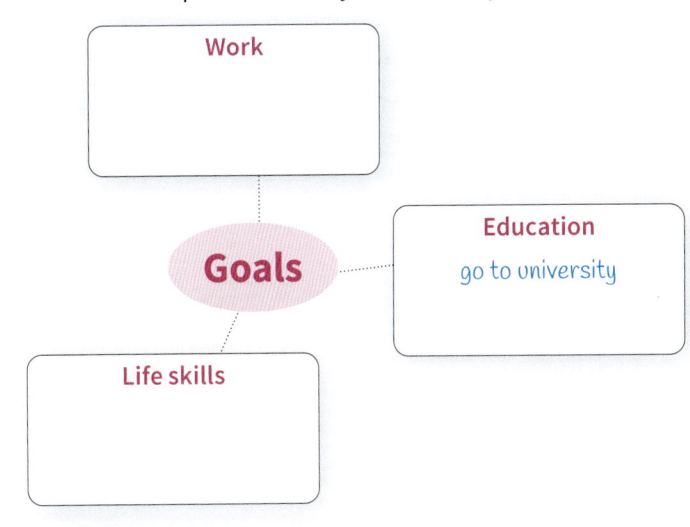

- Work
- Goals
- Education: go to university
- Life skills

9 🔊 **7.02** Listen to a man giving some advice. Where do you think he works? Who do you think he is talking to?

10 🔊 **7.02** Listen again. Answer the questions.
1. Is it easy for students to follow their dreams?
2. Which example of a course does he give?
3. How much money do students earn doing work experience?
4. When can students take classes in life skills?
5. Which three life skills does he talk about?
6. What can the college help students to decide?

11 Work in pairs. Ask and answer the questions.
1. Would you like to go to this college? Why? / Why not?
2. What would you like to study there?

12 **THINK & SHARE** Work in pairs. Ask and answer questions. Give your reasons.

What's the best age to …
- learn to swim / drive?
- start to save / earn a lot of money?
- learn to cook?
- go to college or university?
- get a degree?
- leave home?
- share a house with friends?
- have your own company?
- become a manager?

What's the best age to learn to swim?

I think it's six because …

VOCABULARY BOOSTER Unit 7 87

7.2 GRAMMAR   Use *be going to* to talk about goals and future plans.

Be going to

1 Do you remember the vlog? What dreams did Zara and Callum have? What is their real life like?

2 Look at the dream board on a teenager's social media page. What is she planning to study? Where?

Claudia — 1 day ago

My life goals
- I'm going to college in the USA.
- I'm going to share a house.
- My friends and I aren't going to eat fast food every day.
- I'm going to get a degree in international business.
- I'm not going to spend all day on social media.

Hi there! I'm Claudia. I'm seventeen. I'm Mexican. I always dream big! This is my new dream board. Do you like it?

I want to study Business at the University of Texas in the USA. Is it going to be easy? No, it isn't. Am I going to miss my family? Yes, I am. Especially my little sister, Graciela, because she isn't going to share a house with me there … 😞 But it's going to be really amazing too! I hope that real life is going to be better than my dreams! What do you think?

3 Read the grammar rules. Find all the examples of *be going to* in the text. Complete the examples with the correct form of the verb *be*.

Be going to

▶ **Grammar animation**

We use the verb *be* + *going to* + the infinitive to talk about our plans for the future, our goals and our dreams.

Affirmative
I ¹_____ going to get a biology degree.
She's going to study in the USA.

Negative
My friends and I ²_____ going to eat fast food.
She isn't going to live alone.

Questions
'Is it going to be easy?' 'No, it ³_____.'
'Are you going to share a house?' 'Yes, I am.'
When the main verb is *go*, we often omit *to go*.
I'm going to (go to) college in the USA.

Future time expressions
Future time expressions go at the beginning or at the end of a sentence.
I'm going to finish school soon.

GRAMMAR BOOSTER P144

4 Complete the sentences with the correct form of *be going to* and the verbs in brackets.
1 The students _____ a degree soon. (get)
2 Adam _____ to drive this year. (not learn)
3 My friend _____ a vlog about cooking. (start)
4 I _____ at my parents' company one day. (work)
5 _____ you _____ at home this evening? (stay)
6 Lisa and Ana _____ a house next year. (not share)
7 _____ Ms Lee _____ a manager? (become)
8 _____ we _____ you later? (see)

5 Put the time expressions below in the correct order, starting with the soonest. Can you think of any more?

> in a few minutes   in a minute   in a month   in a year
> in half an hour   in ten days' time   in two years
> next week   the day after tomorrow   this evening
> tomorrow afternoon   tonight

6 Think about your plans. Write five sentences about your plans. Use *be going to* and the future time expressions in Ex 5.

7 💬 Work in pairs. Ask and answer the questions about your future plans, adding appropriate future time expressions. Find out more information.
- visit any relatives? Who … ?
- meet your friends? Who … ?
- study for a test? What … ?
- learn how to do anything? What … ?
- work? Where … ?
- save some money? How much … ?
- chat to friends? Who … ?
- go to university? What / study?

> Are you going to visit any relatives this weekend?
>
> Yes, I am.
>
> Who are you going to visit?
>
> I'm going to visit my aunt and uncle in Buenos Aires.

8 💬 Work with a new partner. Tell them about your partner in Ex 6.

> She's going to visit her aunt and uncle in Murcia.

9 💬 **THINK & SHARE** Work in pairs. Discuss the questions.
1 Is it important to make plans for the future?
2 Do you enjoy making plans?
3 Is it good to 'dream big'?

Recognise different speakers in a discussion about plans and goals.

7.3 LISTENING

New Year celebrations

1 💬 Work in pairs. Look at the photos. How many people are there? What are they celebrating? What can you see in the other photo?

Get fit

Save money

Learn new skills

Help others

Read more

3, 2, 1 – Happy New Year!

Every year, on the night of 31 December, millions of people all over the world set goals for the coming year. These are often about health, money or learning new things. The *Journal of Clinical Psychology* found that only 46% of people achieve their New Year goals.

Dream big

Be happy

2 Read the article. Answer the questions.
  1 When do many people set goals?
  2 What are they often about?
  3 How many people don't meet their goals?

STRATEGY Recognising different speakers

When you listen to a conversation, it helps you understand it better if you know how many people are talking and who they are. The first time you listen, note which people are speaking.

3 🔊 7.05 Read the strategy. Then listen to the conversation. Answer the questions.
  1 How many different voices do you hear?
  2 How many male or female voices are there?

4 🔊 7.05 Listen to the conversation again. Write the person's name next to what they say.
  1 _____ There are going to be some concerts.
  2 _____ There's going to be a big show.
  3 _____ I'm going to join you!
  4 _____ I'm going to stay at home.
  5 _____ Quiet please, Jess!

5 💬 Work in pairs. Ask and answer the questions.
  1 How do people celebrate New Year in your country?
  2 How are you going to celebrate it next year?

6 🔊 7.06 Listen to Jess talking to Simon. Answer the questions.
  1 What are they talking about?
  2 What is Simon going to do?
  3 How many goals has Jess got?

7 🔊 7.06 Listen again. Choose the correct answer: A, B or C.
  1 What is Simon hoping to do next year?
    A He's hoping to have driving lessons.
    B He's hoping to earn some money.
    C He's hoping to buy more things.
  2 How is he going to do this?
    A He's going to go shopping online.
    B He's going to pay by cash.
    C He's going to use his bank card more.
  3 What is Jess's main goal?
    A She's going to read four books each week.
    B She's going to learn how to use computers.
    C She's going to only use her phone in the evenings.
  4 What is Jess's dream for the future?
    A She wants to work for other people.
    B She wants to manage a design company.
    C She wants to start a company and become rich.
  5 When is she planning to achieve this?
    A After she finishes school.
    B After she finishes university.
    C After she finishes travelling.

8 💬 Work in pairs. Ask and answer the questions.
  1 Whose goals do you prefer, Jess's or Simon's?
  2 Did you or your friends and family set any New Year's goals this year?
  3 How easy is it to achieve your goals? Why?

9 Think of five New Year's goals for you. Then write them using the phrases below.
  • My New Year's goals
  • This year, I'm going to …
  • I want to be better at …
  • I hope / plan to …

10 💬 Work in pairs. Share your goals. Explain how you are going to achieve them.

Unit 7   89

7.4 GLOBAL SKILLS — Give a presentation.

My dreams

1 **Work in pairs. Discuss the questions.**
- Do you give presentations at your school?
- How do you prepare for them?
- How do you feel about speaking in front of an audience?

2 **7.07** Listen to a college professor. Put steps A–D in the order that she mentions them.
A Make your presentation interesting. ___
B Give your presentation well. ___
C Decide what to include in it. ___
D Order the information correctly. ___

3 **7.07** Complete the tips. Match them to steps A–D in Ex 2. Then listen again and check.
1 Always speak _____ and clearly.
2 _____ your talk with an introduction.
3 Use _____ to add interest to what you say.
4 While you talk, look at the _____.
5 Think what your _____ points are going to be.
6 _____ your talk with a conclusion.
7 Practise your presentation in front of _____.
8 Decide what topic you'd like to _____ about.

4 **THINK & SHARE** Work in pairs. Discuss the questions.
1 Which of the steps (A–D) in Ex 2 do you find the easiest / the most difficult? Why?
2 Think about the last presentation that you saw. Did the speaker follow the tips in Ex 3? Why? / Why not?

5 Look at these photos from a presentation. What do they show? What do you think this person is going to talk about?

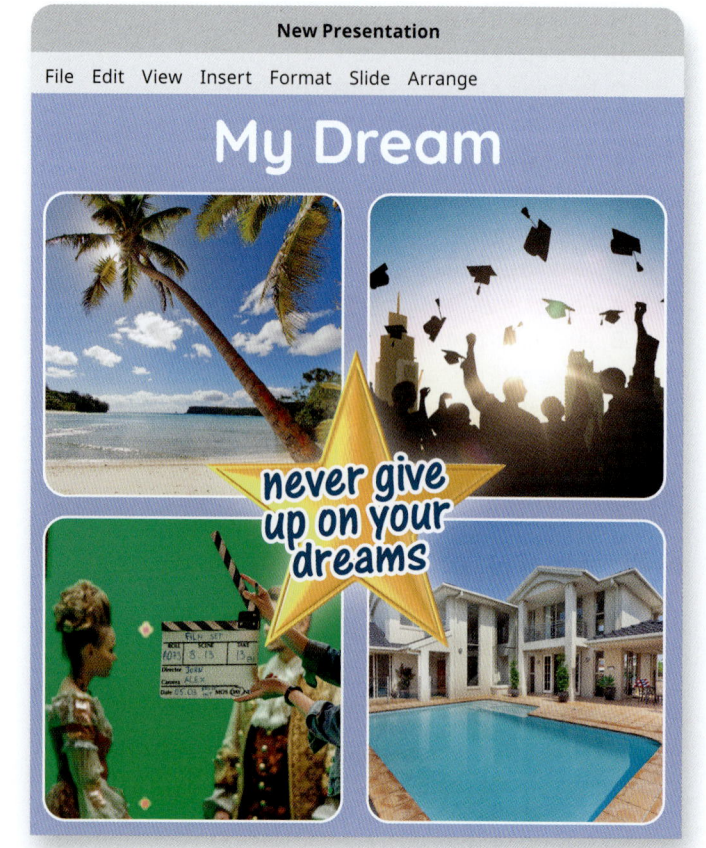

6 **7.08** Listen to Luca's presentation. Check your answers in Ex 5.

7 **7.08** Complete the Phrasebook with the words below. Then listen again and check.

because   finally   first   morning   next
other   photo   talk   thank

PHRASEBOOK Giving a presentation

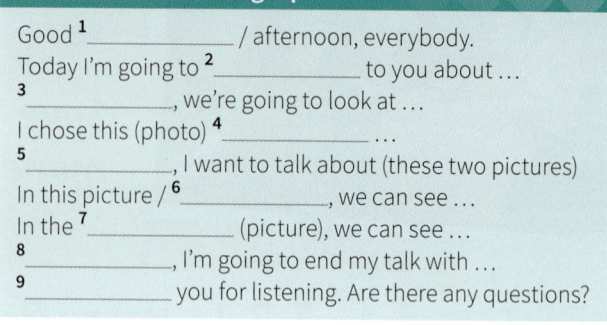

Good [1]_____ / afternoon, everybody.
Today I'm going to [2]_____ to you about …
[3]_____, we're going to look at …
I chose this (photo) [4]_____ …
[5]_____, I want to talk about (these two pictures)
In this picture / [6]_____, we can see …
In the [7]_____ (picture), we can see …
[8]_____, I'm going to end my talk with …
[9]_____ you for listening. Are there any questions?

8 You are going to prepare a short presentation about your dreams and goals. Use the mind map to help you think of things you would like to say.

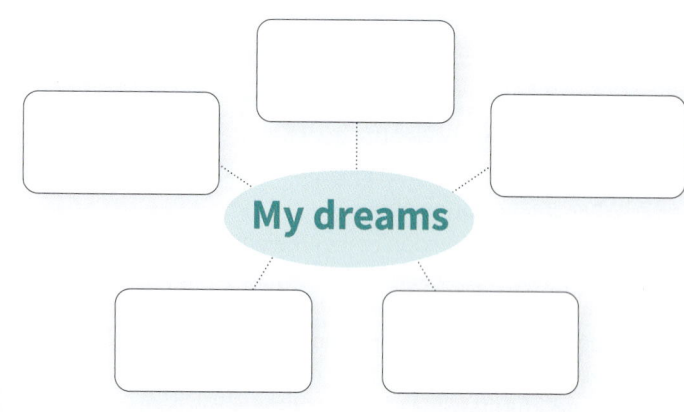

My dreams

9 **Work in pairs.** Ask and answer the questions about your ideas.
- What do you want people to learn about you?
- How are you going to make it more interesting?

10 Write your presentation. Use the steps and tips in Ex 2 and Ex 3, your notes and the Phrasebook to help you.

11 **Give your presentations to the class.** Listen carefully to other presentations and think of …
- one question to ask at the end.
- one thing you really liked about the presentation.

12 **Ask your question at the end of each presentation** and share what you liked about it.

13 Answer the questions about you.
- How did your presentation go?
- What did your audience think of it?
- What can you do to improve next time?

90   Unit 7

Talk about jobs. **7.5 VOCABULARY**

Career choices

1 　 Work in pairs. How many jobs do you know? Write as many as you can think of. You have got two minutes.

2 Look at the web page. Read section A. Who is it for? What is the test going to show you?

3 Now read section B. Tick (✓) the sentences you agree with.

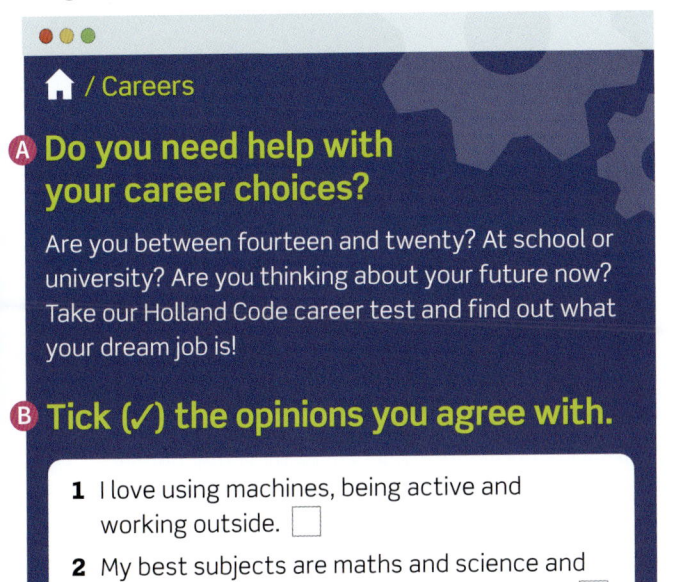

/ Careers

A Do you need help with your career choices?

Are you between fourteen and twenty? At school or university? Are you thinking about your future now? Take our Holland Code career test and find out what your dream job is!

B Tick (✓) the opinions you agree with.

1 I love using machines, being active and working outside. ☐
2 My best subjects are maths and science and I love doing research and solving problems. ☐
3 I enjoy art, music, theatre, books and languages. ☐
4 I like helping or teaching people and working in a team. ☐
5 I'm good at giving directions and pushing people to do things. ☐
6 I like working indoors, following instructions and using computers. ☐

4 Now read section C. What are your possible jobs? Do you agree with your test results?

C Possible career types and jobs

Career types A–F match the numbers in section B. See the numbers you ticked and find out the best jobs for you.

A **Practical**: farmer, pilot, police officer
B **Thinkers**: engineer, doctor, dentist
C **Creative**: designer, journalist
D **Helpers**: teacher, nurse
E **Influencers**: lawyer, businessperson
F **Organisers**: manager, IT technician

influence (n) – to persuade someone to think or do something

5 Look at the chart. Label the career types (practical, etc.) from the text. Add any more jobs you can think of.

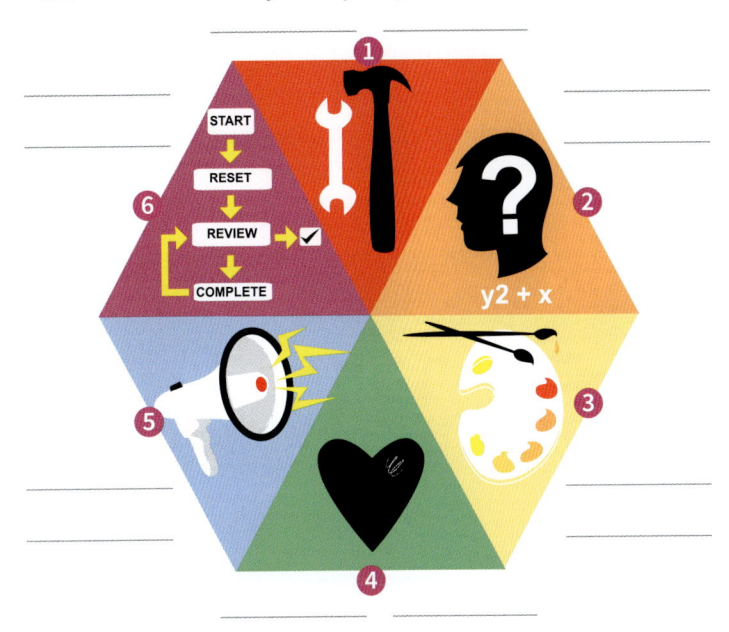

6 **VOCABULARY** Match the jobs in Ex 5 to the definitions.
1 They care for your health. _____, _____, _____
2 They fly planes. _____
3 They work with computers. _____
4 They write articles in newspapers. _____
5 They fight crime. _____, _____
6 They grow plants and/or look after animals. _____
7 They organise other people's work. _____
8 They plan, draw and make things, e.g. clothes or machines. _____, _____
9 They work in business at a high level. _____
10 They work in a school with children. _____

7 　 Work in pairs. Share your test answers. Ask and answer the questions about your three favourite jobs.
1 What do people with these jobs do?
2 Would you like to do any of these jobs?

8 **PRONUNCIATION** 🔊 **7.09** Two sounds which sound very similar are /ə/ and /ɜː/ but one is longer than the other. Listen and repeat.

/ə/	manag**er**, doct**or**
/ɜː/	res**ear**ch, univ**er**sity

9 🔊 **7.10** Complete the table in Ex 8 with the words below. Then listen, check and repeat.

teach**er**　farm**er**　j**our**nalist　lawy**er**
n**ur**se　pil**ot**　p**o**lice　businessp**er**son

10 🔊 **7.11** Listen to people playing the ten questions game. How many questions did he ask before he guessed the answer? What job is it?

11 　 Work in pairs. Think of a job. Play the game. Take turns to ask and answer.

Do you work with animals?　　No, I don't.

7.6 GRAMMAR   Use *will* to talk about the future and make predictions.

Will

1 **THINK & SHARE** Look at the picture. What can you see? What jobs do you think we can do in space? Why do you think that?

2 Read the article about future jobs. Did you guess any of the jobs in space?

Future jobs

Will you work in space one day?

Nobody can predict what will happen in ten years' time, but experts don't think jobs will look like they do now. Studies show that two-thirds of today's children will have jobs that don't exist yet. In fact, many of tomorrow's jobs will come from new discoveries. They will also exist because of problems on Earth such as climate change and pollution. This will certainly lead to new jobs like green-energy technicians.

Companies will probably start offering space travel in ten years too, and this will create more jobs. For example, tourists won't be astronauts, so they'll need space guides. And people won't feel well in space, so they will definitely need doctors, dentists and nurses up there too. One thing is certain: work won't be boring!

pollution – dirty land, water and air
climate change – a change in weather all over the world
green energy – a clean way of making electricity
astronauts – people who travel to and work in space

3 Read the grammar rules. Then find all the examples of *will* / *won't* in the article.

Will

▶ Grammar animation

We use *will* or *won't* to make predictions and guesses about the future.
Affirmative: subject + 'll (will) + the infinitive without *to*.
Negative: subject + won't / (will not) + the infinitive without *to*
Questions: *Will* + subject + the infinitive without *to*
Yes, I will. No, I won't.
We can make predictions with *will* and *probably*, *certainly*, *definitely* or *I think* / *I don't think* …
Experts don't think jobs will look like they do now.
NOT Experts think jobs won't look like they do now.

GRAMMAR BOOSTER   P145

4 Write predictions using *'ll* or *won't* and the verbs below.

| have | not exist | not look | not work | take | travel |

1 I think people _____ to space one day.
2 I _____ as a lawyer when I'm older.
3 In 2050, we _____ holidays in outer space.
4 I believe that phones _____ in fifteen years' time.
5 Robots _____ our jobs in the future.
6 The Earth _____ the same in ten years.

5 Work in pairs. Do you agree or disagree with the statements in Ex 4?

6 Complete the text with *will* and the verbs below.

certainly / need   continue   definitely / live
do   not disappear   not fly   probably / not be
still / design   use

Which jobs will be BIG in the future?

Journalists in scientific magazines think that people [1]_____ longer in the future. These much older people [2]_____ very healthy, so they [3]_____ a lot of doctors and nurses to look after them.

Experts don't think that humans [4]_____ much technical work in the future. For example, people [5]_____ planes; there'll be robot pilots instead. But, at least in the near future, human engineers [6]_____ and build the robots, and of course human technicians [7]_____ them. Most people believe that the internet [8]_____ any time soon, and apps [9]_____ to be important to us.

7 **THINK & SHARE** Work in pairs. Ask and answer the questions. Give reasons.
1 Which jobs will still exist in ten years?
2 Which jobs will disappear in the future?

8 Write questions. Then ask and answer in pairs.
1 go to university or college / the future / ? What subject / study / ?
2 work / ten years' time / ? What job / do / ?
3 live / a different house or flat / ? Where / live / ?
4 become famous one day / ? Why / be famous / ?
5 have children / one day / ? How many / you have / ?
6 travel to space in the future / ? When / go / ?

  Will you go to university or college in the future?

9 Write a paragraph about your predictions for the future. Add an extra sentence for each idea.

7.7 READING

Recognise proper nouns in an article about amazing teenagers.

Teens changing the world

1 Work in pairs. Look at world problems below. Which do you think is the most serious? Give reasons.

climate change   dirty water   diseases   no jobs for young people   not enough food   plastic pollution

YOUNG PEOPLE WILL CHANGE THE WORLD!

When Deepika Kurup visited India as a child, she noticed that many people didn't have clean water. Deepika really wanted to help, so she invented a cheap way to clean water using the sun's light. She then became the USA's Top Young Scientist at fourteen and spoke at the White House. Now, she's studying biology at Harvard University. Over 2 billion people only have dirty water, but Deepika hopes she'll end this.

Rishab Jain from Portland, USA, designed a special computer program for hospitals to help fight cancer more easily. He won the Young Scientist competition, and $25,000. How will he spend this money? He thinks he'll save some for research and he'll give some to his Samyak Science Society that helps poor children to study scientific subjects. Rishab will also spend it on his studies. He plans to get a degree in science or medicine, and he hopes he'll become an engineer or doctor one day.

When Melati and Isabel Wijsen were 12 and 10 years old, they hated all the plastic they saw on the beaches in Bali. So they decided to start a project, 'Bye Bye Plastic Bags'. Today, they meet world leaders, lawyers, and managers, and work with business people and farmers against plastic pollution on their island. Melati has already worked with 500 local businesses to say no to single-use plastic bags. She is going to try and get 1,000 businesses to stop using single-use plastic bags this year. She is now starting a new project, YOUTHTOPIA. Its goal is to help children and teenagers around the world through education.

cancer – a group of serious diseases that affect different parts of the body
single-use – only use once

STRATEGY Recognising proper nouns

You can understand a text better if you can recognise proper nouns. These include names of people or organisations, towns, countries, nationalities and languages. They always begin with a capital letter.

2 Read the strategy. Then quickly find all the proper nouns in the article.

3 🔊 7.14 Read the article. Answer the questions with proper nouns.
1 Which country did Deepika travel to?
2 What competition did she win?
3 Where is she a student now?
4 Where does Rishab come from?
5 What's the name of his organisation?
6 What was the name of the sisters' idea?
7 Where do they live?
8 What's the name of Melati's project?

4 Read the article again. Match the sentence halves. There are three endings that you do not need.
1 Deepika made water safe to drink using only
2 When she was a teenager, she visited the home of
3 Rishab Jain's idea will make jobs easier for
4 He'll use some of his prize money to help
5 Melati and Isabel hope to end the use of
6 Melati's new project aims to help

A doctors and nurses.
B talented teenagers.
C university costs.
D plastic bags.
E young people.
F the US president.
G poor people.
H new technology.
I green energy.

5 **MEDIATION** You are going to give a presentation on teenagers changing the world to a local youth club. Make notes for the presentation, completing the missing information.

Name	Deepika		Melati
Did what?		designed a computer program to help fight cancer	
Wants to … ?	… end dirty water for 2 billion people		… get 1,000 companies to stop using plastic

6 **THINK & SHARE** Work in pairs. Ask and answer the questions. Give reasons.
1 Which idea is the most interesting to you?
2 Which teenager do you admire most? Why?
3 Would you like to take part in a science competition?

7 Think of an incredible young person. Do more research about this person. Then write about …
• what goals they want to achieve.
• how they tried / are trying to do this.
• what they will try to do in the future.

8 Share what you found with the class.

Unit 7   93

7.8 SPEAKING   Compare and contrast photos.

Comparing and contrasting

1 💬 Look at the photos of people working. Write more words to describe them. Then compare your list with a partner.
Picture A: doctors, discuss, clean …
Picture B: outside, show, interesting …
Picture C: country, pick, busy …
Picture D: children, explain, friendly …

A

B

C

D

2 🔊 **7.15** Listen to Suki comparing and contrasting photos in a speaking exam. Which words on your list do you hear? What is the first photo? What is the second photo?

STRATEGY Follow a structure
When you compare photos, follow these steps:
1 Describe what you can see in each photo.
2 Describe the similarities between the two photos.
3 Describe the differences between the two photos.
4 Give your opinion / feelings on the subject.

3 🔊 **7.15** Read the strategy. Does Suki follow the steps in the strategy? Listen again and check.

4 Which steps from the strategy do the things below describe?
A Say how you feel about both photos.
B Find things that exist in both photos.
C Say which photo you prefer and why.
D Describe what the second photo looks like.
E Say what is happening in the first photo.
F Say why the second photo is different.

5 Complete the Phrasebook with the words below.

both but different first
opinion see similar think

PHRASEBOOK Comparing and contrasting photos
A **Describe**
In the ¹_____ photo, there are …
In the second photo, I can ²_____ …
B **Describe the similarities**
Both photos are quite ³_____ because …
⁴_____ photos show (people working together).
C **Describe the differences**
The first photo shows … ⁵_____ the second photo shows …
The two photos are ⁶_____ because …
D **Give your opinion**
In my ⁷_____, it is easier to be a …
I ⁸_____ being (a police officer) is better because …

6 💬 Work in pairs. Prepare to compare two photos. Student A: look at photos A and B. Student B: look at photos C and D. Make a note of the things you can see and any similarities and differences.

7 💬 Now take turns to compare and contrast your two photos. Use the strategy and the Phrasebook to help you. While your partner talks, listen carefully and check that they follow all the steps in the strategy.

8 💬 **THINK & SHARE** Work in pairs. Ask and answer the questions. Give reasons.
1 What are some of the advantages / disadvantages of being (a job in Ex 6)?
2 What is your dream job?
3 What are some of the advantages / disadvantages of your dream job?
4 Do you think you'll do this job one day? How?

9 **REFLECT** Work in pairs. Answer the questions.
1 Did you describe the similarities and differences in the two photos?
2 Which phrases for comparing and contrasting photos did you use?
3 Were your partner's ideas very different to yours? How?

94 Unit 7

7.9 WRITING

Use appropriate tenses in an informal invitation email.

An informal invitation email

1 💬 Work in pairs. Ask and answer the questions.
   1 When do people send invitation emails?
   2 What was the last invitation you received?

2 Read the two invitation emails. Complete the table.

	Email 1	Email 2
Event		
Date		
Time		
Place		

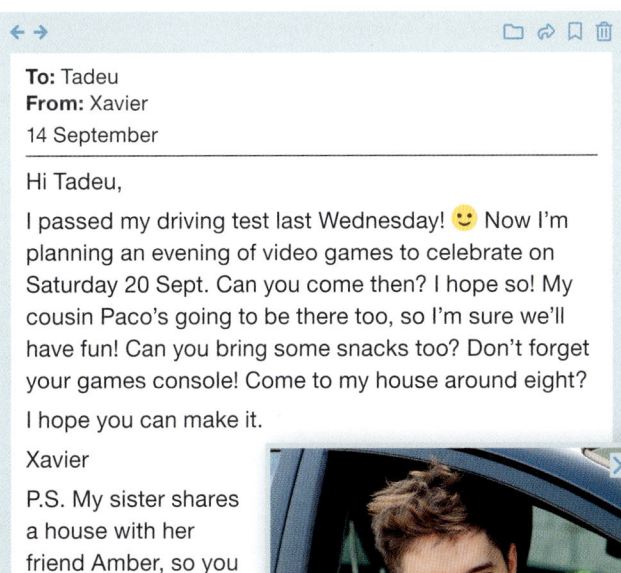

To: Jana
From: Lucia
27 July

Dear Jana,

Thanks for your letter. Sorry I didn't reply sooner.

Good news! I got an offer from Manchester University, so I'm going to study physics there in September. Exciting!!!

On Sunday evening, I'm going to have dinner with my friends to say goodbye. 🙁 That's on 28 August. We're going to go to the pizza restaurant in the square. We're going to meet there at 7.30 p.m. Would you like to join us?

Hope you can come! Please let me know by Thursday!

Take care,

Lucia x

To: Tadeu
From: Xavier
14 September

Hi Tadeu,

I passed my driving test last Wednesday! 🙂 Now I'm planning an evening of video games to celebrate on Saturday 20 Sept. Can you come then? I hope so! My cousin Paco's going to be there too, so I'm sure we'll have fun! Can you bring some snacks too? Don't forget your games console! Come to my house around eight?

I hope you can make it.

Xavier

P.S. My sister shares a house with her friend Amber, so you can sleep in her old bedroom!

STRATEGY Using appropriate tenses

When you write, be careful to use the correct tenses.
1 Past: Use the past simple to say what you did.
2 Present: Use the present continuous to say what you're doing now and the present simple for facts.
3 Future: Use *be going to* to describe your plans or *will* for your predictions for the future.
4 Use the correct time expressions with each tense.

3 Read the **strategy**. Find all the examples of the different tenses in both letters. What are the time expressions?

4 Choose the most appropriate tense.
   1 Ed **gets** / **got** / **'s going to get** a degree in art last year.
   2 Sorry I **don't** / **didn't** / **won't** reply. I was very busy.
   3 Fatima **goes** / **'s going** / **'ll to go** to college this September!
   4 We **plan** / **'re planning** / **'ll plan** to meet at 9 p.m.
   5 I'm sure you **have** / **'ll have** / **had** fun tomorrow!
   6 My brother **lives** / **is going to live** / **will live** with two other students - they really enjoy sharing a flat!
   7 I **hope** / **'m going to hope** / **will hope** you can come.

5 Read the **Language focus**. Find all the examples of contractions in the invitations.

LANGUAGE FOCUS Contractions

We often use contractions in informal writing because it sounds friendlier. Contractions, or 'short forms', usually combine a pronoun / name and a verb, with an apostrophe for the missing letters, e.g. *He is = He's*.

6 Read the invitation. Rewrite it adding contractions wherever possible.

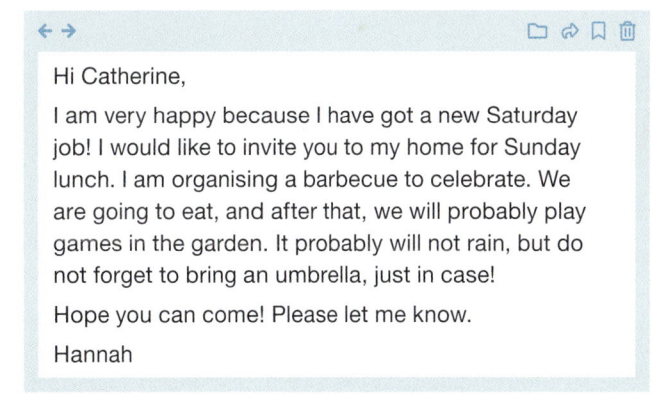

Hi Catherine,

I am very happy because I have got a new Saturday job! I would like to invite you to my home for Sunday lunch. I am organising a barbecue to celebrate. We are going to eat, and after that, we will probably play games in the garden. It probably will not rain, but do not forget to bring an umbrella, just in case!

Hope you can come! Please let me know.

Hannah

---

7 Imagine you are organising a special event / day. Make notes about ...
   • why you are celebrating.
   • details about the event (day, date, time).
   • what you think you'll do there.

8 Write an informal invitation to a friend. Use your notes, the **strategy** and the **Language focus** to help you.

9 ✓ CHECK YOUR WORK
   • Does your invitation include a request to join you?
   • Do you ask for a confirmation?
   • Does your writing include contractions?
   • Does it contain appropriate tenses?

Unit 7   95

7.10 REVIEW

Grammar

1 Complete the dialogue with the verbs below and *be going to* or short answers.

be	do	find	go	not be	not do
pay	save	travel	try		

A What are your plans for next year? **1**_____ you _____ to university after you leave school?

B No, I **2**_____. My brother and I **3**_____ around Europe instead.

A Wow! That sounds expensive! How **4**_____ you _____ for that?

B I've got a weekend job as a waiter, and I **5**_____ as much money as I can. My brother **6**_____ to find work this summer too.

A Really? What **7**_____ he _____?

B Well, he knows how to cook, so he **8**_____ work in a kitchen in a restaurant. My parents don't know about our plans yet.

A **9**_____ they _____ happy with your goal?

B No, they **10**_____! They **11**_____ happy at all! They want me to study medicine and become a doctor, but I **12**_____ that. That definitely isn't the best job for me!

2 Order the words to make sentences and questions.
1. one / will / day / to / space / People / fly
2. in / be / waiters / won't / any / There / space
3. we / don't / will / come / think / We
4. I / you / will / Will / tomorrow / be / Yes, / here / ?
5. they / will / year / work / Where / next / ?
6. won't / probably / My / win / team
7. teacher / won't / become / I / definitely / a
8. think / travel / in / will / 2035 / space / I / exist

Vocabulary

3 Choose the correct answer: A, B or C.
1. Students often … a flat to save money.
   A buy   B live   C share
2. Alex … to drive really fast!
   A studied   B learned   C became
3. My brother goes … university in London.
   A at   B in   C to
4. Top footballers often … rich and famous.
   A become   B spend   C pay
5. You need to learn … speak English well.
   A to   B how   C –
6. My mum got a … in physics in 1998.
   A learn   B work   C degree

4 Complete the sentences with the jobs below.

designer	engineer	farmers	journalist
lawyers	nurses	pilot	police officer

1. The _____ is flying an aeroplane to Madrid.
2. Jackie's a _____ – she makes some brilliant clothes.
3. _____ cared for my aunt when she was in hospital.
4. Rafa is a _____ – he writes for an online magazine.
5. I got lost in the city centre, so I asked a _____ to help me.
6. We buy fresh fruit, milk and eggs from local _____.
7. The _____ designed the machines in this factory.
8. People need _____ to help them win in court.

Cumulative review

5 Complete the presentation with one word in each gap.

Good morning. My name's Sofia. Today I'm **1**_____ to talk about my plans for the future. First, we **2**_____ going to look at three possible career choices for me. I'm very good at computer studies and maths, so I plan **3**_____ use those skills in the future. But, I'm also an active person and I love spending time outside, so I definitely won't become an IT **4**_____ and work with computers all day. Maybe I'll become an international **5**_____ person in an IT company?
I'm also organised, so I hope I'll become a **6**_____ and lead a team one day. Secondly, I love writing and travelling, so I'm going to try to find work as a **7**_____ this year. I can **8**_____ some extra money at the weekend or during the summer writing articles for our local magazine. I think I'll **9**_____ research the job of police **10**_____ too. But I'm not sure because it isn't my dream job.
Next, I want to talk about my studies. I'd like to **11**_____ to college after school, but I don't think I **12**_____ attend a college near my home. I'd like to study in the UK. I certainly won't **13**_____ a degree in English, I'll probably study engineering or maths instead.
And finally, I **14**_____ going to end my talk with my dreams for the future. I hope I'll have my first job **15**_____ five years' time. I don't **16**_____ I'll be rich, but I hope I'll have enough money to live on my own **17**_____ day.

💬 Think & share

6 Read the quote. Then answer the questions.

❝ *What will be will be.* ❞
Anonymous

1. What do you think about the future? Why?
2. What will your life be like in five years' time?
3. What are your plans for the year ahead? Why?
4. What are some good life goals for teenagers like you? Why?

7.11 EXAM SKILLS

Reading

EXAM STRATEGY

When you do a matching task, read the descriptions of the people carefully. Make sure that all the points in the descriptions match what is in the text you choose.

1 Read the strategy above. Then look at the exam task in Ex 2. Underline the key points in each of the descriptions of the people. There is an example to help you.

2 The young people below all want to study courses. There are descriptions of eight courses to take. Decide which course (A–G) would be the most suitable for the young people 1–5. There are three courses that do not match any of the people.

1 ___ Noah is very creative. He loves finding original things to wear. Next year, he's going to create all the costumes for the school concert. He'd like to do a course at the weekend that will help him with that.

2 ___ Rana loves travelling. She already has a travel blog, but would like to improve her skills. She doesn't have much money and would prefer to study from home.

3 ___ Rita makes jewellery and sells it on her website. She would like to improve her IT and maths skills and to make a lot of money one day. She can only study for a few hours every week.

4 ___ Jaime is going to do work experience in a big hotel next summer. When he finishes, he wants to do a degree in business that will help him become a hotel manager in a few years' time. He definitely doesn't want to study online.

5 ___ Karim loves singing and is going to take part in a festival next year. He'd like to learn to play a musical instrument before he goes. He's happy to travel somewhere.

A The business school
We are an online university, and offer a great degree course in business studies. This means you can work and study at the same time. Learn practical skills and watch your business grow. There is also a chance for work experience in local shops and companies.

B Become a star
Our degree in acting is one of the most famous in the world. We also offer short courses and summer schools in this country and other parts of Europe for adults and under 18s. Apply now. You won't be sorry.

C New tastes
Learn to cook food from Japan, India, Greece and many other countries around the world. We offer weekend courses, and evening courses on Tuesdays and Thursdays. This summer, we're going to have a party in a top hotel for all our students.

D Become a writer
Would you like to have a career in writing? Well, you don't need to take long courses or expensive creative writing classes. You can learn online. Our students do 12-week or 18-week courses. They learn how to write different online texts, travel guides and for newspapers.

E New designs
Are you interested in fashion? Do you want to look different from other people? How about learning to make your own clothes? We hold courses in fashion design. Courses last three months and include a three-hour lesson every Saturday.

F Travel the world
Do you want to work in a top London hotel? Or would you prefer to be a manager in a restaurant in Prague? Visit the university website for more information about our courses. All our courses take place at the university.

G The performance school
Are you looking for a creative career or do you just want some fun? You can take acting lessons and music lessons at our six-week summer camp. The camp takes place in a beautiful house in the middle of the country. At the end of the course, students perform. Look on our website for more details.

Speaking

EXAM STRATEGY

Be prepared for the speaking task. Learn phrases for comparing and contrasting ideas.

3 Read the strategy above. Complete the sentences with the words below.

between   both   but   similar

1 _____ photos show people …
2 The photos are _____ because the people …
3 The first job is … , _____ the second job, …
4 One difference _____ the jobs is that …

4 These two photos show two different types of jobs. Compare and contrast the two photos. Include the following points:
- the advantages of both jobs
- the disadvantages of both jobs
- what job you would like to have

Exam skills 97

7 VISION 360° A visit to the museum
Learn about life in Ancient Egypt and create a secret language

Unit 7 360° hotspots ◆ ■ ▲ ★ ♥ ●

1 **THINK & SHARE** Work in pairs. What can we learn about an ancient culture from discovering art and objects from that time? Make a list of your ideas.

EXPLORE 360°
Access the interactive 360° content now!

2 Work in pairs. Look around a room in a museum in Zagreb. Discuss the answers to these questions.
1 When did the museum first open?
   A 1846   B 1864   C 1878
2 What type of object does Petra NOT talk about?
   A paintings   B shoes   C jewellery
3 How many objects can you see there?
   A around 4,000   B around 40,000   C around 400,000

3 ◆ Listen to Petra. Check your answers in Ex 2.

4 **ALL HOTSPOTS** Explore the hotspots. Which hotspot contains information about … ?
1 paintings and furniture
2 beauty and make-up
3 what people ate
4 where you'll find the Egyptian Room
5 a job in the museum
6 a way of writing

5 ■ Listen to an expert talking about hieroglyphs and answer the questions.
1 What do the symbols and pictures mean?
2 Where did they write hieroglyphs?
3 What three things do you find out about scribes?

6 Go online and find out about the Rosetta Stone. Why is it important?

7 Look at the hieroglyphic alphabet. What does this message mean in English?

HIEROGLYPHIC ALPHABET
A	B	C	D	E	F
G	H	I	J	K	L
M	N	O	P	Q	R
S	T	U	V	W	X
Y	Z	CH	KH	SH

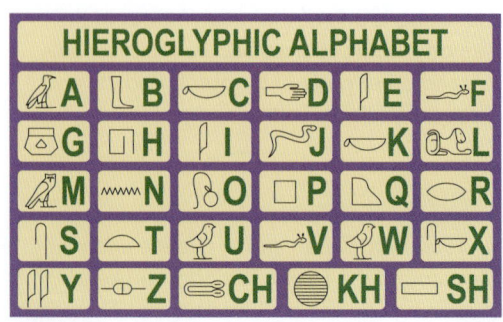

8 ▲ Listen to the description of some everyday objects from Ancient Egypt and answer the questions. Discuss your answers in pairs.
1 What objects show how rich and important the family were?
2 Imagine you're going to paint a picture to show how rich and important a modern person is. Which objects will you include?

Vision 360

Digital literacy 　　　　　　　　　　　　　　　　360° 7

9 Read the fact file. Which person below do you think will be good at the job? Compare your ideas in pairs.

Hugo will get a degree in history next month. His dream is to work for an international company.

Jo works as a police officer, but she's unhappy. She loves history and often visits museums.

Raul's got a degree in English and works as a journalist. He reads history textbooks just for fun.

Tamara is an actor and she's performing in a play about Ancient Egypt next month. She thinks she'll become famous and earn a lot of money.

10 Decide which sentences are true (T) or false (F). Discuss your ideas in pairs.
1 People had a room where they could relax.
2 They couldn't cook meat and fish.
3 Poor people ate fish but not meat.
4 Most children went to school.

11 **THINK & SHARE** Think about your answer to Ex 1 and what you learned about life in Ancient Egypt. Can you add any other ideas to your list?

CREATE ... a secret language

STEP 1
RESEARCH IT!
Go online and find the answers to the questions.
1 What is Obish?
2 What do you do to make new words?
3 How do you say 'fish' and 'meat' in Obish?

STEP 2
You are going to create your own secret language. Choose one of the ideas below or use your own idea.

add a suffix or prefix to existing words
add two letters, e.g. A = C, B = E, C = F
write the letters in a word backwards, e.g. cook → kooc
symbols for words

STEP 3
Practise writing words and write down the rule which explains how your language works.

STEP 4
Write three instructions for the class. Tell them:
• where they will meet
• what they will bring
• what they will wear

STEP 5
Share the messages with the class and try to translate them. Decide on the best language and why.

Vision 360　99

8 A ticket to ride

- **VOCABULARY** Travel and tourism / Types of holidays
- **GRAMMAR** Present perfect: affirmative / Present perfect: negative and questions
- **READING** A travel photographer
- **LISTENING** Adventures on the road
- **GLOBAL SKILLS** Difficult situations
- **SPEAKING** Asking for information
- **WRITING** A postcard
- **DOCUMENTARY** Sky Lodge: an unusual hotel

VOCABULARY BOOSTER P126–127
GRAMMAR BOOSTER P146–147

Getting around

1 💬 Look at the video stills. Answer the questions.
1 What do you think these guest vloggers are going to talk about? Why?
2 Which cities do you think you can see behind them?

2 ▶ 🔊 **8.01** Watch or listen. Check your predictions for Ex 1.

3 ▶ 🔊 **8.01** Watch or listen again. Answer the questions.
1 How long did it take Dan to travel to his city?
2 What famous building did he see in La Boca?
3 How long did Dan's tour last?
4 Where did Lily travel to her city from?
5 What did Lily take to get to TV tower?
6 What countries could she see from the top?

100 Unit 8

Talk about travel and tourism. **8.1 VOCABULARY**

4 REAL ENGLISH Match the **bold** phrases to the meanings.
1 But **where to go**?
2 They're going to tell us **a bit** about their favourite holidays.
3 So, **over to you**, Dan and Lily!
4 It's really easy to **see all the sights**!
5 OK, **now it's my turn**!
6 **Actually**, when we were in Vienna …

A you can start speaking now
B visit the most interesting places
C I'm not sure what places to visit
D in fact
E a little
F I'm going to do it now

5 VOCABULARY Look at the photos and complete the phrases with the words below.

| car   coach   foot   tram   plane   taxi

1 by _____
2 by _____ 
3 by _____ 
4 on _____ 
5 by _____  
6 by _____ 

6 VOCABULARY 8.02 Complete the travel guide with the words below. Then listen and check.

| amazing views   boat trips   catch a flight
| city break   public transport   short journeys
| underground system

Visit Oslo

Attractions   Transport   Where to stay   What's on?

Getting around in Oslo

Oslo, Norway's capital, is a brilliant place to visit for a ¹_____. With a ticket called *Ruter*, you can travel on long and ²_____ on many different forms of ³_____ including Oslo's ⁴_____ (or metro) which has five lines and over 100 stations in the centre. You can also use the ticket on city buses and coaches which take you across Norway. There are also electric trams which go all over the city. These even travel to Oslo Airport if you need to ⁵_____ home. If you prefer to travel by car, you'll find taxis everywhere too. As Oslo is small, you can easily get around by bike or on foot. And when the weather is good, why not try one of the many ⁶_____ to the islands? You'll enjoy ⁷_____ of Oslo and its incredible fjords from the sea.

7 💬 Work in pairs. Which of the places mentioned in this lesson would you most like to visit and why? Which form of transport do you like the most or the least? Why?

8 💬 THINK & SHARE Imagine that you are a guest on Zara and Callum's vlog. In pairs, discuss …
- what the most interesting or important places in your local area are.
- why you recommend that people visit your city / town.
- what is the best way to get around.

VOCABULARY BOOSTER Unit 8 101

8.2 GRAMMAR   Use the present perfect to talk about travel experiences.

Present perfect: affirmative

1 Do you remember the vlog about travel? Which forms of transport and places did they talk about?

2 Read the comments below. Which places do they mention? Which of these places would you like to visit? Why?

▼ Comments

Bence 1 month ago
I'm from Budapest in Hungary and my parents and I have visited Slovakia many times. For us, Bratislava's only a short car journey away, so we can go there on day trips. We've been on some fun city breaks there, but, for me, the Slovak mountains are even better! My family has been snowboarding there five times and we've always had a brilliant time!

Valentina 9 days ago
You've probably heard of Iguazú Falls – the huge waterfalls between Brazil and Argentina. I've seen them twice, but I want to see them again! I've only travelled by plane there. It's a two-hour flight from Buenos Aires, but you can also get there by coach. I've always stayed in Puerto Iguazú because there are regular buses to the falls. There are beautiful walking tours in the park, but the best thing I've done there is the boat trip. The views were amazing!

3 Complete the grammar rules. Use the comments in Ex 2 to help you.

Present perfect: affirmative
▶ Grammar animation
We use the present perfect to talk about life experiences and past events which have a result in the present. We don't say when the event happened – the exact time isn't important.
I / You / We / They + ¹_____ + past participle
He / She / It + ²_____ + past participle
We often use *been* as the past participle of *go* when somebody has gone somewhere and come back. We use *gone* to say they are still there.
He's been to New York. (He went there and returned.)
He's gone to New York. (He's still there now.)
GRAMMAR BOOSTER P146

4 Find more examples of the present perfect in the text. Look at the verbs in these sentences. Which are regular and which are irregular?

5 Write the past participles of the verbs below. Which are regular or irregular?

break	catch	drive	eat	finish	get	give	leave
live	lose	make	meet	play	relax	ride	say
speak	take	tell	try	walk	write

6 Complete the sentences with the present perfect form of the verbs in brackets.
1 They _____ empanadas and they love them. (try)
2 He _____ everyone my secret! (tell)
3 We _____ bikes around Berlin many times. (ride)
4 I _____ the early train home. (catch)
5 Jo doesn't drive, so she _____ by coach. (come)
6 Oh no! You _____ on the wrong tram! (get)

7 Complete the email with the present perfect form of the verbs below.

answer   arrive   be   do   give   send   take   tell   travel

Hi Uncle Omar,
I ¹_____ safely in Santiago and my flight was on time. Celia and her parents met me at the airport. Then we went back to their house. The public transport works well here. I ²_____ on the underground and two buses. I ³_____ even _____ a train today too!
Celia's parents ⁴_____ a lot of nice things for me. Her mum ⁵_____ me a travel guide of Santiago and her dad ⁶_____ me the best way of getting around the city. I'm sharing a room with Celia and she ⁷_____ very kind to me too.
I ⁸_____ lots of messages to people, but so far, only Mum and Dad ⁹_____ me …
Write soon!
Love, Yasmin xx

8 💬 Write three things that you have done, two true and one false. Then share them with your partner. Can they guess which are true?

9 💬 **THINK & SHARE** Complete the experiences for you. Then share your ideas with a partner.
• The most beautiful view / I / see was from …
• The best school trip / we / go on / is …
• The fastest / transport / I / travel / on is …
• The most interesting city / I / visit / is …
• The worst food / I / eat / is …
• The furthest / my family and I / go on foot is …
• The longest journey / I / go on / is …

> The most beautiful view I've seen was from the top of the Eiffel Tower.

10 💬 Can you remember what your partner has said? Tell the class.

102   Unit 8

Understand phrasal verbs for travel. **8.3 LISTENING**

Adventures on the road

1 **THINK & SHARE** Work in pairs. Look at the photos. Answer the questions.
1 What types of transport can you see?
2 What are some of the pros and cons of each one?

STRATEGY Recognising phrasal verbs for travel

Phrasal verbs consist of a main verb and a particle. You need to listen carefully because the particle often changes the meaning of the verb. Recognising phrasal verbs helps you understand what you hear.

2 Read the strategy. Then look at these example sentences. Match the phrasal verbs in **bold** with their meaning.
1 I **got on** the bus and then found my seat.
2 You need to **get off** at the next station.
3 We **set off** for Oxford at eight o'clock.
4 We've got some time. Why don't we **look around** the town?
5 My car **broke down** on the way to work so I was late.
6 'How do you **get around**?' 'I usually take the bus, but I sometimes cycle.'
7 The plane **took off** three hours late.
8 There was a problem with my bike, so I **went back** home.
9 All guests need to **check in to** the hotel before 5 p.m.

a to go to a lot of different places _____
b enter a plane, bus, train _____
c arrive at a hotel to begin your stay there _____
d to stop working because of a problem _____
e to leave the ground and begin to fly _____
f to begin a journey _____
g return the way you have come _____
h to visit a place or building, walking around it to see what is there _____
i leave a plane, bus, train _____

3 🔊 **8.05** Listen to four speakers talking about their travel experiences. Complete the table with the countries below that the people have been to.

| Argentina | Brazil | China | Hungary |
| Indonesia | Russia | Singapore | Türkiye |

Speaker	Places
1	
2	
3	
4	

4 🔊 **8.05** Listen again. Match the statements to the speakers. Write the number of the speaker (1–4).
A travelled across two countries by train ___
B began the journey in England ___
C didn't mind bad weather ___
D had a problem with their car ___
E brought the family together ___
F was taking a break before work ___
G took a plane instead of a boat ___
H started and finished in the same country ___

5 **THINK & SHARE** Work in pairs. Which of the experiences in Ex 3 and Ex 4 would you like to do? Why?

6 Work in pairs. Plan a year's adventure. Think about:
• where you will go.
• how you will travel.
• where you will stay.
• what you would like to see and do.

Unit 8 103

8.4 GLOBAL SKILLS — Deal with difficult situations.

Difficult situations

1 **THINK & SHARE** Read the quotes about dealing with problems. Which one do you prefer? Why?

> A problem is a chance for you to do your best.
> *Duke Ellington*

> If you don't like something, change it; if you can't change it, change the way you think about it.
> *Mary Engelbreit*

> It doesn't matter how slow you go as long as you don't stop.
> *Confucius*

2 🔊 **8.06** Listen to a father and son going on a city break. What difficult situation do they need to deal with? Choose the correct answer: A, B, C or D.
- A They've missed their plane.
- B Their tram has stopped working.
- C They've got on the wrong bus.
- D They've broken their suitcase.

3 🔊 **8.06** Listen again. Look at the list of advice for the situation in Ex 2. Tick (✓) the advice they follow. What do they do in the end?
- A Ask questions and listen to suggestions.
- B Consider your options.
- C Try to stay calm.
- D Decide on an action plan.
- E Find out what the problem is.

4 Read the tips below and match them to a piece of advice in Ex 3.

How to deal with difficult situations

1 ___
Discover what all the facts are first. The longer you ignore a problem, the longer it takes to solve it.

2 ___
Don't be afraid to talk to others and ask them for ideas or help. You are never alone.

3 ___
Brainstorm different ways to deal with the situation; there are often more options than you think.

4 ___
Choose the best way to solve your problem from the different options.

5 ___
If you feel stressed or worried, try talking about it with loved ones. They can help you feel better.

5 💬 Work in pairs. Look at the photo of the girl. Ask and answer the questions.
1. What's her problem?
2. What choices has she got?
3. What do you think is her best action plan?

6 Match the phrases to the tips in Ex 4.
- A We've missed the bus and we're going to be late.
- B Don't worry / panic — I'm sure we can find a solution.
- C What are our options?
- D The next bus is in two hours.
- E Have you got any better ideas?
- F Let's check / find out / ask …
- G What's our plan B?
- H Let's go with your plan.

7 💬 Complete the missing words in the two mini dialogues. Then, in pairs, take turns to practise them.
1. A I ¹_____ lost my hotel keys.
   B Don't ²_____. I'll help you look for them.
   A What are our ³_____ if we can't find them?
   B ⁴_____ tell the hotel manager about it.
   A Oh … I don't want to do that …
   B Have you got any ⁵_____ ideas?
   A No, I haven't …
2. A Somebody's taken my wallet!
   B ⁶_____ calm. Maybe you've left it on the bus.
   A I don't think so.
   B ⁷_____ ask the bus driver if he's found a wallet.
   A What's our plan ⁸_____ if he hasn't got it?
   B We'll go to the police station.
   A OK, let's go with your ⁹_____.

8 💬 Work in pairs. Read the travel problems. Make short dialogues to try and deal with each one. Use the phrases in Ex 6 and Ex 7 to help you.
- Your hotel has cancelled your reservation. You don't have anywhere to stay.
- You're on a walking tour. Your friend has hurt their leg.
- You're on a day trip in the mountains. You've forgotten to bring food or water.
- You've dropped your passport in the hotel pool.

9 💬 Share your ideas as a class.

10 Imagine that one of the situations you discussed in Ex 8 is your best friend's problem. Write a short text message to them and tell them what your classmates think are the best options for dealing with this difficult situation.

In our opinion …

104 Unit 8

Talk about types of holidays.   **8.5 VOCABULARY**

Holidays and places to stay

1 💬 Work in pairs. How many types of holidays can you think of? Where do you sleep in each one?

2 Read the adverts. Match them to the types of holiday.
   A beach holiday
   B city break
   C study trip

3 Read the adverts again. Write Malta (M), Playa del Carmen (P) or Cape Town (C).
   1 Guests pay for everything before the trip. ___
   2 Guests can go online for no extra cost. ___
   3 Guests can bring their own beds with them. ___
   4 The price only includes one meal a day. ___
   5 Guests can improve their language skills. ___
   6 Guests pay extra for activities. ___

4 **VOCABULARY** Write the highlighted words from the adverts in the mind map. Can you add any more words to each group?

   - Types of holidays or activities
   - Places to stay
   - People
   - Verbs
   - Adjectives

---

travel advisor

Plan your trip – book now for the summer!

1 English Summer Camp for 13–17-year-olds, Malta

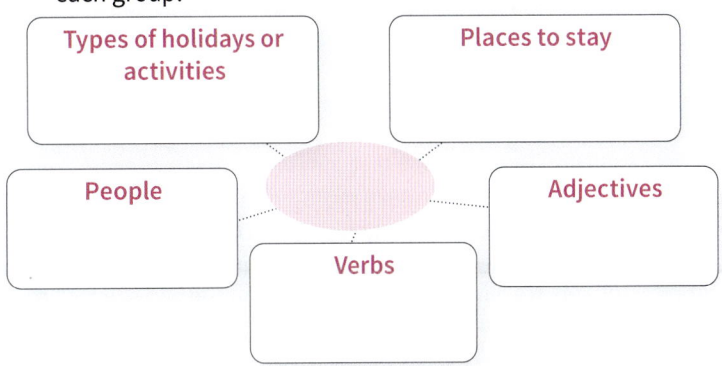

♡ favourite

Go camping, make new friends and practise English. We're based in a modern campsite, ten minutes on foot from the beautiful city of Mdina. Meals, classes, cultural tours and day trips are included*. All our guests have loved their stay!
* sleep in your own tent or rent one from us

2 All-inclusive family resort, Playa del Carmen, Mexico

♡ favourite

Our guests tell us this is the nicest pool they've seen! Our hotel has four other pools, a teenage surf club and a private beach. Leave your money at home* – but don't forget to pack your suncream!
* water sports are included – the people at reception can arrange everything for you

3 Penguin Guest House, Cape Town

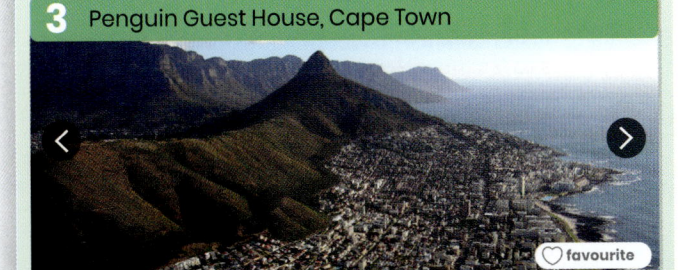

♡ favourite

Our guest house in the centre offers bed and breakfast. Our tour guides are all students who have recently graduated and can show you around the city for low prices. Or, for a little extra, you can have an adventure holiday with surf lessons or hiking on Table Mountain.
* Free Wi-Fi is available.

> **rent** (v) – use for a limited time at a cost
> **resort** – a place where a lot of people go on holiday

---

5 Complete the sentences with the words below.

   | adventure | all-inclusive | campsite | guest |
   | guest house | pack | reception | tour guide |

   1 Large tents are available at our _____.
   2 Our friendly _____ is based in the town centre.
   3 We can arrange a _____ to show you around.
   4 You don't need your wallet on our _____ holiday!
   5 Are you active? These are our top _____ holidays.
   6 You can leave a message with _____ – it's open 24 hours a day.
   7 Dear _____. Welcome to the best hotel in the world!
   8 _____ a good camera. Our safari tours are amazing!

6 **PRONUNCIATION** 🔊 8.07 We pronounce the letter *a* in different ways, e.g. with a short sound /æ/ and a long sound /eɪ/. Complete the table with the words below. Then listen, check and repeat.

   arr**a**nge   av**a**ilable   c**a**mping
   holid**a**y   p**a**ck   pr**a**ctise

   | /æ/ | **a**pple |
   | /eɪ/ | st**a**y |

7 **MEDIATION** Imagine you are on holiday and staying in one of the places in Ex 2. Write a text message to a friend telling them all about it. Use information from the texts.

8 💬 **THINK & SHARE** Work in pairs. Answer the questions.
   1 Which of the three places in the adverts would you most / least like to stay in? Why?
   2 Describe your dream holiday.
      • What type of holiday is it?
      • What place do you stay in?
      • What activities does it arrange for guests?

9 💬 Work in pairs. Write a short advert for your ideal type of holiday and places to stay. Share with the class.

VOCABULARY BOOSTER   Unit 8

8.6 GRAMMAR   Use the present perfect to ask and answer questions.

Present perfect: negative and questions

1 Read the quiz. Choose the best answers for you.

ARE YOU A TOURIST, A TRAVELLER OR AN ADVENTURER?

1 Have you eaten food that you can't pronounce?
   A Yes! I've always loved trying new dishes.
   B Yes, I've had meals at foreign restaurants.
   C No, I haven't. I've never tried any strange food.
2 Have you been on an unplanned journey?
   A Yes, I love going on adventure holidays.
   B No, I've never done that, but I'd like to, with friends!
   C No, I haven't. I arrange all my trips carefully.
3 Have you and your family ever stayed in a tent?
   A Yes, many times. I love camping in nature!
   B Yes, we have. We've stayed in a campsite.
   C No, my family hasn't been camping.
4 Have you ever had an all-inclusive holiday?
   A No, I haven't. I've never stayed in a resort.
   B Yes, but I also like guest houses.
   C Yes, I have. They're wonderful and easy!
5 Has a tour guide told you anything interesting?
   A No they haven't. A tour has never interested me.
   B Yes, I have. I've been on some good tours in museums.
   C Yes, I love hearing what guides have to say.

2 Turn to page 149 and check your quiz score. Do you agree with it?

3 Read the table and complete the examples. Use the quiz to help you.

Present perfect: negative and questions
▶ Grammar animation

Negative
I / You / We / They ¹_____ stayed in a hotel.
He / She / It ² _____ been camping.
Questions
³_____ I / you / we / they eaten foreign food?
Yes, I / we / they have. / No, I / we / they ⁴_____.
⁵_____ he / she / it shown you interesting things?
Yes, he / she / it has. / No, he / she / it ⁶_____.
We can use ⁷_____ (= at any time) in present perfect questions.
We can use ⁸_____ (= at no time) + affirmative verb to give a negative meaning to a sentence.

GRAMMAR BOOSTER P147

4 Complete the sentences.
1 It's a big resort. I / not meet / any other guests here.
2 You / never / stay in a guest house.
3 We / not bring / a tent, so we'll rent one.
4 He / never / be to a campsite. He can't wait to go.
5 Clara / not visit Bali, but she's going to next year.
6 Fan Wang and Bo / not / see a live performance.

5 Order the words to make questions.
1 ever / forgotten / they / passports / their / Have / ?
2 Has / a / marathon / he / ever / run / ?
3 ever / Chinese / Has / sister / food / eaten / your / ?
4 you / Have / been / on / ever / an / holiday / adventure / ?
5 your / trip / Have / a / ever / arranged / friends / day / ?

6 Look at the table. Complete the sentences, questions and short answers using the present perfect.

	Eat sushi	Dance tango	Visit Vietnam
Nina	✓	✗	✗
Lars and Sal	✗	✓	✗
You and I	✓	✗	✓

1 Nina _____ the tango.
2 _____ Lars and Sal ever _____ sushi? _____.
3 _____ you and I _____ Vietnam? _____.
4 _____ Nina ever _____ sushi? _____.
5 You and I _____ the tango.
6 Lars and Sal _____ Vietnam.

7 🔊 **8.10** Listen to the conversation. Where are Sofia and her mother? Where do they want to go?

8 Complete the questions with the correct form of the present perfect.
1 Sofia's mum / lose / anything important / ?
2 What / Sofia / lose / ?
3 Sofia / pack it / in her suitcase / ?
4 she / put it / in her backpack / ?
5 anybody / find / her passport / ?
6 Why / they / not get on / the plane / ?

9 🔊 **8.10** Listen again. Answer the questions in Ex 8. Use short answers.

10 💬 Look at the list of experiences below. Tick (✓) the ones you have had. Then ask and answer with a partner. Give extra information using the past simple.
• lose anything important? What?
• arrange a day trip? Where?
• miss a flight / train? Why?
• go up a mountain? Who?
• stay at a guest house? Which?
• be on an adventure? When?

> Have you lost anything important?
>
> Yes, I have. I lost my house keys on the way to school.

106 Unit 8

Understand topic sentences in an article about a travel photographer.

8.7 READING

A travel photographer

1 💬 Work in pairs. What does a travel photographer do?

STRATEGY Understanding topic sentences

A topic sentence is often, but not always, the first sentence in a paragraph. It introduces the paragraph and tells the reader what it is going to be about. Focusing on topic sentences will help you understand the structure of the text.

2 💬 Read the strategy. In pairs, read the title of the article and the opening paragraph and discuss the questions.
  1 Who is Kevin Faingnaert?
  2 What type of photos does he take?

3 🔊 **8.11** Read the article. Match headings A–G to paragraphs 1–5. There are two headings that you do not need. Use the underlined topic sentences to help you.
  A More than just places
  B A family man
  C The future
  D Experiences
  E Follow your dreams
  F Plan, plan, plan
  G Quality, not quantity

4 💬 Work in pairs. Discuss the questions.
  1 Would you like to have Kevin's job? Why? / Why not?
  2 What countries would you like to travel to? What would you like to photograph?

5 **VOCABULARY** Match the highlighted phrases in the text with the definitions.
  1 creating strong feelings _____
  2 spend time with something or someone so you learn more about them _____
  3 achieve a lot through your work _____
  4 made a great choice after thinking about different options _____

6 Complete the summary of the article with one word in each gap.
Kevin first became interested in ¹_____ in his teens. Since then, he has become a professional ²_____ and has travelled to many different ³_____. His photos of South ⁴_____ are his most well known. He has been on lots of exciting ⁵_____ and has ⁶_____ many people. Kevin likes to know a lot about his subjects ⁷_____ he takes any photos of them, and he ⁸_____ take many pictures.

7 💬 Work in pairs. Read the travel quotes below. Explain what you think each quote means by saying them in your own words.

> Take nothing but pictures; leave nothing but footprints.
> *Anonymous*

> To travel is to live.
> *Hans Christian Anderson*

> Never go on trips with anyone you do not love.
> *Hemingway*

8 💬 **THINK & SHARE** Work in pairs. Which quote do you like the most / least? Why?

Meet Kevin Faingnaert

Have you ever stopped to look at beautiful mountains and lakes? Have you ever taken pictures of interesting people around you? Have you ever waited hours to find the ideal light for a photo? Well, Kevin Faingnaert has. Even if you haven't heard of this adventurer, you've probably seen his pictures online.

1 ____

Ever since Kevin was a teenager, he has loved taking photos. After university, Kevin worked in an office. But when his hobby started to become successful, he left his job and became a travel photographer. For Kevin, it was the best decision he has ever made.

2 ____

He has won awards and worked for many international magazines and airlines. His job has taken him to incredible places such as Spain, Vietnam and Denmark. But the most famous photos he has ever taken are the ones of his South American journey. For this project, he travelled to regions which are a long way from any all-inclusive hotels. He arranged trips across Patagonia and slept in a tent at 5,000 metres in the Andes because there weren't any campsites or guest houses.

cholita – people from the Indian *Aymara* social group

3 ____

Kevin always researches a place before he visits it. He carefully studies maps and checks where the sun will be. Then, when he sees something interesting on tour, he goes on foot or rides a bike around the area looking for ideas. This process helps him find amazing views which nobody has ever seen.

4 ____

However, his photographs of people are his most famous work. It's important for him to get to know the people first and get close to them. In Argentina's capital, he's photographed people dancing the tango. And in Bolivia, he's taken pictures of cholita in their national costumes.

5 ____

He only takes a few photographs when he travels. In fact, he spends most of his time just walking and meeting people. He'll only take out his camera when the weather, the colours and the story are perfect. As he packs both digital and traditional cameras, he always has extra film available.

Kevin's photos are full of emotion, and make you feel like you have visited those places too.

Unit 8

8.8 SPEAKING — Ask for information about a place to stay.

Asking for information

1 **THINK & SHARE** Work in pairs. Look at the photos. Answer the questions.
1 Where do you think the boat is in the first photo?
2 What type of room is it in the second photo?
3 Would you like to stay here? Why? / Why not?

STRATEGY Preparing to talk

Before you ask for information on the phone, e.g. about a place to stay, think of some of the things you want to know. Then write a list of useful questions, e.g. *How far is it from the airport?* This will help you to speak more fluently and understand answers better.

2 Read the strategy. Work in pairs. Imagine you want to go to the places in the photos. What would you like to know about them before you can decide to go or not?

3 Read phrases A–G. Did you have similar ideas in Ex 2? Match the information below to the phrases.

a hundred pounds   boat trips   by tram   double room
every half an hour $50   42 Parkside Rd
in July   next week   on foot   ten minutes by bus
The Holiday Inn   twin room   two people

A name and address
B transport and times
C types of rooms available
D the planned travel dates
E the number of guests
F the price of rooms
G tours

4 Work in pairs. Prepare a list of questions you need to find out the information in Ex 3.

5 🔊 **8.12** Listen to a phone call. Did you hear any of your questions?

6 🔊 **8.12** Listen again. Complete the customer's notes.

Name and address: Falls Hostel [1]_____ Oakwood Road, Niagara, Ontario
Transport to Falls: [2]_____ or by bus.
Tours: boat trips 1 May–[3]_____ Nov, museum (5–7 p.m.)
Dates: rooms free 25 July–[4]_____ August.
Room prices: single $35, twin $[5]_____, family $110.
Phone: N.B. Reception closes at [6]_____ p.m. Call mobile: 905-453-[7]_____

7 Look at the phrasebook. Write C (customer) or R (reception).

PHRASEBOOK Talking about numbers

On the phone, you often need to ask about or understand numbers such as dates, quantities, prices, phone numbers, times, etc.
_____
We're … km (kilometres) away from …
There are buses which leave every … (half an hour).
It takes about … (minutes) on foot / by (train).
We have a double room available. It costs …
_____
There are (five) of us.
We're thinking of coming on … and going back on …
How much does it cost?

8 Work in pairs. Take turns to ask and answer the questions about Falls Hostel.
• Where exactly is the guest house?
• How can I get to the Falls?
• What tours do you arrange?
• Have you got any rooms free in July?
• How much do the rooms cost?

9 🔊 **8.13** Complete the dialogue with the words below. Then listen and check.

€135   10 km   fifth   half   minutes   six   twice   twin

A I'd like some information about your hotel, please.
B Have you ever been to the Netherlands?
A Yes, I've been [1]_____, but I've never visited Amsterdam. Where exactly are you?
B We're [2]_____ away from Amsterdam.
A How long does it take to get to the city centre?
B It takes [3]_____ an hour by bike or 20 [4]_____ by tram. When are you thinking of coming?
A On the [5]_____ of June and going back on the ninth.
B So, four nights. And how many people are there?
A There are [6]_____ of us.
B We have three [7]_____ rooms available.
A How much do they cost?
B Each room costs €45 a night, so [8]_____ in total.

10 Work in pairs. Student A: read cards 1 and 2 on page 150. Student B: read cards 1 and 2 on page 151. Use the prompts to ask and answer questions on card 2. Then complete the information. Use the Strategy and Phrasebook to help you.

11 **REFLECT** Work in pairs. Answer the questions.
1 Did you manage to find out the information you needed?
2 Which phrases from the Phrasebook did you use?
3 Did you get all the numbers and information correct?

108   Unit 8

Decide what to include in a postcard.

8.9 WRITING

A postcard

1 Work in pairs. Ask and answer the questions.
  1 Have you ever sent a postcard? Where from? Who to?
  2 Have you ever received one? Who was it from? Where were they?

2 Read the postcards. What relation are the people to Anya? What do you think they are interested in? Which one sounds more formal or informal?

> Dear Ms Rossi,
> This is our fourth day in Italy. We're staying at a campsite near Lucca. Have you ever been to Tuscany? The old cities are beautiful, and the weather is wonderful! We've visited lots of museums and I've seen some amazing paintings. We haven't been to the Uffizi art gallery in Florence, but we're going to go on a tour on Friday. I hope the tour guides are good! Wish you were here! Give my regards to the other students.
> See you all in the New Year.
> Best wishes,
> Anya

> Hi Grandad,
> So far, we've been in Italy for two weeks. We're staying at a guest house near Milan and it's very hot. We've visited the Ferrari museum in Modena – the fast cars are the best thing I've ever seen! We haven't been to Milan, but hopefully we're going to go to the racing track in Monza this week! Thinking of you.
> See you soon.
> Love from
> Anya xxx
> P.S. Say hi to Auntie Tilly from us.

STRATEGY Deciding what to include

When you write, think about what you need to include and who you are writing for. For example, when you write a postcard, consider who you're writing to and what they're interested in. Then, follow these steps to help you write a postcard:
1 Say hello.
2 Say where you're staying.
3 Say what the weather's like.
4 Say what you've done.
5 Say what you're going to do next.
6 Finish your postcard and say goodbye.

3 Read the strategy. and answer the questions.
  1 What phrases does Anya use to start and end her postcards?
  2 What tenses does she use to describe points 2–5 in the strategy?

4 Read the postcards again. Complete the table about each postcard.

	Postcard 1	Postcard 2
1 Where is she?		
2 What's the weather like?		
3 What has she done?		
4 What are her plans?		

5 Read the Language focus. Find examples of the phrases in the postcards. Which greetings are more formal?

LANGUAGE FOCUS Postcards

Hi, Hello / Dear,
We're staying at … we've visited …
Say hi to … / Give my regards to …
Wish you were here! / Thinking of you.
See you soon. / See you (next week).
Love from / Best wishes

6 Tick (✓) the phrases that Anya uses in her postcards.
I'm having a great time in …
This is our fourth day in …
The weather is wonderful / terrible.
I've only seen …
Say hi / hello to …
Give my love to (Dad).
See you soon.

7 Choose the best alternative.

> Dear Uncle Mike,
> I'm ¹**going to have / having** a brilliant time in Croatia. I ²**'m staying / stay** at an all-inclusive hotel near Zadar. It ³**was / is** very hot and sunny. We ⁴**go / 've been** on boat trips around the islands and we ⁵**'ve swum / 're going to swim** with dolphins! On Friday, we ⁶**'re going to visit / 've visited** Plitvice Lakes National Park.
> Wish you ⁷**are / were** here!
> See you ⁸**later / soon**.
> ⁹**Goodbye / Love from**,
> Victor

8 Imagine you are on holiday. Think of a place and activities. Decide who your postcard is for.

9 Organise your ideas. Use the strategy to help you.

10 Write a postcard in 60–80 words. Use your notes and the Phrasebook to help you.

11 ✓ CHECK YOUR WORK
  • Does your postcard include the necessary information?
  • Have you written a greeting and an ending?
  • Do you include some typical expressions?
  • Are the tenses of the verbs correct?

Unit 8   109

8.10 REVIEW

Grammar

1 Complete the sentences and questions with the present perfect form of the verb in brackets.
   1 We _____ enough warm clothes with us. (not bring)
   2 My classmates and I _____ the past simple. (study)
   3 _____ your parents _____ our teacher? (meet)
   4 My cousin _____ a plane. (never / miss)
   5 _____ you _____ Japanese sashimi? (ever / try)
   6 They _____ to each other all day. (not speak)
   7 I _____ a city break in Vienna. (never / have)
   8 _____ Anna _____ at this restaurant? (eat)

2 Choose the correct answer: A, B or C.
   1 Alisha and I … the bus to school today.
      A have taken   B has taken   C have took
   2 Those boys _____ never paid for lunch!
      A haven't   B has   C have
   3 'Has the teacher come back?' 'No, … .'
      A hasn't she   B she hasn't   C she's not
   4 This is the best city break I …
      A had.   B have had.   C have.
   5 'Have you found it?' 'Yes, … !'
      A have I   B you have   C I have
   6 Which countries … to?
      A has Dan been   B have been Dan   C has been Dan

Vocabulary

3 Are the sentences true (T) or false (F)? Correct the false sentences with one word.
   1 A flight is the time you spend on a train.
   2 Trams usually run under city streets, next to cars.
   3 To go on foot means to walk.
   4 A plane is a big, comfortable bus that travels long distances.
   5 You can go by taxi if you haven't got your own car.
   6 A short holiday in a big town is called a town break.
   7 People often take a train trip along the river.
   8 On a journey, you're travelling from one place to another.

4 Complete the definitions.
   1 You can sleep in this on holiday: t_____.
   2 This means 'to organise': a_____.
   3 What we call people staying in a hotel: g_____.
   4 This type of holiday offers exciting or dangerous experiences: a_____.
   5 This is a short visit, often organised by a tourist agency: t_____.
   6 This type of holiday includes transport, meals, a place to stay and free-time activities: a_____-i_____.
   7 You can stay in a caravan or tent here: c_____.
   8 This means to put clothes, etc in a bag to travel: p_____.
   9 Something that you can get, buy or find: a_____.
   10 This is a type of holiday in a tent: c_____.

Cumulative review

5 Complete the email with the correct form of the words below.

book   buy   ever visit   guest house   never eat
not travel   pack   rain   reception   spend   stay
transport   underground   views   walking tour

Dear Emma,
We're having a great time in London!
My family and I [1]_____ to many capital cities (only Paris and Madrid), but I think this is definitely my favourite one so far! I think it's the most exciting city in the world!
[2]_____ you _____ London?
We [3]_____ two big double rooms in an old [4]_____ in Hammersmith. They don't speak any Hungarian at the [5]_____ desk, so I am practising a lot of English right now! I think it's a very nice hotel; in fact, it's certainly the best place I [6]_____ in.
London's public [7]_____ system is also fantastic. There are lots of buses and trains, and it's got the largest [8]_____ system in Europe; 'the tube' is 402 km long and has got nearly 300 stations.
I like the food, but my dad says it's nothing special. It's our fifth day here, and he [9]_____ real fish and chips … So, maybe we'll have that for dinner this evening.
The weather is pretty terrible. It [10]_____ all day, every day, so unfortunately, a [11]_____ hasn't been possible. We [12]_____ a lot of time inside museums and shops. I forgot to [13]_____ an umbrella, so I [14]_____ a new one with the British flag on it (the Union Jack).
Tonight, we're going to the UK's most popular tourist attraction: the London Eye. Over 3 million people visit it every year. It's 135 metres tall, so there are going to be some incredible [15]_____ from the top. Please don't rain!
Thinking of you.
See you soon,
Laci

Think & share

6 Read the quote. Then answer the questions.

  I haven't been everywhere, but it's on my list.
  Susan Sontag

   1 What are some of the most interesting places in the world? Why?
   2 What types of holidays and places to stay are best for young people? Why?
   3 What different types of transport have you used? Where were they?
   4 What are some of the pros and cons of each type?

8.11 EXAM SKILLS

Listening

EXAM STRATEGY

When you have a task with missing information, read the text carefully before you listen. Try to predict what the missing information might be, for example, a number, a place, a time, etc.

1 Read the strategy above. Then look at the exam task in Ex 2. Match gaps 1–5 in the sentences to the types of information (A–E).
   ___ A form of transport
   ___ B name of month
   ___ C number
   ___ D activity
   ___ E amount of time

2 🔊 8.14 For each question, listen and write the correct answer in the gap. Write one or two words, or a number, a date or a time.

You will hear a radio presenter talking about city breaks.

City breaks in Seville, Spain

You can go on this break at the beginning of ¹_____.
You will stay in a beautiful hotel for ²_____.
You can walk from the Parque de Maria Luisa to the city in ³_____ minutes.
Price includes: flight, hotel, breakfast.
You can pay extra to see the city on a ⁴_____.
You can travel to Ronda by ⁵_____.

Use of English

EXAM STRATEGY

When you have multiple-choice options for a text with missing words, read the text again after you have chosen the answers. Check the options that you've chosen are correct and the ones that you've left are definitely wrong.

3 Read the strategy above. Then read the text and the options below. One of the chosen answers is incorrect. Which one? What should the answer be?

> I ¹___ on many school trips. Last year we ²___ by coach to Pisek. The problem was that on the way home, the coach broke ³___. We waited three hours for someone to fix it.
>
> 1 A went   B am going   C going   (D) have been
> 2 A have travelled B travel   (C) travelled   D will travel
> 3 A back   B down   (C) off   D on

4 Read the blog below and choose the correct answer (A, B, C or D) for each gap.

Explore Venice

Have you ¹_____ been to the Italian city of Venice? It's a very beautiful and interesting place. Venice is made up of small islands so there is a lot of water. There are no cars, but there are lots of boats and it's easy to see the city ²_____ foot. When you walk, and you don't drive or travel ³_____ bus or train, you see many things that tourists don't usually see. I've ⁴_____ some of the most beautiful buildings and interesting cafés and shops this way. As a result, I try not to use public transport in a new place. Of course, it's wonderful to get ⁵_____ the city on the water too. I've ⁶_____ taken a boat taxi in Venice, but I've been in a gondola. ⁷_____ you heard of these long, black boats? They're very famous in Italy. I enjoyed my gondola trip, but it ⁸_____ also very expensive.

	A	B	C	D
1	never	than	got	ever
2	at	on	by	down
3	by	in	off	around
4	find	finding	to find	found
5	around	back	by	off
6	got	never	no	been
7	Do	Are	Have	Will
8	has been	is going to be	will be	was

Writing

EXAM STRATEGY

Before you start writing, read the task carefully and make notes about each piece of information you need to include.

5 Read the strategy above. Then look at the exam task in Ex 6. Match notes A–D below to the questions (1–4) in the first task option.
   A coach broke down / people angry
   B last summer / early morning
   C waited six hours / someone fixed coach / went back to Zagreb
   D on holiday / on coach / Croatia / trip from Zagreb to lakes

6 Choose one of the tasks – the description OR the article – then write your text.

Description
Your English teacher has asked you to write a description of an interesting travel experience you have had. It can be real or invented. Think about these points.

1 Where were you?
2 When was it?
3 What happened?
4 What happened in the end?

Article
You have seen the following advert in an online magazine for English language students. Write an article for the magazine.

My favourite place
We want you to write an article about the best place you have ever been to. What was it like? Why was it so wonderful? How much do you enjoy travelling?

1.1 VOCABULARY BOOSTER

Daily routines

1 GET STARTED 🔊 **1.03** Match the activities below to the photos. Listen and check.

| drink   eat   meet my friends   sleep   study   work

1 _____
2 _____
3 _____
4 _____
5 _____
6 _____

2 💬 Work in pairs. Ask and answer the questions.
1 What do you do after school?
2 What do you do at the weekend?

3 PRACTISE Complete the words with the missing letters.
1 On Friday after school, I r___ ___ ___x with my family. I don't do homework.
2 We v___ ___g about things like books and music. People watch us talking about them online.
3 I l___ ___ ___ ___n to m___ ___ ___c on my phone all the time. I really like rap.
4 I w___ ___ ___h T___ with my sister after dinner.
5 I g___ to b___d early because I g___ ___ u___ at 5.30 a.m. every morning.
6 I h___ ___e b___ ___ ___ ___f___ ___t at home with my brothers and sisters before I go to school.
7 I b___ ___ ___h my t___ ___ ___h before I g___ to b___ ___ at night.
8 I b___ ___ ___h my h___ ___r on the bus to school, not at home. My friend Adah helps me because my hair is very long!

4 💬 Choose the correct alternative. Which sentences are true for you? Compare with a partner.
1 I **do / have** a shower in the evening, not in the morning.
2 I **get / take** dressed after I have breakfast.
3 I **go / have** lunch at school and dinner at home.
4 I **do / take** the bus to my friend's house at the weekend.
5 I **go / have** guitar lessons on Tuesdays after school.
6 I **go / go to** school at 8.30 a.m. and I **go / go to** home at 4 p.m.
7 I **do / get** my homework after dinner.

5 EXTEND 🔊 **1.04** Complete the definitions with the phrases below. Listen and check.

| check your timetable   get out of bed
  get ready for tomorrow   have a lie-in
  have a rest   wake up late

1 When you're tired, you often sit or lie down and _____.
2 When you _____, you check that you have everything you need for the next day, for example clothes and books for school.
3 You _____ to get information about the lessons, sports and other things you need to do the next day or in the next week.
4 When you _____, you stay in bed in the morning because you don't have to get up early.
5 When you _____, you need to get ready very quickly so that you aren't late for school.
6 You don't need to _____ early at the weekend because there's no school.

6 💬 Work in pairs. Ask and answer the questions.
1 Where do you have a rest?
2 What do you get ready the evening before school?
3 How important is it to check your timetable?
4 Do your parents have a lie-in at the weekend? Why / Why not?

1.5 VOCABULARY BOOSTER

Free-time activities

1 **GET STARTED** 🔊 1.10 Look at the pictures and complete the phrases about free-time activities with the words below. Listen and check.

| check   coffee   cook   letter
| listen   read   shopping   talk

1 go for a _____
2 go _____ 
3 _____ a book 
4 _____ your favourite meal  
5 write a _____ 
6 _____ to the radio 
7 _____ to a friend 
8 _____ your emails 

2 Work in pairs. Which of the activities in Ex 1 do you do …
- every day? _____
- sometimes? _____

3 **PRACTISE** Match 1–8 to A–H to make complete sentences.
1 Every weekend, we **go**
2 My dad wants to get fit so he **goes for**
3 My sister **rides**
4 I **read**
5 When it rains at the weekend, we **play**
6 We **listen to**
7 Please **tidy**
8 My sister wants to **design**

A **your room**. All your clothes and books are on the floor!
B **a board game** indoors.
C **a run** every morning before work.
D **a comic** on the bus home from school.
E **for a walk** in the park with our friends.
F **music** in the car.
G **a bike** to school.
H **a website**.

4 Complete the sentences with the words below.

| draw   learn   make   take

1 When I spend time with my family I _____ a lot of photos.
2 I _____ pictures to help me remember new words.
3 We _____ a cake for our friends when they visit us.
4 All the children _____ a language at school.

5 **EXTEND** 🔊 1.11 Complete the phrases with the verbs below. Listen and check.

| check   do   go (×2)   hang out with
| learn   listen   take

1 _____ it easy
2 _____ your friends
3 _____ to the library
4 _____ a musical instrument
5 _____ online
6 _____ your social media
7 _____ to a podcast
8 _____ yoga

6 Complete the text with words and phrases from Ex 5.
At the weekend I ¹_____ and I don't do much. I ²_____ in my room – for example, an interesting discussion, or sometimes something that makes me laugh. Then after lunch, I ³_____ my friends. Sometimes we ⁴_____, but we don't read books there. They have really good wi-fi and lots of computers so it's a great place to ⁵_____ online. We usually watch videos and ⁶_____ our social media there.

I have a brother but he's very different from me. He doesn't stop. He learns two ⁷_____ so he practises a lot! He has a guitar and there's a piano at home as well. He also does ⁸_____ every Saturday afternoon. Now he can stand on his head!

Word skills

RECOGNISING WORD TYPES

7 Look at the words in **bold** in the pairs of sentences and answer the questions.
   A My friends **help** me.
   B I ask my friends for **help**.
   C His **work** is very interesting.
   D They **work** in a school.

1 Is **help** in A a verb or a noun?
2 Is **help** in B a verb or a noun?
3 Is **work** in C a noun or a verb?
4 Is **work** in D a noun or a verb?

8 Choose the correct alternative to complete the rule about word types.
The same word **can / can't** be more than one part of speech.

2.1 VOCABULARY BOOSTER

Crazy about sport

1 **GET STARTED** 🔊 **2.03** Match the words below to the photos. Listen and check.

| basketball   cycling   game   horse-riding
| rugby   running   sports   team

1 _____
2 _____
3 _____
4 _____
5 _____
6 _____
7 _____
8 _____

2 💬 What do you do to stay healthy? Write three sentences with words from Ex 1. Tell your partner.

3 💬 **PRACTISE** Work in pairs. Complete the mini quiz.

What's the sport?

1 You usually do this with music.
   A snowboarding   **B** dance classes   **C** surfing

2 It's a team sport with a ball and two goals. There are eleven players in each team.
   A tennis   **B** volleyball   **C** football

3 You do this in the sea, in a river or in a pool.
   A swimming   **B** skateboarding   **C** snowboarding

4 The weather is very important when you do this sport.
   A doing a workout   **B** windsurfing   **C** going to the gym

5 This is a game for two or four players. You can play inside or outside.
   A tennis   **B** diving   **C** dance classes

4 Complete the sentences with the words below.

| athlete   diving   fit   gym   skateboarding
| snowboarding   surfing   volleyball   workouts

1 We hardly ever go to the _____ because we like to do exercise outdoors.
2 In winter, Pasha goes _____ in the mountains with his friends.
3 Lisa is very _____ because she goes to dance classes and the gym.
4 I like sports that you play in a team, like football and _____.
5 When I go swimming, I usually practise some _____ as well.
6 Sonya does two or three _____ in the gym every week.
7 In the summer when he can't go snowboarding, Max goes _____ in the park near his house instead.
8 When we go to the beach, we often go swimming or _____ in the sea.
9 Sandro is an amazing _____. He can run very fast.

5 **EXTEND** 💬 **2.04** Work in pairs. Match the words to their definitions. Listen and check.

| a match   a racket   fishing   golf
| hiking   hockey   skiing   table tennis

1 another word for a sports game _____
2 you use this to hit the ball in sports, e.g. tennis _____
3 you need a small white ball and a long metal stick for this sport _____
4 going for long walks in the country _____
5 a sport you do in the snow on a mountain with two sticks _____
6 a sport you do near water _____
7 a sport also called ping pong! _____
8 this sport has two teams of eleven players with wooden sticks and a ball _____

6 Complete the sentences with words and phrases from Ex 5.

1 It's important to have good walking boots when you go _____.
2 My brother loves team sports, so he plays _____ at the weekend.
3 When I play _____, I often lose my ball in the trees. I'm not very good, but it's great fun!
4 We go _____ in the mountains in the winter and surfing at the beach in the summer.
5 My dad goes _____ because it's relaxing. Sometimes he catches dinner!
6 I've got my _____ because I'm playing tennis later today.
7 We watched the football _____ on TV.

Vocabulary booster

2.5 VOCABULARY BOOSTER

How to eat well

1 GET STARTED 🔊 2.13 Match the words below to the photos. Listen and check.

| butter   cake   coffee   fruit   juice   salad
| sandwich   sugar   tea   vegetables

1 _____
2 _____
3 _____
4 _____
5 _____
6 _____
7 _____
8 _____
9 _____
10 _____

2 💬 Number the food in Ex 1 from food you like a lot (1) to food you do not like very much (10). Compare with a partner.

3 PRACTISE 💬 Work in pairs. Choose the incorrect alternative.
1 You put **tomatoes** / **lettuce** / **cola** in a salad.
2 There's a lot of sugar and fat in **ice cream** / **chocolate** / **meat**.
3 People often drink **cola** / **ice cream** / **water** with their meals.
4 You get food like **chicken** / **fish** / **bread** from animals.
5 You make **avocado** / **cheese** / **yoghurt** from milk.
6 **Apples** / **Broccoli** / **Carrots** are vegetables.
7 **Strawberries** / **Beans** / **Bananas** are fruits.

4 💬 Work in pairs. Ask and answer the questions.
1 What do you usually have for breakfast?
2 What do you have for lunch at the weekend?
3 What do you usually eat when you have a snack?
4 What food do you eat every day?
5 What food do you never eat?

5 EXTEND 🔊 2.14 Match the words below to the definitions. Listen and check.

| a biscuit   honey   lamb   a lemon
| nuts   jam   a melon   toast

1 you make this from fruit and sugar and put it on bread
2 meat from a young sheep
3 bees make this from flowers and it's very sweet
4 you need some bread to make this
5 A big round fruit with a hard skin. It can be yellow or green.
6 a yellow fruit, you often use the juice in cooking
7 small hard fruits that are usually brown
8 a small sweet snack that you often have with a cup of tea or coffee

6 💬 Work in pairs. Ask and answer the questions. Use words from Ex 5.
1 Which types of food have a lot of sugar or fat?
2 Which types of food grow on trees?
3 What can you put on toast?
4 Which types of food are healthy?

Word skills

COMPOUND NOUNS

7 Look at the words below. Which three are NOT compound nouns? Why?

| biscuits   cheeseburger   ice cream
| lunchtime   olive oil   orange juice
| lunch box   vegetables   yoghurt

8 Make more compound nouns with the words below. Which three do we write as one word?

| beef   milk   fruit   cheese
| cake   burger   chocolate   salad

Vocabulary booster 115

3.1 VOCABULARY BOOSTER

What's your style?

1 GET STARTED 🔊 **3.03** Match the words below to the photos. Listen and check.

| a bag | boots | brown | a coat |
| green | grey | a jumper | white |

1 _____ 2 _____
3 _____ 4 _____
5 _____ 6 _____
7 _____ 8 _____

2 💬 Work in pairs. Ask and answer the questions.
1 What do you wear every day?
2 What do you wear at weekends?
3 What do you wear when you go to a party?

3 PRACTISE Look at the photos below and complete the words with the missing letters.

1 a d___k t___
2 a sh___t s___ ___t
3 b___ ___t ___ ___l s___ ___s
4 a c___ ___m j___ ___ ___ ___t
5 d___ ___k t___ ___ ___ ___ ___s
6 a c___ ___ ___ ___r___ ___l tie
7 a p___ ___k T-s___ ___ ___ ___
8 a b___ ___ ___t ___ ___l s___ ___ ___t

4 💬 Look at the clothes in Ex 1 and Ex 3. What do you often / sometimes / never wear? Compare in groups.

I often wear …
I sometimes wear …
I never wear …

5 EXTEND 🔊 **3.04** Match the clothes to the definitions. Listen and check.

| a cap | a belt | gloves | a scarf | shorts |
| a swimsuit | trainers | a uniform |

1 you wear these shoes for sports, or with informal clothes _____
2 you wear them on your hands in winter _____
3 you wear it around your neck when you're cold _____
4 you wear this at the beach to go swimming _____
5 children often wear this at school, and people sometimes wear one at work _____
6 baseball players wear this hat _____
7 you wear these trousers in hot weather or when you do sport _____
8 you wear this around the middle of your body _____

6 Complete the text with words from Ex 5.
Everyone at my school wears a ¹_____. The younger boys wear ²_____, a white shirt, a tie and a jumper. When they are twelve, they can wear trousers. They wear a ³_____ on their head especially when it's hot and sunny outside. The girls wear a skirt, a white shirt and a jumper. Everybody wears black shoes. We can only wear ⁴_____ when we do sports or exercise. In winter when it's cold, everybody wears their school ⁵_____ around their necks. It's red, blue and purple. I always wear ⁶_____ too, so my hands are warm!

7 💬 Work in pairs. What do children usually wear to school in your country?

3.5 VOCABULARY BOOSTER

Describing character

1 **GET STARTED** 🔊 3.11 Choose the correct option in **bold** to complete sentences a and b. Listen and check.
   1 good / bad
      a My best friend always helps me because she is a _____ person.
      b When we're _____ in class our teacher gives us more homework.
   2 interesting / boring
      a My little brother is so _____! He talks about trains all the time!
      b Sofia tells me lots of great things I don't know – she's very _____!
   3 sad / happy
      a When I'm _____ my mum always asks me how she can help.
      b My dad laughs a lot because he's a very _____ person.
   4 nice / horrible
      a My sister is _____ because she gives me clothes and make-up.
      b Nobody in our class is _____ – we are all good friends.

2 **PRACTISE** Match the sentences.
   1 Mario always makes people laugh.
   2 Katya isn't afraid of anything.
   3 Everything Yuka says is true.
   4 Kamal is never rude.
   5 Rita never gets angry when she needs to wait.
   6 Enrique doesn't laugh very often.
   7 People think Frank is a bit stupid, but it isn't true.
   8 Everybody likes Valerie and she has lots of friends.
   9 It's very easy to talk to Mark.
   10 Marina prefers listening to other people. She doesn't talk a lot.
   11 Anton helps me all the time.

   A She's very **popular**.
   B He's always very **kind**.
   C She's always very **patient**.
   D He's very **funny**.
   E She's very **quiet**.
   F She's very **honest**.
   G He's actually really **clever**.
   H She's very **brave**.
   I He's a really **friendly** person.
   J He's very **serious**.
   K He's always very **polite**.

3 💬 Write two true sentences and two false sentences about you. Use words from Ex 2. Read them to your partner. Take turns to say which are true and which are false.

4 **EXTEND** 🔊 3.12 Complete the definitions with the words below. Listen and check.

   | brilliant   caring   confident   creative
   | hard-working   organised   relaxed   shy

   1 A _____ person spends a lot of time studying or working, they aren't lazy.
   2 A _____ person is kind and helpful, and they often look after people who need help.
   3 A _____ person is very good at all the things they need to do.
   4 An _____ person plans everything they need to do, and they often like everything to be very tidy.
   5 A _____ person believes they can do things.
   6 When someone is _____, they don't have anything to worry about.
   7 A _____ person often feels nervous when they meet and speak to new people.
   8 _____ people are good at things like art, writing, making films.

5 💬 Think of somebody you know for the words in Ex 4. Then work in pairs and tell your partner about them. Give reasons.

   My grandmother is very caring. She looks after all her grandchildren, cooks lovely food and makes everybody feel great.

Word skills

WORD BUILDING: ADJECTIVES

6 <u>Underline</u> the adjectives in the sentences and answer the questions below.
   • My brother is serious and hardly ever laughs.
   • This film is so funny! We can't stop laughing!
   • Your bedroom is so untidy!
   • Don't be so unkind. Think before you speak.

   Which adjectives …
   1 have a prefix?
   2 are opposites?
   3 have a negative meaning?

7 Write the opposite of the adjectives below. Use a prefix if possible.

   | clever   friendly   noisy   popular

   _____
   _____
   _____
   _____

Vocabulary booster 117

4.1 VOCABULARY BOOSTER

Come on in

1 GET STARTED 🔊 **4.03** Match the words below to the photos. Listen and check.

| bath   bed   desk   door   shower
| table   toilet   window

1 _____
2 _____
3 _____
4 _____
5 _____
6 _____
7 _____
8 _____

2 💬 Work in pairs. Ask and answer the questions.
1 Which things would you find in the bedroom?
2 Which things would you find in the bathroom?
3 Which things would you find in any room in the house?

3 PRACTISE Read the advertisements and choose the correct alternative.

This is a lovely ¹**flat / floor** with a ²**balcony / kitchen** where you can sit, have a drink and look at the sea. There is a big ³**bathroom / living room** with two comfortable ⁴**bedrooms / sofas** to sit on, and beautiful carpets on the ⁵**floor / sink**. There are two ⁶**bedrooms / fridges** with large double beds, and both have windows with a view of the sea. Each bedroom also has a ⁷**bathroom / dining room** with a bath and shower.

This house is very good for big parties. It has a huge living room and a fantastic ⁸**bedroom / dining room** with a long table, where lots of people can have dinner. There is a very large ⁹**balcony / kitchen** as well, with three ¹⁰**floors / fridges** for all your food, and two ¹¹**sofas / sinks** for washing dishes. Upstairs there are five bedrooms and five bathrooms.

4 💬 Work in pairs. Look at the photos in Ex 3. Where would you like to stay on holiday? Why?

5 EXTEND 💬 🔊 **4.04** Work in pairs. Match the words to their definitions. Listen and check.

| basin   bin   cooker   dishwasher   furniture
| lamp   stairs   washing machine

1 a machine for washing plates, glasses, cups, etc.
2 a sink in the bathroom
3 it gives us light – you have a lot of these in your house, on tables, desks, by your bed, etc.
4 you put things you don't want in it – there's usually one in the kitchen, bathroom and every bedroom
5 you use it to cook food
6 a machine for washing clothes
7 chairs, sofas, tables, beds, etc.
8 you use these to go from one floor to another

6 💬 Work in pairs. Imagine your perfect home. Describe it to your partner.

My perfect home is a large flat near the city centre. There's a big balcony with a view of …

118 Vocabulary booster

4.5 VOCABULARY BOOSTER

Places in the world

1 GET STARTED 🔊 4.13 Match the words below to the photos. Listen and check.

| bank   car park   cinema   city   hospital   restaurant
| road   shop   supermarket   village

1 _____
2 _____
3 _____
4 _____
5 _____
6 _____
7 _____
8 _____
9 _____
10 _____

2 💬 Write three sentences about the place where you live with words from Ex 1. Compare in groups.

There isn't a train station in my village but there's a bus station.

3 PRACTISE Choose the correct alternative.
1 There's almost no water in a **desert** / **rainforest**.
2 When you study **architecture** / **oceans**, you learn how to design and make buildings.
3 A **square** / **street** is an open area in a town, usually with buildings on all four sides.
4 **A street** / **An architecture** is a small road in a town or city with lots of buildings or houses.
5 A **forest** / **river** is an area with lots and lots of trees.
6 There are more **lakes** / **oceans** in Canada than any other country in the world.
7 Cyprus, Sicily, Malta and Tahiti are all **beaches** / **islands**.
8 The Nile in Africa, the Amazon in South America and the Ganges in India are all **rivers** / **lakes**.

4 Complete the text with the words below.

| beaches   buildings   islands   Ocean   rainforests

Hawaii is a group of ¹_____ in the middle of the Pacific ²_____. The capital, Honolulu, is a big city with many tall ³_____ everywhere. But Hawaii isn't just famous for its capital city, it's also famous for its beautiful ⁴_____. Tourists go there to sit in the sun and swim in the sea. They can also visit the ⁵_____ to see the amazing plants and trees, and all the animals and birds of every colour that live there. It's a fantastic place to go on holiday!

5 EXTEND 🔊 4.14 Match the words to their definitions. Listen and check.

| coast   countryside   field   hill
| stream   valley   waterfall   wood

1 land that is higher than the land near it, but smaller than a mountain _____
2 the land next to or near the sea or ocean _____
3 an area of low land between hills or mountains _____
4 a place where a river falls from a high place _____
5 land outside towns and cities, with fields, forests, etc. _____
6 an area of trees, smaller than a forest _____
7 a very small river _____
8 land used to grow things or keep farm animals e.g. sheep, cows, etc. _____

6 💬 Rewrite the sentences so they are true for you. Compare in groups.
1 I live in a small village near the coast.
2 There are lots of hills and mountains near my home.
3 I often go to a waterfall.
4 I live in a valley near a river.
5 I can see a stream from my house.
6 I live near a beautiful wood.

Word skills

SPELLING AND PRONUNCIATION

7 Are the sentences true (T) or false (F)?
1 You always pronounce every letter in English words. There are no letters that we don't pronounce. ___
2 The same letter or group of letters is not always pronounced the same way. ___

8 Choose the correct alternative.
1 The pronunciation of *ch* in *architecture* and *beach* is **the same** / **different**.
2 In *cupboard*, you don't pronounce the letter **b** / **p**.
3 The pronunciation of *oo* in *floor* and *door* is **the same** / **different**.
4 In *listen*, you don't pronounce the letter **s** / **t**.

9 Can you think of any more examples like the ones in Ex 8?

Vocabulary booster   119

5.1 VOCABULARY BOOSTER

I'm into art

1 GET STARTED 🔊 **5.03** Complete the phrases with the words below. Listen and check.

| act | band | dance | movie |
| paint | sing | story | ticket |

1	watch a _____	at the cinema / on TV
2	_____	a song / very well / in a group
3	_____	with someone / to music / at a party
4	_____	a picture
5	buy a _____ to see	a film / a play
6	tell / listen to / write	a _____
7	_____	in a film / in a play
8	play music in / sing in	a _____

2 💬 Write three true sentences with words from Ex 1. Compare in groups.

My sister sings in a band.
My mother paints very well.
We watch lots of movies on TV.

3 PRACTISE Choose the correct alternative.
1 Coachella, Glastonbury and Benicassim are all famous music **exhibitions** / **festivals**.
2 We watched a film in the park on a very big **painting** / **screen**.
3 **Hip-hop** / **Rock** started in the 1970s - the artists usually speak very quickly to the music instead of singing.
4 We saw a wonderful dance **event** / **show** at the theatre last week.
5 I often go to **concerts** / **exhibitions** to listen to music. My favourites are Mozart and Beethoven.
6 You play a **drum** / **screen** by hitting it with your hands or a stick.
7 There is a wonderful **exhibition** / **event** of modern art at the museum at the moment.
8 There's a famous **painting** / **show** of sunflowers by Van Gogh at the National Gallery in London.

4 Complete the sentences with the phrases below.

| crowded streets | cultural events |
| incredible artists | street theatre |

1 They planned lots of _____ _____ in the city, including exhibitions, films and street theatre.
2 People enjoy watching _____ during the festival because it's fun, it's outdoors and it's free.
3 Lots of _____ go to the Edinburgh Festival every year to act in plays, sing, dance and play music.
4 The _____ were full of tourists and artists during the festival.

5 EXTEND 🔊 **5.04** Match the words below to the photos. Listen and check.

| art gallery | ballet | classical music | film star |
| jazz | opera | painter | pop music | singer |

1 _____ 2 _____ 3 _____

4 _____ 5 _____ 6 _____

7 _____ 8 _____ 9 _____

6 💬 Work in pairs. Ask and answer the questions.
1 Do you ever go to museums or galleries to look at paintings? When?
2 Do you ever listen to opera or classical music? Do you have a favourite?
3 Do you know anybody who likes ballet? Who?
4 Do you have a favourite painter? Who?
5 Which film stars do you like?
6 What kinds of music do you like? Who are your favourite artists?

5.5 VOCABULARY BOOSTER

Entertainment

1 **GET STARTED** 🔊 5.11 Complete the sentences with the words below. Listen and check.

| dangerous   exciting   great   long   relaxing   short

1 I make _____ videos on my phone – they usually last about 10 or 15 minutes.
2 It's very _____ to watch nature programmes about animals and birds – I sometimes go to sleep on the sofa!
3 I hate _____ films that are more than two hours. It's boring.
4 We watch film actors do some _____ things like jumping out of planes, but it isn't real, and they don't hurt themselves!
5 I like watching action films because lots of _____ things happen all the time.
6 The Harry Potter movies are my favourite – they're _____!

2 💬 Work in small groups. Which sentences in Ex 1 do you agree with?

3 **PRACTISE** Match 1–6 to A–F to make complete sentences.
1 I liked the original film of *The Jungle Book* from 1967 more
2 Everybody likes films with romantic endings
3 My parents think *The X Factor* is a wonderful show
4 That new film has good reviews
5 I started to watch that film but I stopped
6 There are lots of excellent performances in the film of the musical *Les Miserables*

A and they watch it every week.
B because all the actors are great singers.
C than the one from 2016.
D because of the terrible acting.
E where the characters get together.
F but it was nothing special.

4 💬 Complete the questions with the words below. Then work in pairs and ask and answer the questions.

| boring characters   brilliant songs
| loud music   reviews   TV series

1 Which _____ do you enjoy watching the most?
2 Do you ever read _____ of films and TV series before you watch them?
3 Which movies aren't very interesting because they have _____?
4 Which musicals have _____ that you want to listen to again and again?
5 Do your parents ever get angry if you listen to _____?

5 **EXTEND** 🔊 5.12 Match the words to their definitions. Listen and check.

| all right   awful   beginning   cool
| end   marvellous   middle   unusual

1 very good, wonderful _____
2 OK but not very good _____
3 very bad, terrible _____
4 start, first part _____
5 part between the start and the finish _____
6 final part _____
7 not common, not normal _____
8 good, fashionable, modern or popular _____

6 Complete the sentences with words from Ex 4.
1 I like films with good stories that have a clear _____, a middle and an _____.
2 The clothes in that film are fantastic. The actors look so _____!
3 That movie is _____ but it isn't great.
4 I love that book. It's a _____ story.
5 It's a very _____ film. It's different from all the other films I usually watch.
6 I hate that show. It's _____!

Word skills

COLLOCATIONS WITH *HAVE* AND *TAKE*

7 Complete the sentences with *have* or *take* in the correct form.
1 We always _____ the bus to school.
2 They _____ breakfast at 7.30 a.m.
3 'Do you _____ notes in class?' 'Yes, we do.'
4 I _____ a PE lesson this afternoon.

8 Complete the rule and advice with the words below.

| together   two   use

- A collocation is ¹_____ or more words that we often ²_____ together
- Learn the words in collocations with *have* and *take* ³_____.

9 Complete the phrases with the words below.

| care   a cup of tea   fun   a picture

1 have _____, _____
2 take _____, _____

6.1 VOCABULARY BOOSTER

Phone zombies

1 GET STARTED 🔊 6.02 Match the words below to the photos. Listen and check.

| a computer   a message   an app   an email
| a photo   a radio   a smartphone   the internet

1 _____
2 _____
3 _____
4 _____
5 _____
6 _____
7 _____
8 _____

2 Work in pairs. Ask and answer the questions.
1 How often do you send text messages to your friends?
2 Does anyone ever send you emails? Who?
3 How often do you use a computer?
4 Does anyone in your family listen to the radio? Who? What do they listen to?
5 Do you use the internet every day? What do you use it for?
6 Do you download a lot of apps? Why / Why not?
7 Is it a good idea for children under ten to have a smartphone? Why? / Why not?

3 PRACTISE Complete the words with the missing letters.
1 Computers, mobile phones and tablets are all d___ ___ ___ ___l d___ ___ ___ ___s.
2 We have a desktop computer at home that everybody in my family uses, but I also have a l___ ___ ___ ___p that I take to school with me.
3 My phone has a very good b___ ___ ___ ___y so I can use it all day.
4 I often post on a g___ ___ ___p c___ ___ ___t with my friends after school. We're all in our own houses, but we can still talk to each other!
5 I love listening to my m___ ___ ___ c l___ ___ ___ ___ ___y. I add new songs to it all the time.
6 Can I connect to your B___ ___ ___ ___ ___th s___ ___ ___ ___ ___r? I'd like to listen to some music.

4 Complete the text with the words below.

| check   through   text   off   on

As soon as I wake up in the morning, I have a shower and then I have breakfast. After that, I turn ¹_____ my phone to ²_____ my messages. But before I leave the house, I always ³_____ my friend Tom. He lives on the same road as me so we usually walk to school together. I don't scroll ⁴_____ my social media in the morning because it makes me late for school. Then when I get home, I always listen to music on my Bluetooth speaker. But before I go to bed, I always turn ⁵_____ my phone. A good night's sleep is very important!

5 EXTEND 🔊 6.03 Check the meaning of the verbs and phrases below. Then complete the questions. Listen and check.

| click   keyboard   passwords   record
| save   shut down   type

1 Do you always remember your _____ for different things?
2 Do you think it's a good idea to _____ your computer every night?
3 Do you always remember to _____ your work on your computer?
4 How many fingers do you use to _____ messages on your phone?
5 Before you _____ on something, do you always check you know what it is and that it's safe?
6 Do you ever _____ conversations, lessons or music on your phone?
7 Do you prefer to type on a screen or on a _____?

6 Work in pairs. Ask and answer the questions in Ex 5. Give reasons for your answers.

122 Vocabulary booster

6.5 VOCABULARY BOOSTER

Everyday items

1 **GET STARTED** 🔊 **6.08** Match the words below to the photos. Listen and check.

| a clock   a cup   a glass   glasses   a knife
| a newspaper   paper   a pen   a pencil   a plate

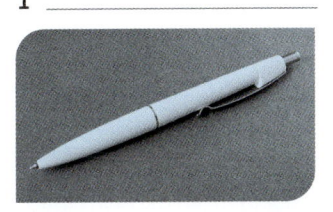

1 _____
2 _____
3 _____
4 _____
5 _____
6 _____
7 _____
8 _____
9 _____
10 _____

2 Work in pairs. Which of the things in Ex 1 do you have …
- in your bedroom?
- in your bag?
- with you now?

3 **PRACTISE** Complete the definitions with the words below.

| cash   bank card   make-up   mirror   charger   wallet

1 You use a _____ to check your hair is tidy.
2 You use a _____ to get money from your account out of a machine.
3 People use _____ to help them look more attractive.
4 When your phone battery dies, you need to use a _____.
5 Most people keep their money and bank cards in a _____, and they keep it in their pocket or bag.
6 Sometimes small shops don't take cards, so you need to use _____ to pay for things.

4 Choose the correct alternative.
1 My hair looks terrible. I need a **comb** / **charger**!
2 I always have my **wallet** / **water bottle** with me so that I don't get thirsty.
3 People usually look in the **dictionary** / **mirror** to check that they look OK.
4 Before there were cameras on phones, most people used a **dictionary** / **digital** camera.
5 I always look up words I don't know in my **mirror** / **dictionary**.
6 I never carry much **make-up** / **cash** with me these days. I pay for everything with my **bank card** / **camera**.

5 **EXTEND** 🔊 **6.09** Match the words below to the photos. Listen and check.

| a backpack   a hairbrush   a calculator   an ID card
| a purse   scissors   a toothbrush   a notebook

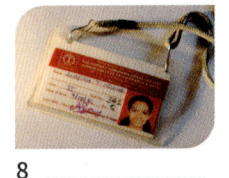

1 _____
2 _____
3 _____
4 _____
5 _____
6 _____
7 _____
8 _____

6 💬 Work in pairs. Ask and answer the questions.
1 Which of the things in Ex 5 do you usually take to school?
2 Which do you never take to school?
3 What's in your backpack or school bag today?

Word skills

TO + VERB OR VERB + -ING

7 Choose the correct alternative to complete the sentences.
1 <u>Would</u> you <u>like</u> **paying** / **to pay** by card?
2 I <u>enjoy</u> **scrolling** / **to scroll** through social media after school.
3 My sister <u>wants</u> **buying** / **to buy** a new laptop.

8 Tick (✓) the correct statement about the <u>underlined</u> verbs in Ex 7.
1 After some verbs, we usually use *to* + verb. After other verbs, we usually use verb +*-ing*. ☐
2 After the verbs, we can use *to* + verb or verb +*-ing*. Both are correct. ☐

9 Complete the sentences with *to* + verb or verb + *-ing* and your own ideas.
1 I love _____.
2 I'd like _____.
3 I decided _____.

Vocabulary booster 123

7.1 VOCABULARY BOOSTER

Dream big

1 **GET STARTED** 🔊 7.03 Complete the phrases about life goals with the verbs below. Listen and check.

| do   get   have (×2)   leave (×2)   live   travel

1 _____ school
2 _____ in a different country
3 _____ children
4 _____ a big family
5 _____ a course
6 _____ home
7 _____ a good job
8 _____ around the world

2 💬 Complete the questions with one word from Ex 1. Then work in pairs and ask and answer the questions.
1 Do you want to _____ a course in the holidays? Why? / Why not?
2 What's the best way to _____ around the world?
3 Is it common to _____ a big family in your country?
4 Do most young people _____ home when they _____ a job after university?
5 Would you like to _____ in a different country after you _____ school?
6 What's the best age to _____ children, in your opinion?

3 **PRACTISE** 💬 Work in pairs. Complete the texts with the words below.

A

| an actor   cook   drama school   earn   famous   a house

Soroush would love to be in films and on TV in the future. So when he leaves school, he wants to go to ¹_____ and become ²_____. He'd like to leave home and share ³_____ with some of the other students. In the holidays, he wants to learn to ⁴_____ so that he can get a job in a restaurant. He wants to ⁵_____ money and study at the same time. Soroush's dream is to become ⁶_____ one day. He wants everybody to know his name!

B

| company   degree   drive   manager   rich   save   university

Elisa is 17 and she lives in a small town in Argentina. She has two jobs at the weekend and she works very hard! She wants to ⁷_____ money so she can leave home and move to Buenos Aires. She wants to go to ⁸_____ there and get a ⁹_____ in business. After that, she'd like to work for a big ¹⁰_____. She wants to become a ¹¹_____ and have lots of people working for her. Elisa's dream is to become very ¹²_____ so she can buy a big house for her family and get an expensive car. She just needs to find time to learn to ¹³_____ first!

4 Rewrite the sentences so they are all true for you.
1 I don't want to go to college or university.
2 I'd like to share a flat with friends in the future.
3 I don't want to learn to drive.
4 I'd like to work for a big company.
5 I want to get a degree in maths.
6 I don't want to become famous.

5 💬 Work in pairs and compare your sentences. Give reasons for your answers.

6 **EXTEND** 🔊 7.04 Complete the sentences with the phrases below. Listen and check.

| get a better phone   get married
  move to a new school   pass an exam
  play for a team   start my own business
  take up a hobby   write a book

1 I want to _____ _____ in the holidays. I think I'd like to learn to design and make my own clothes.
2 We need to _____ in every school subject at the end of the year.
3 My dream is to _____ that everybody wants to read.
4 I don't want to work for a company or another person. I want to _____ instead.
5 I need to save some money to _____. The one I've got is too old and the battery is no good.
6 I don't want to _____ and have children until I'm at least 30. I want to travel and see the world first.
7 When I go to university, I'd really like to _____, either football or volleyball.
8 My parents want me to _____ next year, but I'm worried about making new friends.

7 💬 Work in pairs. Write questions with the phrases in Ex 5. Find a new partner and ask and answer your questions.

Would you like to take up a hobby? What?
Do you want to start your own business after you leave school? What type of business?

124 Vocabulary booster

7.5 VOCABULARY BOOSTER

Career choices

1 GET STARTED 🔊 **7.12** Match the jobs below to the pictures. Listen and check.

| bus driver   chef   cleaner   factory worker
| office worker   photographer   shop assistant   waiter

1 _____
2 _____
3 _____
4 _____
5 _____
6 _____
7 _____
8 _____

2 💬 Work in pairs. Which jobs in Ex 1 would you like to do? Put them in order from the best (1) to the worst (8). Compare in groups.

3 PRACTISE Complete the jobs with the missing letters.
1 The d_____s and n_____s at the hospital will help you get better when you are sick.
2 L_____rs and p_____ o_____rs fight crime.
3 When you have a problem with your computer, you can call an IT t_____n.
4 My mother is a b_____s p_____n. She has her own company.
5 My uncle is a p_____t. He flies planes all over the world.
6 To have healthy teeth, it's important to go to the d_____t once or twice a year.
7 You need a really good e_____r to design and build a bridge.
8 I want to be a newspaper j_____t and write stories about important people.
9 A young Japanese d_____ created these clothes - they look fantastic!
10 F_____s have to work hard to look after their animals and the food they grow.

4 EXTEND 🔊 **7.13** Complete the definitions with the words below. Listen and check.

| architect   boss   builder   cook   hairdresser
| programmer   personal assistant   receptionist

1 A _____ cuts hair.
2 A _____ builds houses and other buildings.
3 A _____ helps someone who does an important job.
4 An _____ designs buildings and draws the plans for them.
5 A _____ prepares food for people to eat e.g. in a school or hospital.
6 A _____ is the first person you see when you go into a big company or hotel.
7 Your _____ tells you what to do at work.
8 A _____ writes computer programs.

5 💬 Work in pairs. Ask and answer the questions about the jobs in Ex 3 and Ex 4.
1 Who sometimes works outside?
2 Who usually works inside?
3 Who works in a kitchen?
4 Who helps to make people look nice?
5 Who works in a hotel?
6 Who helps someone to do their job better?
7 Who looks after other people?
8 Which of the jobs would you like to do? Which ones would you hate to do?

Word skills

PHRASES WITH *GET*

6 Complete the sentences below with one word.
1 I _____ to university by car.
2 My parents _____ a lot of letters.
3 Can you _____ something for dinner from the supermarket?
4 We always _____ to school early.

7 Which phrase in Ex 6 means:
buy something   _____
travel somewhere   _____
receive something _____
arrive somewhere   _____

Vocabulary booster **125**

8.1 VOCABULARY BOOSTER

Getting around

1 GET STARTED 🔊 8.03 Match the words below to the photos. Listen and check.

| a bike   a bus   an airport   a station |
| a ticket   a train   to drive   to walk |

1 _____
2 _____ 
3 _____ 
4 _____ 
5 _____ 
6 _____ 
7 _____ 
8 _____ 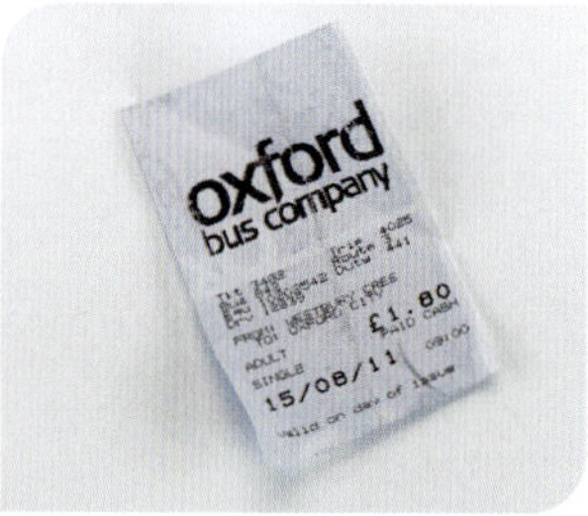

2 💬 Work in pairs. Ask and answer the questions.
1 Do you ever ride a bike? When? Where do you go?
2 When was the last time you took a train? Where did you go?
3 Do you know anybody who drives to work? Who? How far do they drive?
4 How do you get to the local supermarket from your house?
5 When was the last time you were in a bus station? Why were you there?
6 How far away from an airport do you live? How do people usually get there?
7 Are bus and train tickets too expensive in your local area? Why? / Why not?

3 PRACTISE 💬 Choose the correct alternative to complete the questions about your local area. Then work in pairs and answer the questions.
1 How good is the **journey** / **public transport** in your local area?
2 Can you travel on electric vehicles like **trams** / **flights**?
3 Do people usually travel to other parts of the country by **coach** / **tram**? When did you last travel this way?
4 How often do you go somewhere **by** / **on** car?
5 Can you go to your friends' houses **in** / **on** foot? Why? / Why not?
6 Is there **a coach** / **an underground system** in your capital city? Do you ever use it? When?
7 How long is the **journey** / **travel** from your house to school?

4 Complete the text with the words below.

| boat trips   city break   short journey |
| catch a flight   amazing views |

I've been to lots of new and interesting places with my family. Last Saturday, for example, we went to the mountains near my town, so it was a
¹_____. We got up very early and came back home late, but we had a great time. We spent the day walking and when we got to the top of the mountain, we saw some ²_____. We could even see the sea, and it's very far away. We love the sea and in the summer we often go on ³_____. Sometimes, we go away for the weekend. Last year, we went on a ⁴_____ to Rome. It's my favourite place in the whole world. I haven't been on any really long journeys yet, but next year, we're going to Australia. I'm really excited, but I'm also a bit worried because we have to ⁵_____ that is twenty hours long – that's almost a whole day! I don't know if I can sit on a plane for such a long time.

5 EXTEND 🔊 8.04 Check the meaning of the words and phrases below. Complete the sentences. Listen and check.

| bus stop   get lost   late   on time |
| platform   seat   soon   the way |

1 The bus usually gets here at 8 o'clock. It's 8 o'clock now and the bus isn't here. It's _____.
2 Marina is never late for school. She's always _____ or a bit early.
3 Run! Our train leaves very _____, in just a couple of minutes!
4 You can go to the city centre by bus. There's a _____ over there.
5 I don't know _____ to your house. Can you tell me how to get there?
6 When the bus is busy, you can't get a _____ and you have to stand.
7 My train to work leaves the station from _____ five every morning.
8 When I _____ and I don't know the way, I always ask someone to help me find the place I'm looking for.

6 💬 Work in pairs. Write questions with the words and phrases in Ex 5. Ask and answer the questions in groups.

126 Vocabulary booster

8.5 VOCABULARY BOOSTER

Holidays and places to stay

1 **GET STARTED** 🔊 8.08 Complete the dialogue with the words below. Listen and check.

| beach holiday   beds   fly   hotel   pool
| problem   room   sea   summer holidays

A What did you do in the ¹_____ last year?
B We went on a ²_____ and stayed in a very nice ³_____ with a big swimming ⁴_____.
A What was the best thing about your hotel?
B We had a great ⁵_____ with a view of the ⁶_____, and we slept well because the ⁷_____ were very comfortable.
A Was there anything you didn't like?
B Well, we had a ⁸_____ with the shower on the first day. There wasn't any hot water!
A Oh dear!
B Well, it was OK because we had hot showers the next day.
A Are you going to go there again this year?
B Yes, I think so. But we aren't going to drive. We're going to ⁹_____ because it's quicker.

2 💬 Write two true and two false sentences about your holidays using words from Ex 1. Work in pairs. Read your sentences to a partner. Take turns to guess which are true and which are false.

3 **PRACTISE** Complete the texts with the words below.

A

| adventure   all-inclusive   book   reception

I love ¹_____ holidays where you pay for everything before you go and you don't need to worry about how much things cost. But I also really like ²_____ holidays, like the one we had last year when we went hiking in the mountains. It was a very active holiday. We stayed in a small hotel with a pool, so we could go for a swim after walking all day. The hotel ³_____ was open from 6 a.m. until 10 p.m. so it was easy to ⁴_____ a local guide or a boat trip on the lake near the hotel. We went swimming there too. It was fantastic but very cold!

B

| available   camping   campsite   pack   tents

My family goes ⁵_____ every summer. We never sleep in hotels or guest houses. We always sleep in ⁶_____. We book the same ⁷_____ every year because it has amazing views and it's near the beach. They have lovely hot showers and there are washing machines ⁸_____ for washing your clothes. The only thing I don't like about camping is getting everything ready before we go. We have to ⁹_____ our bags and all our food for the trip, and then get everything in the car.

C

| arranges   guests   guest house   tour guide

Last weekend, I went on a fantastic city break with my family. We stayed in a wonderful ¹⁰_____ in the city centre. It was very small and there weren't any other ¹¹_____, just us. The owner is a very nice woman and she ¹²_____ everything for her guests. We wanted to see all the sights, so she found a brilliant ¹³_____ who took us everywhere. It was great, but we were very tired when we got back to the guest house!

4 **EXTEND** 🔊 8.09 Match the words to the definitions. Listen and check.

| accommodation   a day trip   an apartment
| a passport   a reservation   a suitcase
| a visitor   a youth hostel

1 a seat on a coach, train or plane; a table at a restaurant; or a room in a hotel that you already booked
2 you use this to carry clothes when you are travelling
3 a place to live or stay in
4 you usually need one to travel to another country
5 a visit that is completed in one day
6 a flat that you rent for a holiday; you can cook your own food there because it always has a kitchen
7 a cheap place to stay, usually for young travellers
8 a person who doesn't usually live or work in that place

5 💬 Work in pairs. Ask and answer the questions.
1 When was the last time you and your friends or family had a reservation for something? What was it for?
2 Do you think it's easy to pack a suitcase when you go on holiday? Why? / Why not?
3 What kind of accommodation do you usually stay in on holiday?
4 Are there any countries you can visit without a passport? Which ones?
5 When was the last time you went on a day trip? Where did you go?
6 Do visitors often come to your house? Are they mostly friends or family? Do they ever stay?

Word skills

PHRASAL VERBS

6 Look at the sentences and underline the phrasal verbs.
• We want to look around the museum this morning.
• It's safer to sit down on the bus!
• We went to New York last year. I want to go back next year.
• Before we set off I'm going to look at an online map.

7 Which phrase in Ex 6 means:
return _____
leave on a journey _____
see everything in a place _____
not stand _____

8 💬 Work in pairs. Make phrasal verbs with the verbs and particles below. You can use the same particle more than once. Then answer the questions.
Verbs: *go, get, find, look, turn*
Particles: *on, off, up, out, down, back, around*
1 How many different phrasal verbs can you make?
2 Can you write a sentence with each phrasal verb?

Vocabulary booster 127

GRAMMAR BOOSTER

0.1 Present simple the verb *be*

Affirmative and negative

We use the verb *be* to talk about people and things.
The affirmative forms of the verb *be* are *am*, *is* and *are*.

Affirmative		
Subject	The verb *be*	
I	am	
You	are	
He / She / It	is	English.
We	are	
You	are	
They	are	

TIP

In spoken or informal written English, we use the short forms of the verb *be*: *am* = 'm, *is* = 's and *are* = 're.
Hello! I'm Simon.

We form the negative by adding *not* after the correct form of the verb *be*.

Negative		
Subject	the verb *be* + *not*	
I	am not	
You	are not	
He / She / It	is not	English.
We	are not	
You	are not	
They	are not	

TIP

We usually use the short negative forms of the verb *be* in conversation: *am* = 'm not, *is* = isn't and *are* = aren't.
She isn't 18.

Questions and short answers

We form *yes / no* questions by placing the correct form of the verb *be* before the subject.

Questions		
The verb *be*	Subject	
Am	I	
Are	you	
Is	he / she / it	English?
Are	we	
Are	you	
Are	they	

We form short answers with the correct form of the verb *be* in the affirmative and the verb *be* + *not* in the negative.

Short answers	
Affirmative	Negative
Yes, I am.	No, I'm not.
Yes, he / she / it is.	No, he / she / it isn't.
Yes, we / you / they are.	No, we / you / they aren't.

TIP

In positive short answers, we don't use short forms.
'Are you a student?' 'Yes, I am.' (NOT ~~Yes, I'm.~~)

1 Complete the sentences with the affirmative form of the verb *be*.
1 I _____ in Class Seven.
2 We _____ from Japan.
3 Today _____ a school day.
4 My friends _____ in the classroom.
5 Kenji _____ my best friend.
6 You _____ in Class Six.
7 She _____ 18 years old.
8 They _____ from China.

2 Make the sentences negative.
1 Julio is British.   5 My parents are teachers.
2 I am from London.   6 She is at home.
3 We are sixteen.   7 He is from Spain.
4 You are Scottish.   8 They are happy today.

3 Complete the dialogues with the correct form of the verb *be*.
1 A _____ you Swiss?
    B No, I _____ not. I _____ from Austria.
2 A _____ Luke British?
    B Yes, he _____. He _____ from Manchester.
3 A Hi. _____ you a new student?
    B Yes, I _____. I _____ Maria. Hi!
4 A _____ your friends at school today?
    B No, they _____. They _____ at home.
5 A _____ your phone in your bag?
    B No, it _____. It _____ in my pocket.

4 Complete the dialogue with the correct form of the verb *be*. Use contractions where possible.
A [1]_____ you and Lena in the same English class?
B No, we [2]_____. We [3]_____ in different classes. I [4]_____ in Class 2 and Lena [5]_____ in Class 3.
A [6]_____ your teachers from England?
B No, they [7]_____. My teacher is Canadian and Lena's teacher [8]_____ from Ireland.
A Oh, Mr Duffy [9]_____ Irish. [10]_____ he Lena's teacher?
B Yes, he [11]_____.
A He [12]_____ my sister's teacher too!
B I know! Your sister and Lena [13]_____ in the same English class.

128 Grammar booster

GRAMMAR BOOSTER

0.2 Singular and plural nouns

We use *a / an* with singular nouns only.

> **TIP**
>
> We use *a* before singular nouns that start with a consonant. If the noun starts with a vowel sound, we use *an*.
>
> a book   an apple
>
> If a singular noun has an adjective starting with a vowel, we also use *an*.
>
> a house – an old house.

We add *-s* to form the plural of most nouns: apple → apples, book → books, student → students.

If a noun ends in *-s*, *-ch*, *-sh* or *-x*, we add *-es*: bus → buses, beach → beaches, dish → dishes, box → boxes.

If a noun ends in *-f* we change *f* to *v* and add *-es*: knife → knives

To form the plural of nouns ending in *-y* after a consonant, we change *-y* to *-ies*: baby → babies.

Some plural nouns are irregular. We don't form the plural with *-s* or *-es*: man → men, child → children.

This / that / these / those

We use *this* (singular) and *these* (plural) for things that are close to us. We use *that* (singular) and *those* (plural) for things that are further away.

> This is my book and that is your book over there.
> These apples are good, but those are not.

Imperatives

We use imperatives to tell someone to do something. We often use them to give directions and instructions.

> Close the door, please.
> Go straight on as far as the traffic lights, then turn left.

We form the affirmative imperative with the infinitive without *to*.

Affirmative

Verb	
Run!	
Cross	the road.
Help	me!
Go	left.
Be	quiet!

> **TIP**
>
> There is no subject in imperative sentences.
>
> Come here! (NOT ~~You come here!~~ or ~~Come you here!~~)
>
> However, we can add the name of the person we are talking to at the beginning or end of the sentence.
>
> Simon, come here!   Come here, Simon!
>
> We can also add *please* to sound more polite.
>
> Please come here.   Come here, please.

We form the negative imperative with *don't* and the infinitive without *to*. We sometimes use the full form *do not* in writing.

Negative

Don't	Verb	
	run!	
	cross	the road.
Don't	ask	me.
	go	left.
	be	late!

1 Write the plural form of the words.

1. bag _____
2. wife _____
3. video _____
4. story _____
5. fox _____
6. woman _____
7. life _____
8. child _____
9. watch _____
10. person _____
11. book _____
12. boy _____
13. library _____
14. hat _____
15. lunch _____
16. match _____
17. man _____
18. phone _____
19. half _____
20. diary _____

2 Choose the correct alternative.

1. **This** / **These** is a black bag.
2. **That** / **Those** are red apples.
3. **These** / **This** tablets are new.
4. **That** / **Those** headphones are cool.
5. **That** / **Those** is a good video.
6. **These** / **This** book is great.

3 Write the missing sentences.

singular	plural
That man is old.	1 _____
2 _____	These books are new.
Is that child Spanish?	3 _____
4 _____	Are these apples from France?
This is a bad game.	5 _____

4 Complete the sentences using the imperative form of the verbs below.

> be   close   do not eat   not go
> open   sit   not talk   turn

1. Hello, Class 3. Please _____ down.
2. Ssssh! _____ and _____ quiet!
3. _____ your books and _____ to page 7.
4. Please _____ chocolate in the lesson.
5. _____ your homework!
6. _____ the door when you leave.
7. _____ to bed late during the week.

Grammar booster   **129**

GRAMMAR BOOSTER

0.3 Have got

We use *have got* to talk about things that people own or have. The form for the third person singular is *has got*. The short forms are: *have got* = *'ve got* and *has got* = *'s got*.

Affirmative		
Subject	have got / has got	
I / You / We / They	have got	a new phone.
He / She / It	has got	

We form the negative by adding *not* after *have got / has got*.

Negative		
Subject	haven't got / hasn't got	
I / You / We / They	haven't got	a new phone.
He / She / It	hasn't got	

We form questions by placing *have / has* before the subject.

Questions			
Have / Has	Subject	got	
Have	I / you / we / they	got	a new phone?
Has	he / she / it		

Short answers	
Affirmative	Negative
Yes, I / you / we / they have.	No, I / you / we / they haven't.
Yes, he / she / it has.	No, he / she / it hasn't.

Possessive 's

We add *'s* to a noun to show possession or a relationship.
 the girl's rucksack   Nikola's brother

With plural nouns and nouns ending in *-s*, we sometimes only add an apostrophe (') but *'s* is more common.
 my parents' car   James's book

Possessive adjectives

Subject pronouns	Possessive adjectives
I	my
you	your
he	his
she	her
it	its
we	our
you	your
they	their

We use possessive adjectives to talk about possession.
 I've got a new phone. It's my phone.
 It's John's book. It's his book.

1 Choose the correct alternative.
 1 We **'ve got / 's got** a new TV.
 2 Dan **'ve got / 's got** two sisters.
 3 I **'ve got / 's got** a baby brother.
 4 **Have / Has** Lucy got a tablet?
 5 My friend **haven't got / hasn't got** a phone.
 6 **Have / Has** you got a school bag?
 7 They **haven't got / hasn't got** a big family.
 8 I **haven't got / hasn't got** an umbrella.

2 Complete the dialogues with the correct form of *have got* or short answers.
 1 A _____ you _____ a sister?
   B Yes, I _____. I _____ two sisters and a brother!
 2 A _____ your friend _____ a tablet?
   B No, he _____, but he _____ a new phone.
 3 A _____ you _____ a blue bag?
   B No, I _____. I _____ a yellow bag.
 4 A _____ your grandparents _____ a big house?
   B No, they _____. They _____ a small house.
 5 A _____ your aunt _____ a new car?
   B Yes, she _____. And my cousin _____ her old one now.
 6 A _____ your phone _____ a good camera?
   B No, it _____. But it _____ a good battery. It lasts for two days!

3 Look at the first sentence. Complete the second sentence so it means the same as the first sentence. Use the possessive *'s*.
 1 Martina has got a brother called Simon.
   Simon is _____ brother.
 2 My parents have got a new car.
   It's my _____ new car.
 3 My sister has got her own bedroom.
   It's my _____ bedroom.
 4 Lewis has got a guitar.
   It's _____ guitar.
 5 Briony has got lots of books.
   They're _____ books.
 6 Agnes has got some comics in her bag.
   They're _____ comics.

4 Choose the correct alternative.
 Hi. [1]**My / I** name's Tomek and I'm fifteen.
 I [2]**'s got / 've got** a sister. [3]**Her / She** name is Anna.
 [4]**Her / She** is twelve. I [5]**hasn't got / haven't got** a brother.
 My [6]**parents' / parent's** names are Kasia and Marek.
 [7]**They're / Their** teachers. [8]**They're / Their** school is near [9]**our / we** house. [10]**We / Our** live in a city. [11]**It's / Its** name is Kraków. [12]**It's / Its** in Poland.

130   Grammar booster

GRAMMAR BOOSTER

0.4 Can

We use *can* to talk about abilities. It has only one form and we use it for all persons (*I, you, he*, etc.).

Affirmative		
Subject	can	Verb
I / You / He / She / It / We / They	can	speak English.

The negative form of *can* is *cannot*. In spoken or informal written English, we use the short form *can't*.

Negative		
Subject	can't	Verb
I / You / He / She / It / We / They	can't	speak English.

We form questions by placing *can* before the subject.

Questions		
Can	Subject	
Can	I / you / he / she / it / we / they	speak English?

We make short answers with *can* in the affirmative and *can't* in the negative.

Short answers	
Affirmative	Negative
Yes, I / you / he / she / it / we / they can.	No, I / you / he / she / it / we / they can't.

> **TIP**
> We don't repeat the other verb in short answers.
> '*Can you cook?*' '*Yes, I can.*' (NOT *Yes, I cook.*)

Object pronouns

Personal pronouns can be used as the subject or object of a sentence.

Cara's my favourite singer. → *She's my favourite singer.*
　　　　　　　　　　　　　　　　subject

I really like Cara. → *I really like her.*
　　　　　　　　　　　　　　object

Subject pronouns	Object pronouns
I	me
you	you
he	him
she	her
it	it
we	us
you	you
they	them

1 Look at the table. Then complete the sentences with *can* or *can't*.

	run fast	play the guitar	speak German	solve difficult maths problems
Ben	✓	✓	✗	✗
Clara	✓	✗	✗	✓

1 Ben and Clara _____ run fast.
2 Ben _____ play the guitar.
3 Clara _____ play the guitar.
4 Ben and Clara _____ speak German.
5 Ben _____ solve difficult maths problems.
6 Clara _____ solve difficult maths problems.

2 Complete the questions and answers with the correct form of *can*.

1 A _____ (you / speak) French?
　B Yes, I _____.
2 A _____ (Rosie / run) fast?
　B No, she _____.
3 A _____ (I / dance) well?
　B Yes, you _____.
4 A _____ (your parents / make) videos?
　B Yes, they _____.
5 A _____ (David / draw) well?
　B No, he _____.

3 Write true sentences using the correct form of *can* and the verbs in brackets.

1 Babies _____. (walk)
2 Computers _____ music. (play)
3 Dogs _____. (dance)
4 My teacher _____ English. (speak)
5 I _____. (read and write)
6 I _____ ten languages. (speak)

4 Choose the correct alternative.

1 We're friends. **I** / **My** like you and you like **my** / **me**!
2 **They** / **Their** are amazing pictures! Look at **they** / **them**!
3 Look, there's Ella. **She** / **Her** 's my cousin. Can you see **she** / **her**?
4 Is **he** / **his** your brother? What's **him** / **his** name? I like **him** / **he**!
5 **It's** / **Its** a good book. I like **it** / **its**.
6 Our teachers give **we** / **us** lots of homework. Sometimes **we** / **us** haven't got time to finish it all.

5 Complete the missing object pronouns.

1 That's my phone! Give it to _____!
2 Look, there's Harry! Let's call _____!
3 I don't like coffee. In fact, I hate _____!
4 She's cool. I like _____.
5 They're new students. Do you know _____?
6 What's your name? I don't know _____.
7 We're hungry. Give _____ some food.

Grammar booster　131

GRAMMAR BOOSTER

1.2 Present simple: affirmative

We use the present simple to talk about habits, daily routines and things that happen regularly:

I take the bus to school.

Ali gets up at half past five.

We also use it to talk about general facts.

I come from Scotland.

Marcello likes pasta.

The affirmative form of the present simple is the infinitive without *to*. To make the third person singular (*he / she / it*), we add *-s*. However, some verbs take *-es* or *-ies*:

- If a verb ends in *-o, -sh, -ch, -x* or *-ss*, we add *-es*: *go → goes, brush → brushes, watch → watches, relax → relaxes, miss → misses*
- If a verb ends in *-y* after a consonant, we leave out the *-y* and then add *-ies*: *study → studies, cry → cries*

Affirmative

Subject	Verb	
I	live	
You	live	
He / She / It	lives	in Edinburgh.
We	live	
You	live	
They	live	

TIP

The third person singular of the verb *have* is *has*.

Zara has dinner at half past seven.

1 Choose the correct alternative.
1. I **take** / **takes** the bus to school.
2. School **start** / **starts** at 8.30 a.m.
3. We **have** / **has** lunch at school.
4. My sister **do** / **does** her homework on the bus.
5. You **like** / **likes** the same music as me.
6. All my friends **watch** / **watches** videos on their phones.
7. I **listen** / **listens** to music in bed.
8. Toby **cook** / **cooks** on Sundays.

2 Complete the sentences with the correct form of the verbs in brackets.
1. Chidi _____ (hate) mornings. He _____ (get up) late. He _____ (love) his bed!
2. I _____ (like) Friday evenings. I _____ (have) dinner with my family and then we _____ (relax) together.
3. Maya _____ (have) a music lesson every Saturday. She _____ (go) to her teacher's house. She _____ (want) to be in a band.
4. Rafa and Carlos _____ (play) video games and they _____ (make) funny videos. Lots of people _____ (watch) them.

3 Complete the sentences with the correct form of the verbs below. There is one extra verb.

| brush   do   get   go   have   listen to   watch

1. My brother _____ a lot of TV.
2. I _____ my homework before dinner.
3. They _____ a shower after football practice.
4. We _____ to school at 8.30.
5. Suzie _____ her teeth after breakfast.
6. You _____ great music!

4 Complete the text with the correct form of the verbs below.

| do   go   listen   love   play (x2)
| practise   say   tell   think

My sister and I are very different! She ¹_____ studying and she always ²_____ very well at school. She also ³_____ the piano and she ⁴_____ every day before and after school. But I ⁵_____ it's very important to spend lots of time relaxing. I ⁶_____ video games online every evening and I ⁷_____ to music at the same time. But my sister ⁸_____ to bed really early at 9 p.m., and that's when my parents ⁹_____ me my music is too loud! They ¹⁰_____ I go to bed too late but the evening is the best time to be online with my friends!

1.4 Prepositions of time

We use *on* with dates and days of the week: *on 25 June, on Monday*.

We use *at* with times: *at 11 o'clock, at half past two*.

We use *in* with months, seasons, years and parts of the day: *in January, in the summer, in 2015, in the morning*.

TIP

We say *at the weekend* (NOT ~~in the weekend~~) and *at night* (NOT ~~in night~~).

1 Match 1–5 to A–E.
1. I brush my teeth in
2. My mum has lunch at
3. I can meet you at
4. I sleep very well at
5. The school holidays start in

A 7.30 p.m. outside the cinema.
B night because I'm always tired after a long day!
C the morning after breakfast.
D July and I can't wait!
E 1 p.m. when she's at work.

2 Complete the sentences with *on*, *at* or *in*.
1. The party is _____ Saturday.
2. My birthday is _____ May.
3. The concert finishes _____ 8 p.m.
4. I relax _____ the weekend.
5. I do my homework _____ the evening.
6. There is no school _____ the afternoon.
7. I go to my grandma's house _____ the summer.

132 Grammar booster

GRAMMAR BOOSTER

1.6 Present simple: negative and yes/no questions

We form the present simple negative with *do not* or *does not* and the infinitive. In spoken or informal written English, we use the short forms *don't* or *doesn't*.

Negative			
Subject	don't / doesn't	Verb	
I	don't		
You	don't		
He / She / It	doesn't	live	in Edinburgh.
We	don't		
You	don't		
They	don't		

We form present simple *yes / no* questions with *do* or *does*.

Questions			
Do / Does	Subject	Verb	
Do	I		
Do	you		
Does	he / she / it	live	in Edinburgh?
Do	we		
Do	you		
Do	they		

TIP

For negative and questions, we don't add *-s* to the verb for *he / she / it*.
Luke doesn't play the piano. (NOT ~~Luke doesn't plays the piano.~~)
Does Luke play the piano? (NOT ~~Does Luke plays the piano?~~)

We make short answers with *do* or *does* in the affirmative and *don't* or *doesn't* in the negative.

Short answers	
Affirmative	Negative
Yes, I / you / we / they do.	No, I / you / we / they don't.
Yes, he / she / it does.	No, he / she / it doesn't.

TIP

In short answers, we don't use the main verb.
'Do you speak English?'
'Yes, I do.' (NOT ~~Yes, I speak.~~)

1 Complete the sentences with the present simple negative form of the verbs in brackets.
1 Jacinta cooks, but she _____ cakes. (make)
2 Josep _____ the bus every day. (take)
3 I _____ my room every week. (tidy)
4 My friends _____ their bikes to school. (ride)
5 We've got a piano, but we _____ it. (play)
6 My dad _____ board games. (like)
7 That bus _____ to our school. (go)
8 My mum _____ books. (read)
9 We _____ for a walk at weekends. (go)

2 Write questions in the present simple. Complete the short answers.
1 you / take / lots of selfies?
_____
Yes, I _____.
2 Katya / listen to / audiobooks?
_____
Yes, she _____.
3 you and your friends / go / to the gym?
_____
No, we _____.
4 your parents / read / comics?
_____
No, they _____.
5 I / speak / good English?
_____
Yes, you _____.
6 Aziz / do / his homework with his friends?
_____
No, he _____.
7 your mum / draw / lots of pictures?
_____
No, she _____.
8 you and Masood / go / for a run every day?
_____
Yes, we _____.

3 Match 1–5 to A–E. Then complete the questions and answers.
1 _____ (Zoltan / like) Italian food?
2 _____ (you and your sister / read) a lot?
3 _____ (your parents / listen to) music?
4 _____ (you / speak) French?
5 _____ (Beata / play) chess?

A Yes, they _____. But they _____ (not play) musical instruments.
B No, I _____. And I _____ (not speak) German.
C Yes, he _____. But he _____ (not like) pizza.
D No, she _____. She _____ (not like) board games.
E Yes, we _____. But we _____ (not read) comics.

GRAMMAR BOOSTER

2.2 Adverbs of frequency

We use adverbs and expressions of frequency to say how often we do something, or how often something happens.

```
0%                    50%                    100%
never  hardly ever  sometimes  often  usually  always
```

The normal position of an adverb of frequency is:
- immediately after the verb *be*.
  Faisal is often tired in the morning.
- immediately before most other verbs.
  Zara always does 60 minutes of exercise.
- The adverbs *sometimes*, *usually* and *often* can also go at the beginning or end of a sentence.
  Sometimes, Tom plays football.
  Usually, he plays video games.
  He doesn't play basketball very often.

Expressions of frequency

Expressions of frequency like *every day, once a week, five times a year,* etc. go at the beginning or end of a sentence.
Every week, we go swimming.
My friend does karate twice a week.

Question words

We use question words to ask for information about:

people	*Who is she? Who do you like?*
things	*What is this? What does this mean?*
places	*Where am I? Where do you live?*
date / time	*When is the first lesson? What time does it start?*
manner / way	*How are you?*
frequency	*How often do you play sport?*
age	*How old are they?*
reason	*Why are you here? Why do you go to the gym?*
alternative	*Which classroom are you in? Which sport do you prefer?*
possession	*Whose bag is this?*

TIP
The question word always comes at the beginning of the sentence. Usually, it is directly followed by the verb, but the question words *what*, *which* and *whose* are sometimes followed by a noun.

1 Choose the correct alternative.
1. I **go never** / **never go** swimming.
2. Jasper **is hardly ever** / **hardly ever is** late for school.
3. You **usually don't play** / **don't usually play** football.
4. Lotta **runs often** / **often runs** in the morning.
5. We **are always** / **always are** tired after school.
6. I **sometimes do** / **do sometimes** a workout before school.

2 Write sentences in the present simple with the adverb in brackets in the correct place.
1. Josh / go / to the gym on Fridays. (always)
2. I / dance. (never)
3. We / see / our cousins. (hardly ever)
4. Sasha / do / yoga on Saturdays. (usually)
5. I / be / hungry. (always)
6. They / play / tennis. (often)
7. I / play / football. (sometimes)

3 Put the words in the correct order to make sentences.
1. brush / twice / day / my / I / teeth / a
2. a / they / week / dance / go / class / to / once
3. times / exams / we / three / year / a / have
4. don't / go / school / day / I / every / to
5. month / and / go / I / my / once / the / to / a / cinema / family

4 Look at the answers and complete the questions. Use the words below.

| How old   What   Where   Who   Whose   Why

1. A _____ time does our PE lesson start?
   B It starts at 11.00.
2. A _____ is the sports teacher?
   B Mr Thomas.
3. A _____ do you do yoga?
   B Because it's good for me!
4. A _____ bike is that?
   B It's mine.
5. A _____'s the swimming pool?
   B It's near our school.
6. A _____ is your brother?
   B He's twelve.

5 Match 1–7 to A–F.
1. Where are you?
2. How old is your teacher?
3. What time do you get up?
4. When is your guitar lesson?
5. How are you?
6. Whose shoes are these?
7. Which is your favourite subject?

A on Thursday
B about 40
C fine, thanks
D they're Kirsty's
E English of course!
F at home
G at 7.30 a.m

134 Grammar booster

GRAMMAR BOOSTER

2.6 There is / there are, some, any

Affirmative	There is an apple on the desk. There are some eggs.
Negative	There isn't an apple on the desk. There aren't any eggs.
Questions	Is there an apple on the desk? Are there any eggs?
Short answers	Yes, there is. / No, there isn't. Yes, there are. / No, there aren't.

We usually use *some* in affirmative sentences. We use it with plural countable nouns and uncountable nouns.

There are some crisps in the bowl.
There's some butter on the table.

We usually use *any* in negative sentences and questions. We use it with plural countable nouns and uncountable nouns.

He doesn't want any milk. We haven't got any sandwiches.
Are there any apples? Is there any coffee?

We don't use *some* or *any* with singular countable nouns. We use *a* or *an*.

Do you want a snack?

A lot of, much and many

We use *a lot of* in affirmative sentences.

There's a lot of rice. There are a lot of bananas.

We use *a lot of, much* and *many* in negative sentences.

We use *much* with uncountable nouns, and *many* with countable nouns.

There isn't much rice.
There isn't a lot of rice.
There aren't many bananas.
There aren't a lot of bananas.

We use *How many … ?* with plural countable nouns. The answer is often a number.

How many tomatoes do you need? Three.

We use *How much … ?* with uncountable nouns. The answer is often a quantity.

How much sugar have we got? Two kilos. / A lot. / Not much.

1 Complete the sentences with *is(n't), are(n't), some* and *any*.

```
water       ✓
tomatoes    ✓
bread       ✗
strawberries ✗
meat        ✓
rice        ✓
```

1 There _____ _____ water.
2 There _____ _____ tomatoes.
3 There _____ _____ bread.
4 There _____ _____ strawberries.
5 There _____ _____ meat.
6 There _____ _____ rice.

2 Choose the correct alternative.

1 Can I have **a / some** more bread, please?
2 Are there **some / any** potatoes in the cupboard?
3 We haven't got **some / any** eggs in the fridge.
4 You need to buy **some / any** rice from the shop.
5 There aren't **many / much** people here.
6 I don't eat **many / much** meat.
7 My mum drinks **many / a lot of** tea.
8 How **much / many** cheese would you like?
9 A How many apples have you got?
   B **A lot / Many**.
10 A How much ice cream do you want?
   B **A lot / Much**!

3 Complete the sentences with the words below.

| a   a lot   an   any   are   aren't   is
| isn't   many   much   some (x2)

1 _____ there any nuts in this cake?
2 How _____ bananas are there?
3 There is _____ of cheese on this pizza!
4 Is there _____ apple in your lunch box?
5 I'm a vegetarian. I don't eat _____ meat.
6 There _____ any tomatoes.
7 How _____ pasta is there?
8 _____ there any sugar?
9 There's _____ strawberry for you!
10 There is _____ bread.
11 There _____ much water.
12 There are _____ eggs.

4 Complete the questions and answers. Write one word in each space.

1 A How _____ bread is there?
  B Not _____. But there's _____ rice.
2 A Are there _____ vegetables?
  B Yes, there _____. There's _____ broccoli and there _____ some carrots.
3 A _____ there any meat in this dish?
  B No, there _____. There are _____ beans and a _____ of vegetables.

Grammar booster **135**

GRAMMAR BOOSTER

3.2 Present continuous

We use the present continuous to talk about things that are happening at the moment of speaking.

I'm watching a video.
Ian is talking to his cousin.
They're wearing new clothes.

We also use it to talk about things that are happening around now (*today, this week*, etc.).

We aren't going to school this week. We're on holiday!

We form the present continuous affirmative with the correct form of the verb *be* and the *-ing* form of the main verb. In spoken or informal written English, we use the short forms *'m, 's* or *'re*.

Affirmative		
Subject	The verb *be*	*-ing* form
I	am ('m)	talking.
You	are ('re)	
He / She / It	is ('s)	
We / You / They	are ('re)	

In some cases, there are spelling changes:
- If the verb ends in *-e*, we leave out the *-e* before we add *-ing*: *write → writing, dance → dancing*
- If the verb has only one syllable and ends in one vowel (*a, e, o*, etc.) + one consonant (*t, n, p*, etc.) we double the consonant: *run → running, chat → chatting*
- If the verb ends in *-ie*, we change the *-ie* to *-y*: *lie → lying, die → dying*

To form the present continuous negative, we add *not* after the correct form of the verb *be*. In spoken or informal written English, we use the short forms *'m not, isn't* or *aren't*.

Negative		
Subject	The verb *be* + *not*	*-ing* form
I	am not ('m not)	talking.
You	are not (aren't)	
He / She / It	is not (isn't)	
We / You / They	are not (aren't)	

We form present continuous questions by placing the correct form of the verb *be* before the subject.

Questions		
The verb *be*	Subject	*-ing* form
Am	I	talking?
Are	you	
Is	he / she / it	
Are	we / you / they	

We make short answers with the correct form of the verb *be* in the affirmative and the verb *be* + *not* in the negative.

Short answers	
Affirmative	Negative
Yes, I am.	No, I'm not.
Yes, he / she / it is.	No, he / she / it isn't.
Yes, we / you / they are.	No, we / you / they aren't.

TIP
In positive short answers, we don't use short forms.
'Is he having lunch?' 'Yes, he is.' (NOT ~~Yes, he's.~~)

1 Write the *-ing* form of the verbs.
1 do _____
2 go _____
3 have _____
4 play _____
5 make _____
6 wear _____
7 stop _____
8 tie _____
9 take _____
10 give _____
11 hit _____
12 carry _____

2 Complete the sentences with the present continuous form of the verbs below.

| chat | not do | not go | not have |
| make | play | take | wear |

1 Kelly _____ a photo with her phone.
2 I _____ online to some friends.
3 _____ (you) your new jeans?
4 The boys _____ loud rock music.
5 We _____ to the park.
6 _____ (they) a video?
7 I _____ my homework right now.
8 Jack _____ lunch at the moment.

3 Match 1–6 to A–F.
1 Are you having a good time, Maria?   A No, she isn't.
2 Is she wearing a hat?   B Yes, we are.
3 Are you and Natalia going to the cinema? C No, he isn't.
4 Is your brother playing his guitar? D Yes, I am!
5 Are your friends eating their lunch? E Yes, it is.
6 Is it raining at the moment?   F No, they aren't.

4 Complete the questions and answers. Write the present continuous form of the verbs, or short answers.

1 A _____ (Rosa / watch) TV?
   B No, she _____. She _____ (study).
2 A _____ (you / write) a story?
   B Yes, I _____. I _____ (write) a story about school.
3 A _____ (Joe / wear) his new shirt?
   B Yes, he _____. But he _____ (not wear) his new jeans.
4 A _____ (your parents / shop)?
   B Yes, they _____. They _____ (buy) some food.
5 A _____ (you and I / do) the same project this term?
   B No, we _____. We _____ (do) different projects.

136 Grammar booster

GRAMMAR BOOSTER

3.6 Present simple and present continuous

We use the **present simple** to talk about habits, daily routines, opinions, facts and general truths.

We use the **present continuous** to talk about things that are happening now or around now.

I wear school uniform from Monday to Friday, but today I'm wearing jeans because it's Saturday.

We use the two tenses with different adverbs and time expressions.

Present simple	Present continuous
adverbs of frequency (*always, never, sometimes, often*, etc.)	(right) now
once / twice a day / week / month / year	at the moment
three times a day / week / month / year	today
every morning / day / week / month / summer / year	this morning / week / month / year
on Tuesdays / school days	these days

Dynamic and stative verbs

Dynamic verbs describe actions: *walk, play, sing, eat*, etc. We can use dynamic verbs in the present simple and continuous.

I usually have sandwiches for lunch, but today I'm having pizza.

Stative verbs describe states, opinions, or possession: *be, think, want, prefer, like, love, hate, understand, believe, agree, know, have got, need, own, belong*, etc. We don't normally use stative verbs in continuous tenses.

I'm not playing because I don't like this game.
(NOT *I'm not playing because I'm not liking this game.*)

1 Match 1–6 to A–F.
1 My big sister usually helps me
2 Arthur is driving to work
3 I get dressed
4 My family are going on holiday
5 I often walk to school, but I take the bus
6 He's having a lie-in because

A to Malta this year.
B before breakfast every morning.
C he doesn't have school today.
D at the moment.
E when it's raining.
F with my homework.

2 Complete the sentences with the correct form of the verbs in brackets.
1 Look! Bako _____ (run) to school. He's late!
2 I _____ (not like) Tuesdays. We always _____ (get) a lot of homework.
3 'What _____ (your dad / do)?' 'He's a teacher.'
4 'Hi! Where _____ (you / go)?' 'We _____ (go) to the shops.'
5 Sssh! The baby _____ (sleep) and you _____ (play) loud music.
6 My friends often _____ (play) video games, but at the moment they _____ (listen) to music.
7 'What _____ (you / do) right now?' 'Well, I _____ (not / have) any homework so I _____ (watch) a film.'
8 I usually _____ (play) video games on Saturdays, but I _____ (want) to do more exercise so today, I _____ (play) football with my friends!

3 Choose the correct alternative.
Hi, I'm Zak. I'm from New York, USA. I ¹**like** / **'m liking** New York, but I'm not there right now. I ²**stay** / **'m staying** with my friend Liam in London, England. Liam ³**lives** / **'s living** near the River Thames. Every morning, we ⁴**go** / **'re going** for a run near the river. We ⁵**sometimes stop** / **'re sometimes stopping** at Liam's favourite café. We ⁶**sit** / **'re sitting** there now, and we ⁷**have** / **'re having** a snack. I ⁸**don't eat** / **'m not eating** much because I'm not hungry. We ⁹**don't do** / **'re not doing** this every day because we haven't got lots of money!

4 Complete the questions and answers. Use the present simple or present continuous form of the verbs in brackets.
1 A What _____ (you / do) right now?
  B I _____ (write) a message.
2 A _____ (Harry / study) at the moment?
  B No, he isn't. He _____ (chat) to friends.
3 A _____ (you / often / post) photos online?
  B No, I don't. But I _____ (use) social media all the time!
4 A How often _____ (you / look) at your phone?
  B Once or twice an hour. I _____ (look) at it now!
5 A Why _____ (you / laugh)?
  B Because I _____ (think) this book is funny.
6 A Listen! _____ (those people / speak) German?
  B I _____ (not know). Maybe they _____ (speak) Dutch.
7 A What _____ (you / think) about?
  B I really _____ (want) an ice cream! It's so hot!
8 A _____ (you / believe) her?
  B No, I _____. She _____ (lie).

Grammar booster 137

GRAMMAR BOOSTER

4.2 Comparative adjectives

We use comparative adjectives when we compare two or more people, animals or things. We often use *than* in sentences with comparative adjectives.

Your house is older than ours.
London is bigger than Manchester.
Cars are more expensive than bikes.

For short adjectives, we usually form the comparative with *-er*. For long adjectives, we usually form the comparative with *more* + adjective.

Adjectives with …	Comparative form
one syllable: add *-er*	long → longer
one syllable ending in *-e*: add *-r*	nice → nicer
a vowel and a consonant at the end: double the consonant and add *-er*	big → bigger
two syllables ending in *-y*: remove *-y* and add *-ier*	funny → funnier
three or more syllables: put *more* before the adjective	difficult → more difficult
irregular forms	good → better bad → worse far → further / farther

TIP
The adjective *far* has two comparative forms: *further* and *farther*. We can use both to talk about distance, but we only use *further* to mean 'additional', or when we talk about the degree or extent of something.
I live further / farther away from school than you.
For further information, please call 2018 05963.

TIP
For some adjectives with two syllables, we can form the comparative with *-er* OR *more*:
clever → cleverer OR more clever
quiet → quieter OR more quiet
simple → simpler OR more simple
However, for adjectives with two syllables ending in *-y*, we always use *-ier*:
happy → happier
funny → funnier
easy → easier

1 Write the comparative form of the adjectives below.
1 fast _____
2 sad _____
3 funny _____
4 wet _____
5 horrible _____
6 safe _____
7 cold _____
8 beautiful _____
9 strange _____
10 crazy _____
11 happy _____
12 bad _____
13 good _____
14 far _____,

2 Complete the sentences with the comparative form of the adjectives below.

| cheap   close   comfortable   difficult
| easy   friendly   good   high   slow

1 I never get good marks in science, but I always do well in maths. I think maths is a lot _____ than science.
2 Come and sit here – the sofa is _____ than those chairs!
3 A mountain is _____ than a hill, so it's usually _____ to climb one.
4 The bus costs £15, but the train is £28, so the bus is a lot _____.
5 When you're in Europe, America is _____ than Australia.
6 Well done, you're the winner! You're _____ than everyone else!
7 You can run really fast! I'm a _____ runner than you.
8 Gaby is a lot _____ than her sister, Martha. Gaby always says hello, but Martha never says anything!

3 Complete the sentences. Use the comparative form of the adjectives and *than*.
1 Summer is (hot / winter) _____.
2 80% is (good / 50%) _____.
3 Belgium is (small / China) _____.
4 A potato is (big / a tomato) _____.
5 Is chocolate (nice / cheese)? _____.
6 People are (clever / animals) _____.
7 A test result of 25% is (bad / 50%) _____.
8 Computers are usually (expensive / phones) _____.

4 Complete the dialogues. Write the comparative form of the adjectives. Add *than* if necessary.
1 A Is English _____ your language? (easy)
  B Yes, it is. My language is _____! (difficult)
2 A Which is _____ – a wet day or a cold day? (bad)
  B Cold days are _____ wet days! (good)
3 A Your bedroom is _____ mine! (tidy)
  B Yes, but your room is _____. (interesting)
4 A Our flat is _____ from town than yours. (far)
  B That's true. But your flat is _____ to the school. (close)
5 A The city centre is _____ at the weekends. (busy)
  B That's right. I prefer it during the week when it's _____. (quiet)

138 Grammar booster

GRAMMAR BOOSTER

4.6 Superlative adjectives

We use superlative adjectives to describe one thing in a group of three or more people, animals or things. We always use the definite article *the* or a possessive pronoun before superlative adjectives.

Alaska is one of the coldest places on earth.
This is my best selfie.

For short adjectives, we usually form the superlative with *-est*. For long adjectives, we usually form the superlative with *most* + adjective.

Adjectives with …	Superlative form
one or two syllables: add *-est*	old → oldest
three or more syllables: put *most* or *least* before the adjective	dangerous → most dangerous
irregular forms	good → best bad → worst far → furthest / farthest

We can form negative superlatives with *least*.

It's the least expensive phone in the shop.
What's your least interesting lesson?

TIP
We don't normally use *least* with short adjectives.
Which place has the least comfortable climate: Yakutsk, London or Machu Picchu?
(NOT ~~Which place has the least nice climate: Yakutsk, London or Machu Picchu?~~)

TIP
After superlative adjectives, we often use *in* + a group or a place.
Grandma is the oldest person in my family.
New York is one of the most famous cities in the world.

1 Write the superlative form of the adjectives below.
1. fast _____
2. sad _____
3. funny _____
4. wet _____
5. horrible _____
6. safe _____
7. cold _____
8. beautiful _____
9. strange _____
10. crazy _____
11. happy _____
12. bad _____
13. good _____
14. far _____

2 Complete the sentences with positive superlatives.
1. What's the _____ (beautiful) place in your country?
2. Tom is the _____ (cool) person in our class!
3. What's your _____ (good) subject?
4. What is the _____ (unusual) building in your town?
5. I'm the _____ (bad) singer in our family.
6. My sister is the _____ (happy) person ever!
7. We've got the _____ (nice) teacher in the world!
8. What's the _____ (funny) show on TV?

3 Complete the sentences with the superlative form of the adjectives below.

| bad   comfortable   dangerous   expensive (x2)   good

1. I think *The Lord of the Rings* is the _____ film ever! It's my favourite movie of all time.
2. This is the _____ watch in the shop. All the others are cheaper.
3. 22% is the _____ mark in the class. You can do a lot better than this.
4. We don't have much money so we need to buy the _____ car we can find.
5. My mum is the _____ driver I know. She never looks at the other cars on the road!
6. These shoes are the _____ pair I've got. I can walk in them all day and my feet never get tired.

4 Complete the sentences and questions using the words below.

| big / lake   famous / city   difficult / language
| good / books   exciting / places   high / mountain

1. Mount Everest is _____ in the world.
2. Beijing is _____ in China.
3. Lake Baikal, in Russia, is _____ in the world.
4. Times Square is one of _____ in New York.
5. Is Japanese _____ in the world?
6. I think the Harry Potter books are _____ ever!

5 Complete the text with the words below.

| driest   dry   in   least   of   one
| popular   the   wettest

The ¹_____ place on Earth is also ²_____ of the coldest. It's in Antarctica. It almost never rains there, so it's actually a desert. The Atacama Desert in South America is very ³_____ too, of course. It's ⁴_____ oldest desert ⁵_____ the world, and one ⁶_____ the hottest. What about the ⁷_____ place? That's a small town in north-east India. It has about 12 metres of rain every year! It probably has the ⁸_____ comfortable climate ever – but never mind, it's one of the most ⁹_____ places for tourists in the area – they love it!

Grammar booster   139

GRAMMAR BOOSTER

5.2 Past simple: regular verbs

Affirmative

We use the past simple to talk about past events, finished actions and states.

We enjoyed the concert last night.
Lucy played the drums.
They loved music.

We often use the past simple with past time expressions, such as *yesterday* (*morning / afternoon / evening*), *last* (*night / Tuesday / week / weekend / month / winter / year*), *the day before yesterday*, (*three days / a week / two months / a month / five years*) *ago*, *in 1998*, etc. These time expressions usually go at the beginning or end of the sentence.

We add *-ed* to form the past simple affirmative of most regular verbs.

Affirmative		
Subject	Verb + -ed	
I		
You		
He / She / It	played	tennis yesterday.
We		
You		
They		

In some cases, there are spelling changes:
- Verbs ending in *-e*: add *-d*: *live → lived, dance → danced*
- Verbs ending in a consonant + *-y*: change the *-y* to *-i* and then add *-ed*: *try → tried, cry → cried*
- Verbs that have one syllable and end in one vowel (*a, e, o,* etc.) + one consonant (*t, n, p,* etc.): double the consonant: *stop → stopped, chat → chatted*

Some verbs are irregular and have different forms for the past simple, for example *have → had, go → went*.

TIP
The form of the past simple is the same for all persons (*I, you, he,* etc.). It doesn't change in the third person singular.

1 Write the past simple form of the verbs.
1. like _____
2. carry _____
3. stop _____
4. enjoy _____
5. worry _____
6. stay _____
7. watch _____
8. hate _____
9. happen _____
10. study _____
11. cry _____
12. chat _____

2 Complete the sentences with the correct form of the verbs in brackets.
1. Aart _____ (change) his phone number a month ago.
2. My dad _____ (study) English at university.
3. We _____ (visit) the museum last week.
4. Our friends _____ (arrive) in Greece two days ago.
5. I _____ (cook) some eggs for breakfast yesterday.
6. We _____ (enjoy) the concert last night.
7. Mai _____ (like) the film yesterday.
8. We _____ (finish) all our homework yesterday.

3 Complete the sentences with the correct form of the verbs below.

| arrive   chat   cry   happen   hate   miss   start |

1. 'What _____?' 'I _____ the bus so I was late'.
2. That film is so sad. I _____ at the end!
3. I _____ carrots when I was younger, but I eat them all the time now.
4. I can't play any songs yet because I only _____ guitar lessons a few weeks ago.
5. Gemma was at the station when my train _____.
6. My mum _____ to my granddad on the phone for an hour last night!

4 Read the notes about what Priti did yesterday. Then write sentences.

Day   Week   Month   Year

- 8.00: cook breakfast
- 9.00: travel to London
- 10.30–11.30: walk around the streets
- 11.30–12.30: shop
- 12.30–2.30: visit a museum
- 2.30–4.30: watch a film at the cinema
- 6.30: arrive back home

1. *Priti cooked breakfast at 8.00 a.m.*
2. _____
3. _____
4. _____
5. _____
6. _____
7. _____

5 Choose the correct alternative.
1. I missed school the day before **today / yesterday** because I was sick.
2. They arrived three hours **last / ago**.
3. We listened to a great podcast last **night / evening**.
4. My brother passed all his exams **last year / year ago**.
5. We played a game of tennis **last / yesterday** afternoon.
6. I started school **in / ago** 2005.

GRAMMAR BOOSTER

5.6 Past simple: the verb *be* and *can*

The verb *be*: affirmative, negative and questions

The past forms of the verb *be* are *was* (singular) and *were* (plural).

Angela was late for class yesterday morning.
Jakub and Antoni were at the cinema on Monday.

Affirmative (the verb *be*)		
Subject	*was / were*	
I / He / She / It	was	at home last night.
We / You / They	were	

> **TIP**
> We use *was / were* with *born*.
> *I was born in 2003.* (NOT ~~I'm born in 2003.~~)

The past simple negative forms of the verb *be* are *was not* and *were not*. In spoken or informal written English, we use the short forms *wasn't / weren't*.

Negative (the verb *be*)		
Subject	*wasn't / weren't*	
I / He / She / It	wasn't	at home last night.
We / You / They	weren't	

We form past simple questions with the verb *be* by placing *was* (singular) or *were* (plural) before the subject.

Questions (the verb *be*)		
Was / Were	Subject	
Was	I / he / she / it	at home last night?
Were	we / you / they	

We make short answers with *was / were* in the affirmative and *was / were + not* in the negative.

Short answers (the verb *be*)	
Affirmative	Negative
Yes, I / he / she / it was.	No, I / he / she / it wasn't.
Yes, we / you / they were.	No, we / you / they weren't.

Can: affirmative, negative and questions

The past simple affirmative form of *can* is *could*, and the negative form of *can* is *could not*. In spoken or informal written English, we use the short form *couldn't*. It is the same for all persons (*I, you, he,* etc.).

Subject	*could/ couldn't*	Infinitive without *to*	
I / He / She / It	could / couldn't	swim	when I / he / she / it was five.
You / We / They	could / couldn't	swim	when you / we / they were five.

We form past simple questions by placing *could* before the subject.

Questions (*can*)		
Could	Subject	
Could	I / you / he / she / it / we they	swim?

We make short answers with *could* in the affirmative and *could + not* in the negative.

Short answers (*can*)	
Affirmative	Negative
Yes, I / you / he / she / it / we / they could.	No, I / you / he / she / it / we / they couldn't.

1 Rewrite the sentences in the past.
1 Jack is at the theatre.
2 We're late for the concert.
3 I can't hear the music.
4 Ben can play the guitar.
5 My friends are in a band.
6 It isn't a very good song.
7 Suzie can speak Italian.
8 My parents can't dance.
9 The children aren't tired.
10 They can't see the problem.
11 He isn't happy about the cost.
12 We can't swim very well.

2 Complete the dialogues with the words below. You can use some of them more than once.

| could   couldn't   was   wasn't   were   weren't

1 **A** Where ¹_____ you last night?
  B I ²_____ at the cinema.
  A What ³_____ the film like?
  B It ⁴_____ brilliant.
2 **A** ⁵_____ you understand our maths homework last night?
  B No, I ⁶_____! It ⁷_____ really difficult.
  C I know! My dad tried to help me, but even he ⁸_____ do it!
3 **A** ⁹_____ you at the concert last night?
  B No, we ¹⁰_____. We ¹¹_____ get any tickets.
  A What ¹²_____ the problem?
  B Well, I tried to pay by card and then I remembered there ¹³_____ any money in my bank account!
  A Oh no! But you ¹⁴_____ with Hassan so he ¹⁵_____ pay with his card instead, right?
  B No! He ¹⁶_____ remember his bank card number! I ¹⁷_____ very happy with him!

3 Complete the text with the past simple form of *can* and the verb *be*.

Felix Mendelssohn is very famous because he wrote beautiful music. He ¹_____ born in 1809 in Hamburg, Germany. His parents ²_____ very rich, and they loved art and music. Felix ³_____ very talented. He ⁴_____ play the piano when he ⁵_____ very young, and he ⁶_____ write music too. Soon he ⁷_____ very famous. His sister Fanny ⁸_____ also very talented, but she ⁹_____ (not) famous. Felix and Fanny ¹⁰_____ (not) very old when they died. Felix ¹¹_____ 38, and Fanny ¹²_____ 41.

Grammar booster 141

GRAMMAR BOOSTER

6.2 Past simple: irregular verbs

Affirmative

Some verbs have irregular past simple (affirmative) forms.

You need to learn these forms by heart. See the list of the most used irregular verbs below. There is a fuller list on page 148.

do → did   I did my homework yesterday.
find → found   I found £10 on the ground.

be	was / were	/wɒz/ /wə(r)/
become	became	/bɪˈkeɪm/
begin	began	/bɪˈɡæn/
break	broke	/brəʊk/
bring	brought	/brɔːt/
build	built	/bɪlt/
buy	bought	/bɔːt/
catch	caught	/kɔːt/
come	came	/keɪm/
do	did	/dɪd/
draw	drew	/druː/
eat	ate	/eɪt/
fall	fell	/fel/
fight	fought	/fɔːt/
find	found	/faʊnd/
get	got	/ɡɒt/
give	gave	/ɡeɪv/
go	went	/went/
have	had	/həd/
make	made	/meɪd/
meet	met	/met/
read	read	/red/
see	saw	/sɔː/
send	sent	/sent/
speak	spoke	/spəʊk/
take	took	/tʊk/
teach	taught	/tɔːt/
think	thought	/θɔːt/
throw	threw	/θruː/

The affirmative form of the past simple is the same for all persons, singular and plural (*I, you, he, we*, etc.).

I took her phone to school.
We took some great photos.
The Olympics took place last year.

> **TIP**
> Remember that the past simple of the verb *be* is *was / were*. It behaves differently from other verbs.

1 Complete the past simple forms with the missing vowels (a, e, i, o, u).

	Past simple
1 be	w___s / w___r___
2 meet	m___t
3 fall	f___ll
4 get	g___t
5 lose	l___st
6 say	s___ ___d
7 can	c___ ___ld
8 have	h___d
9 write	wr___t___
10 leave	l___ft
11 sell	s___ld
12 go	w___nt

2 Write the past simple form of the verbs in brackets.
1 Yesterday, my phone _____ (fall) on the floor and the screen _____ (break).
2 Sam _____ (send) a message to Amy and then he _____ (speak) to her.
3 My friend _____ (make) a robot and _____ (bring) it to school.
4 I _____ (find) my laptop and _____ (put) it in my bag.
5 My friends _____ (buy) a card for me when I _____ (be) ill.
6 The boy _____ (say) 'hello' and _____ (tell) me his name.

3 Make sentences with the past simple form of the verbs below.

| begin   buy   do   draw   go   meet   read   think

1 Toby _____ pictures of all his classmates.
2 You're late! The film _____ five minutes ago.
3 Kia _____ to the library at lunchtime.
4 We _____ a charger from the phone shop.
5 I _____ an interesting story yesterday.
6 I _____ my friends after school last Friday.
7 Kim _____ of a brilliant idea last week.
8 Jan _____ his homework on the bus this morning.

4 Complete the text with the past simple form of the verbs below.

| be   come   drink   eat   get
  have   go   run   see   speak

I ¹_____ a horrible morning yesterday. I ²_____ up late. I ³_____ some milk, ⁴_____ a banana and ⁵_____ to the bus stop to go to school. When the bus ⁶_____, I ⁷_____ to the driver to say hello as usual but he just looked at me strangely and asked, 'Do you know what day it is?' Then suddenly, I remembered. It ⁸_____ Saturday and there's no school! So I ⁹_____ home again, and luckily, nobody from my school ¹⁰_____ me.

142 Grammar booster

GRAMMAR BOOSTER

6.6 Past simple: irregular verbs
Negative, questions and short answers

Negative	Questions
I didn't go.	Did I go?
He / She / It didn't go.	Did he / she / it go?
We / You / They didn't go.	Did we / you / they go?
Full form	**Short answers**
didn't = did not	Yes, I did. / No, I didn't.

The forms are the same for all persons, singular and plural (*I, you, he, she, it, we, they*).

In negative sentences, for regular and irregular verbs, we use:
I, you, he, she, it, we, they + *didn't* + the infinitive without *to*.
We DO NOT use the past simple form of the main verb.
 I didn't see you.
 NOT ~~I didn't saw you.~~

In questions, for regular and irregular verbs, we use:
Did + *I, you, he, she, it, we, they* + the infinitive without *to*.
We DO NOT use the past simple form of the main verb.
 Did he go to school?
 NOT ~~Did he went to school?~~

Time expressions usually go at the end of the question.
 Did you go to the cinema last weekend?
 Did she have breakfast this morning?

We can put a question word before *did* to ask for more information.
 What did you do last weekend?
 When did you buy that phone?

1 Match 1–7 to A–G. Then complete the answers.
1 Did your sister have a good time?
2 Did you forget to do your homework again, John?
3 Did the teacher get angry?
4 Did your aunt and uncle drive here?
5 Did I tell you my good news?
6 Did you and Hugo buy any new clothes at the shops?
7 Did your phone break when you dropped it?

A Yes, we _____. Would you like to see them?
B Yes, he _____. He wasn't very happy about it!
C No, I _____. Here it is.
D No, it _____. I was really lucky.
E Yes, she _____. She thought it was great.
F No, you _____. What is it?
G No, they _____. They took the train.

2 Put the words in the correct order to make sentences or questions.
1 birthday / her / party / have / on / a / did / she / ?
2 they / go / to / did / the / concert / last / week / ?
3 city / we / centre / didn't / to / last / weekend / the / go
4 go / after / you / where / did / school / ?
5 the / at / didn't / Eva / morning / this / I / see / stop / bus
6 afternoon / to / didn't / have / this / to / museum / time / they / the / go
7 he / money / do / with / what / did / the / ?
8 to / way / it / here / didn't / find / take / long / the

3 Complete the sentences with the negative form of the verbs below.

| buy   do   go   have   know   write

1 I _____ a letter, I sent a message.
2 Valeria _____ her homework last night. She watched TV.
3 We _____ the answer so we looked online.
4 The tablet was expensive so I _____ it.
5 They _____ to school. They stayed at home.
6 Lorenzo _____ pizza for lunch, he had pasta!

4 Complete the questions.
1 A _____ your first phone?
  B I got my first phone when I was 11.
2 A _____ you?
  B My friends met me at the bus stop.
3 A _____ yesterday?
  B Sam bought a phone charger.
4 A _____ home early?
  B I went home early because I had lots of homework.
5 A _____?
  B I saw Gert last Tuesday.
6 A _____?
  B She went skateboarding in the park after school.

5 Complete the dialogues with the past simple form of the verbs in brackets. Then complete the short answers.
1 A _____ (Emma / take) her laptop on holiday?
  B No, she _____. She _____ (leave) it at home.
2 A Which songs _____ (you / download)?
  B I _____ (not / download) any songs. I _____ (not / want) to pay!
3 A _____ (you / enjoy) the film last night?
  B I _____ (not watch) it. I _____ (go) to bed early.
4 A _____ (your parents / go) to the concert yesterday?
  B Yes, they _____. They _____ (think) it was great.
5 A _____ (Tom / post) his photos online?
  B Yes, he _____. I _____ (see) them this morning.

Grammar booster 143

GRAMMAR BOOSTER

7.2 Be going to

We use *be going to* to talk about plans and intentions for the future.

'What are you going to do when you leave school?'
'I'm going to travel.'

We form affirmative sentences with the correct form of the verb *be* + *going to* + the infinitive without *to*. We usually use short forms of the verb *be* with *going to*.

Affirmative

Subject	The verb *be*	*going to*	Infinitive without *to*
I	'm		
You	're		
He / She / It	's	going to	learn to drive.
We	're		
They	're		

To form the negative, we add *not* after the correct form of the verb *be*.

Negative

Subject	The verb *be* + *not*	*going to*	Infinitive without *to*
I	'm not		
You	aren't		
He / She / It	isn't	going to	learn to drive.
We	aren't		
They	aren't		

We form questions by placing the correct form of the verb *be* before the subject.

Questions

The verb *be*	Subject	*going to*	Infinitive without *to*
Am	I		
Are	you		
Is	he / she / it	going to	learn to drive?
Are	we		
Are	they		

We make short answers with the correct form of the verb *be* in the affirmative and the verb *be* + *not* in the negative.

Short answers

Affirmative	Negative
Yes, I am.	No, I'm not.
Yes, he / she / it is.	No, he / she / it isn't.
Yes, we / you / they are.	No, we / you / they aren't.

If there is a question word (*what, who, when, where, how, why*, etc.), it comes at the beginning of the sentence, before the verb *be*.

When are you going to learn to drive?

When we use *be going to* to talk about plans, we often use future time expressions:

I'm going to make a cake tomorrow.
She's going to visit her grandparents next week.

next week, in a month, in a minute, this evening, in two years, in ten days' time, tomorrow afternoon, the day after tomorrow, in half an hour, in a few months, in a year, tonight, in a few minutes, this afternoon

1 Put the words in the correct order to make sentences.
1. to / October / to / go / Amy / university / next / is / going
2. going / to / flat / We / share / a / not / are
3. TV / going / this / I / am / watch / evening / to
4. next / Roy / study / not / maths / term / is / to / going
5. to / going / tomorrow / My / are / my / teacher / parents / talk / to / afternoon
6. going / leave / I / to / am / year / not / school / next

2 Complete the sentences with the correct form of *be going to* and the verbs in brackets.
1. What _____ (you / do) next summer?
2. I _____ (go) to work with my mum next week.
3. _____ (you and your friends / play) video games at the weekend?
4. My cousins _____ (not visit) us next week.
5. Where _____ (your brother / study) next year?
6. We _____ (not get) jobs this summer.
7. I _____ (not take) the bus to school tomorrow.
8. _____ (Tobias / play) his guitar at the concert tonight?

3 Complete the questions, short answers and sentences with the correct form of *be going to* and the verbs in brackets. Then match 1–5 to A–E.
1. When _____ (you / do) your homework?
2. _____ (Ellie / go) to college next term?
3. _____ (you / make) a vlog?
4. What _____ (we / have) for lunch?
5. How _____ (they / travel) to France?

A No, I _____. But I _____ (post) some photos online.
B Mum _____ (make) sushi.
C They _____ (go) by train.
D Yes, she _____. She _____ (study) drama.
E I _____ (do) it on Saturday afternoon.

144 Grammar booster

GRAMMAR BOOSTER

7.6 Will

We use *will* to make predictions and guesses about the future. We often use it with *I think* or *I don't think*.

I don't think it will rain in the afternoon.
I think the weather will be nice.

We form the affirmative with *will* + the infinitive of the main verb.

Affirmative

Subject	will	Infinitive without *to*
I / You / He / She / It / We / They	will	be late for school.

TIP
In spoken English, we often use '*ll*, the short form of *will*, after pronouns.
She'll get a good job.

To form the negative, we add *not* after *will*. In spoken or informal written English, we use the short form *won't*.

Negative

Subject	will + not	Infinitive without *to*
I / You / He / She / It / We / They	won't	be late for school.

We form questions by placing *will* before the subject.

Questions

Will	Subject	Infinitive without *to*
Will	I / you / he / she / it / we / they	be late for school?

We make short answers with *will* in the affirmative and *won't* in the negative.

Short answers

Affirmative	Negative
Yes, I / you / he / she / it / we / they will.	No, I / you / he / she / it / we / they won't.

We use the adverbs *certainly* and *definitely* to say we are sure about something. We use *probably* when we aren't 100% sure.

The adverbs *certainly*, *definitely* and *probably* go after *will* but before *won't*.

He'll certainly / definitely pass his exams.
We probably won't go on holiday this year.

1 Complete the sentences with the correct form of *will* and the verbs in brackets.

1 Andy _____ (be) a farmer like his dad.
2 Jen _____ (probably / study) physics at university.
3 I don't think people _____ (eat) much meat in the future.
4 _____ (machines / control) humans in the 22nd century?
5 I _____ (certainly / not / become) an astronaut.
6 Where _____ (we / be) in ten years' time?

2 Complete the text with the correct form of *will* and the words in brackets.

¹_____ (humans / live) on Mars one day? Some people think it ²_____ (happen), but it ³_____ (certainly / not happen) in the near future. Astronauts ⁴_____ (probably / travel) there soon, but it ⁵_____ (certainly / not be) possible to live there. I think one day people ⁶_____ (build) cities on Mars, but I don't think it ⁷_____ (be) in my lifetime. Perhaps my great grandchildren ⁸_____ (be) the first Martians!

3 Complete the sentence with *I'll* + a verb from below.

| answer   be (x2)   email   go   have   stay   turn (x2)

1 'There's somebody at the door.' 'OK, _____ it.'
2 'Would you like to come with us?' 'No thanks, I think _____ here.'
3 'Don't forget to send me that link to the website.' 'Sure, _____ you later.'
4 'Did you have time to fix my bike?' 'No, I didn't, but _____ a look now.'
5 'I can't hear the TV' '_____ it up then.'
6 'Oh no, there's no milk in the fridge!' 'Don't worry, _____ to the shop right now. I _____ back in 15 minutes.'
7 'It's a bit dark in here.' '_____ on the lights.'
8 'Do you need any help with that?' 'It's OK thanks, _____ fine.'

4 Read the situations. Then write sentences beginning with *I think I'll … or I don't think I'll …* and your own ideas.

1 The weather forecast for tomorrow is very good.
2 I want to stay at home this evening.
3 I need a new phone, but I haven't got enough money to buy one.
4 It's late and I'm really tired.
5 There's nothing on TV tonight.
6 I need to go to the city centre.
7 I like these shoes, but the shop doesn't have my size.
8 I don't want to go to the cinema on my own.

5 Write your own predictions about the things below using *will / won't* and *certainly*, *probably* and *definitely*.

1 people live on the moon in twenty years' time
2 scientists find life on Mars soon
3 people have holidays in space one day
4 aliens invade Earth
5 Earth become hotter in the future
6 people stop driving cars

Grammar booster 145

GRAMMAR BOOSTER

8.2 Present perfect: affirmative

We use the present perfect to talk about life experiences.

I have been to Egypt and I have seen the pyramids.
She has had three different jobs this year – she has worked as a waitress, a shop assistant and a secretary.

We also use it to talk about past events which have a result in the present. We don't say when the event happened – the exact time isn't important.

Gustav has eaten the whole chicken! (= There's no chicken left for me.)
We have packed our bags. (= The bags are packed now.)

We form the present perfect affirmative with *have / has* and the past participle of the main verb.

Affirmative		
Subject	have / has	Past participle
I	have	climbed the Eiffel Tower.
You	have	
He / She / It	has	
We	have	
They	have	

Past participles

Regular past participles end in *-ed*. They have the same form as the past simple: *visit → visited*, *play → played*, *stop → stopped*, *study → studied*

Irregular past participles don't end in *-ed*. Some of them are the same as the past simple, and some are different. See the list of common irregular verbs and their past participles on page 148.

be → was / were → been
write → wrote → written
make → made → made
have → had → had

1 Write the past participles of the verbs.
1 be _____
2 forget _____
3 take _____
4 make _____
5 have _____
6 go _____, _____
7 put _____
8 do _____
9 find _____
10 become _____
11 meet _____
12 see _____
13 eat _____
14 bring _____

2 Complete the sentences with the present perfect form of the verbs in brackets.
1 Oh no! Tom _____ (fall) off his bike.
2 I _____ (finish) my homework at last.
3 My parents _____ (go) to the shops.
4 I need an umbrella. It _____ (start) to rain.
5 You _____ (write) a very good story.
6 Maisie _____ (make) a chocolate cake.

3 Complete the sentences with the present perfect form of the verbs below.

| be   begin   buy   eat   find   have   meet   take

1 They _____ each other before.
2 I _____ a really awful day!
3 Paula _____ the bus to school today.
4 We _____ there before so we don't want to go again.
5 He told me he _____ an expensive new car.
6 You _____ your glasses! Where were they?
7 Shhh! The film _____!
8 I _____ at a Japanese restaurant once before but I didn't really like it.

4 Complete the situations with the phrases below. Use the present perfect form of the verbs.

| do our homework   lose my phone   miss the bus
have their lunch   pass her exams

1 Maya is happy because she _____.
2 I can't text because I _____.
3 We're relaxing because we _____.
4 They aren't hungry because they _____.
5 I'm going to be late because I _____.

5 Complete the text with the present perfect form of the verbs in brackets.

It's the end of the summer holidays. Jerome [1]_____ (have) a great time. He and his parents [2]_____ (be) to Budapest on holiday. They're home again now and Jerome [3]_____ (begin) to learn Hungarian because he wants to go back there next year. He [4]_____ (download) an app and he [5]_____ (learn) some new phrases. He [6]_____ (find) a Hungarian penfriend too. They [7]_____ (send) some emails and they [8]_____ (share) some photos. Maybe they'll meet in Hungary next year!

146 Grammar booster

GRAMMAR BOOSTER

8.6 Present perfect: negative and questions

To form the present perfect negative, we add *not* after *have / has*. In spoken or informal written English, we use the short forms *haven't* or *hasn't*.

Negative		
Subject	have / has + not	Past participle
I	haven't	
You	haven't	
He / She / It	hasn't	booked a holiday.
We	haven't	
They	haven't	

We form present perfect questions by placing *have / has* before the subject.

Questions		
Have / Has	Subject	Past participle
Have	I	
Have	you	
Has	he / she / it	booked a holiday?
Have	we	
Have	they	

We make short answers with *have / has* in the affirmative and *have / has + not* in the negative.

Short answers	
Affirmative	Negative
Yes, I / you / we / they have.	No, I / you / we / they haven't.
Yes, he / she / it has.	No, he / she / it hasn't.

TIP

In positive short answers, we don't use short forms.
'Have you met my brother?' 'Yes, I have.' (NOT ~~Yes, I've.~~)

If there is a question word (*what, who, when, where, how, why*, etc.), it comes at the beginning of the sentence, before *have / has*.

- Where have you been?
- Who has remembered suncream?
- How many books have you read?

TIP

We don't usually ask present perfect questions with *when*. We use the past simple instead.
When did he fly to Spain? (NOT ~~When has he flown to Spain?~~)

Ever and *never*

We use the present perfect affirmative + *ever* to ask questions about life experiences. *Ever* means 'at any time in your life'.

- Have you ever slept in a tent?
- Have you ever climbed a mountain?
- Has Josie ever flown in a plane?

We use the present perfect affirmative + *never* to talk about life experiences we have not had.

- I have never climbed a mountain.
- Josie has never flown in a plane.

TIP

We don't use *not* and *never* together.
I've never eaten Indian food.
(NOT ~~I haven't never eaten Indian food.~~)

1 Complete the sentences with the correct present perfect form of the verbs in brackets.
1 Bruno _____ (not take) any photos.
2 I _____ (not pack) a sun hat.
3 _____ (you / bring) a camera?
4 Where are they? Where _____ (they / go)?
5 We _____ (not buy) many souvenirs.
6 _____ (Beate / visit) the museum?
7 Which activities _____ (you / do) today?
8 What _____ (Jin / tell) you about his holiday?

2 Complete the questions and short answers with the present perfect form of the verbs in brackets. Then match 1–5 to A–E.
1 _____ (you / ever / meet) a famous person?
2 _____ (Sam / ever / swim) in the sea?
3 _____ (you / arrange) a holiday for next year?
4 _____ (your grandparents / ever / use) a computer?
5 _____ (I / give) you my email address?

A Yes, we _____. We're going to go to Italy.
B Yes, you _____. But I haven't got your phone number.
C No, he _____. He's never learned to swim.
D No, I _____. But I'd like to meet Ariana Grande.
E Yes, they _____. They love online shopping!

3 Complete the text.
Hi Amelia,
How are you? We're on holiday in Mexico. I've [1]_____ been here before, but my parents [2]_____ been here twice. We arrived this morning so we [3]_____ had much time for sightseeing. Dad [4]_____ booked a nice restaurant for this evening. The weather isn't great, which is strange! So far it [5]_____ stopped raining, but there are lots of museums. Have you [6]_____ heard of the Frida Kahlo Museum? It's got lots of amazing paintings and we [7]_____ decided to go there – I'll tell you all about it. Oh, the sun [8]_____ come out. I'm going to go out!
See you soon,
Gemma

Grammar booster 147

IRREGULAR VERBS

Base form	Past simple	Past participle
be	was / were	been
become	became	become
begin	began	begun
blow	blew	blown
break	broke	broken
bring	brought	brought
build	built	built
burn	burned / burnt	burned / burnt
buy	bought	bought
can	could	been able to
catch	caught	caught
choose	chose	chosen
come	came	come
cost	cost	cost
cut	cut	cut
do	did	done
draw	drew	drawn
drink	drank	drunk
drive	drove	driven
eat	ate	eaten
fall	fell	fallen
feel	felt	felt
fight	fought	fought
find	found	found
fly	flew	flown
forget	forgot	forgotten
get	got	got
give	gave	given
go	went	gone
grow	grew	grown
have	had	had
hear	heard	heard
hide	hid	hidden
hit	hit	hit
keep	kept	kept
know	knew	known
lay	laid	laid
lead	led	led
learn	learned / learnt	learned / learnt

Base form	Past simple	Past participle
leave	left	left
lend	lent	lent
lose	lost	lost
make	made	made
mean	meant	meant
meet	met	met
pay	paid	paid
put	put	put
read	read	read
ride	rode	ridden
ring	rang	rung
run	ran	run
say	said	said
see	saw	seen
sell	sold	sold
send	sent	sent
shake	shook	shaken
show	showed	shown / showed
shut	shut	shut
sing	sang	sung
sit	sat	sat
sleep	slept	slept
smell	smelled / smelt	smelled / smelt
speak	spoke	spoken
spell	spelled / spelt	spelled / spelt
spend	spent	spent
stand	stood	stood
steal	stole	stolen
swim	swam	swum
take	took	taken
teach	taught	taught
tell	told	told
think	thought	thought
throw	threw	thrown
understand	understood	understood
wake	woke	woken
wear	wore	worn
win	won	won
write	wrote	written

148 Irregular verbs

EXTRA ACTIVITIES

Page 31, Ex 8

Imagine you need to fill in the customer survey form for your local gym. Complete the form in 60–80 words.

MOVE IT!
FITNESS AND SPORTS CENTRE

Gym membership form – personal details
Please fill in all parts of this form.

Gender: M / F
Surname:
First name:
DOB (DD/MM/YYYY):
Address:
Postcode:
Email:
Tel:
Job:
When would you like to use the gym?

PTO

MOVE IT!
FITNESS AND SPORTS CENTRE

1 What physical activities do you enjoy doing?

2 How many times a week do you go to the gym?

3 How long do you exercise for per workout?

4 How many hours of exercise do you do a week?

5 Please give details about the type / frequency of exercise.

6 Please give details about your average daily diet.

Page 36, Ex 6

Choose one of the people. Do not tell your partner. Then ask and answer *yes/no* questions to find out who it is.

Is it a boy? — Yes, it is.
Is he wearing a T-shirt? — Yes, he is.
Is he dancing? — No, he isn't.

Page 106, exercise 2

Check your quiz score. Do you agree with it?

ANSWER KEY

More As – You're an adventurer! You like trying new things and love having exciting new experiences.
More Bs – You're a traveller! You're friendly and like going on trips and meeting people.
More Cs – You're a tourist! You're organised and enjoy arranging holidays and booking activities.

EXTRA ACTIVITIES

Page 14, Ex 9

Ask questions in the present simple to complete your table.

> Does Mia read comics?   Yes, she does.

Student A

	like cake	read comics	take photos
Mia		✓	
Nils	✗		✓
Mum and Dad		✗	
My friends	✗		✓
Your partner?			

Page 28, Ex 9

Ask and answer questions about the bento boxes.

STUDENT A

> Is there any meat in your bento box?   Yes, there is.
> How much is there?   Not much. There's some …

Page 61, Ex 11

You each have information about a different cultural event. Ask your partner about their event and complete the fact file.

Student A

LATITUDE FESTIVAL

'MORE THAN JUST A MUSIC FESTIVAL'

13–16 July
Henham Park, Suffolk, England (UK)

MUSIC CONCERTS WITH WORLD-FAMOUS BANDS

DANCE SHOWS, ART EXHIBITIONS AND LOTS OF STREET THEATRE

Open to everybody, but under sixteen-year-olds can't go at the weekend without an adult!

Festival name: _____
When? _____
Where? _____
Who for? _____
What happens? _____
_____

Page 108, Ex 10

Use the prompts on card 2 to make questions about your partner's holiday. Then ask and answer to complete the missing information.

Card 1 – Student A

Answer Student B's questions about this resort.

Sunset All-Inclusive Resort, Vietnam

Address: 458 Au Co Road – 1 km from Hoi An.
• town centre – 15 mins walk.
• Da Nang train station – 29 min coach, $10
• Cua Dai Beach 19 mins walk / 4 mins car
All-Inclusive, pool, trips to islands, tours in Hoi An.
Prices: twin room: $127, family room: $229
Mobile: (+353) (01) 629 7008

Card 2 – Student A

Ask Student B questions about this campsite.

Colibri Camping

| Where exactly? |
| How far / How long does it take? |
| • La Paz park? |
| • Cable car? |
| • El Alto Airport? |
| Trips? |
| Cost? |
| Phone? |

150   Extra activities

EXTRA ACTIVITIES

Page 14, Ex 9

Ask questions in the present simple to complete your table.

> Does Mia like cake?   Yes, she does.

Student B

	like cake	read comics	take photos
Mia	✓		✗
Nils		✗	
Mum and Dad	✓		✗
My friends		✓	
Your partner?			

Page 28, Ex 9

Work in pairs. Ask and answer questions about the bento boxes.

STUDENT B

> Is there any meat in your bento box?   Yes, there is.
> How much is there?   Not much. There's some …

Page 61, Ex 11

You each have information about a different cultural event. Ask your partner about their event and complete the fact file.

Student B

The Chicago International Children's Film Festival

'The world's largest film festival for young people.'
1–10 November
Theaters all over Chicago city center (USA)
250 international films and videos for 2–16-year-olds
Artists from 40 countries talk about how to make the best videos. Painting classes.

Festival name: _____
When? _____
Where? _____
Who for? _____
What happens? _____
_____

Page 108, Ex 10

Use the prompts on card 2 to make questions about your partner's holiday. Then ask and answer to complete the missing information.

Card 1 – Student B

Answer Student A's questions about this campsite.

Colibri Camping, Bolivia

Address: Calle 94, Camino al Rio – 6 km from La Paz.
• El Alto Airport – 40 mins bus, $5
• La Paz park – 19 mins walk, 4 mins drive
• Cable car – 25 mins bus
Green campsite, free Wi-Fi, hot showers, walking tours in city, trips to mountains.
Prices: tent: $13, twin room: $25 a night
Phone: 00 591 74395698

Card 2 – Student B

Ask Student A questions about this resort.

Sunset All-Inclusive Resort

| Where exactly? |
| How far / How long does it take? |
| • town centre? |
| • beach? |
| • train station? |
| Trips? |
| Cost? |
| Phone? |

Extra activities   151

OXFORD
UNIVERSITY PRESS

Great Clarendon Street, Oxford, OX2 6DP, United Kingdom

Oxford University Press is a department of the University of Oxford. It furthers the University's objective of excellence in research, scholarship, and education by publishing worldwide. Oxford is a registered trade mark of Oxford University Press in the UK and in certain other countries

© Oxford University Press 2022

The moral rights of the author have been asserted

First published in 2022

2026 2025 2024
10 9 8 7 6

No unauthorized photocopying

All rights reserved. No part of this publication may be reproduced, stored in a retrieval system, or transmitted, in any form or by any means, without the prior permission in writing of Oxford University Press, or as expressly permitted by law, by licence or under terms agreed with the appropriate reprographics rights organization. Enquiries concerning reproduction outside the scope of the above should be sent to the ELT Rights Department, Oxford University Press, at the address above

You must not circulate this work in any other form and you must impose this same condition on any acquirer

Links to third party websites are provided by Oxford in good faith and for information only. Oxford disclaims any responsibility for the materials contained in any third party website referenced in this work

ISBN: 978 0 19 406355 5   STUDENT BOOK WITH ONLINE PRACTICE PACK COMPONENT

Printed in China

This book is printed on paper from certified and well-managed sources

ACKNOWLEDGEMENTS

The publisher would like to thank the following for the permission to reproduce photographs: 123RF (Amy Muschik, Anton Starikov, Fabian Schmidt, Jacek Chabraszewski, Michael Turner, Olga Popova, Oliver Hoffmann, Thanapol Kuptanisakorn, Wavebreak Media LTD); Alamy (360Cities, Aflo Co. Ltd., Ammentorp Photography, Andrew Paterson, Anthony Kay/Rail, Arcaid Images, Arina Habich, Artem Merzlenko, B Christopher, Ben Molyneux, Cavan Images, Chas Spradbery, Chris Howes/Wild Places Photography, David R. Frazier Photolibrary, Inc., Dennis MacDonald, Dinodia Photos, dpa picture alliance, Duffie, Gonzales Photo, Jake Lyell, Jim West, Joe Tree, Kirsty McLaren, Martin Dalton, OJO Images Ltd, Oleksiy Maksymenko Photography, PA Images, Panther Media GmbH, paul eccleston, redsnapper, richard sowersby, Science Photo Library, Sipa US, Steve Skjold, Tetra Images, Tito Slack, travelpix, UrbanImages, Vintage_Space, Wavebreakmedia Ltd UC26, WENN Rights Ltd, Zoonar GmbH); Bye Bye Plastic Bags; Corbis (Adie Bush, Kevin Dodge, Steve Prezant); Dillon Photography (Michael Dillon); Getty Images (BananaStock, bradleyhebdon, Creatas, Digital Vision, fstop.123, grahambedingfield/E+, kazunoriokazaki/E+, Marc Debnam, Martin Deja, Peter Cade, SDI Productions/E+, Star Tribune, UpperCut, vgajic/E+, Westend61); Kamae Design; Kevin Faingnaert; Oxford University Press (Gareth Boden, Mark Mason); Rankin; Rishab Jain; Shutterstock (1981 Rustic Studio kan, 4 PM production, A. and I. Kruk, Africa Studio, Ahturner, Aizzul A Majid, AJR_photo, Aleksey Troshin, Alex from the Rock, Alex Jackson, Alex Staroseltsev, AlinaMD, Alpay Erdem, Andrea Izzotti, Andrew Mayovskyy, Andrew Roland, Andrey_Popov, APN Photography, archideaphoto, ariadna de raadt, Arsenie Krasnevsky, arslaan, Art Konovalov, Artazum, AS photostudio, aslysun, AV_photo, AVA Bitter, baibaz, BarbaraGoreckaPhotography, bellena, BernatRV, bikeriderlondon, Billion Photos, Bohbeh, BonNontawat, Bram Smits, BrAt82, Brester Irina, CandyBox Images, Carlos Amarillo, Cesar Quesada Contreras, Chauveau Nicolas/Sipa, Christian Bertrand, Christopher Meder, Cincila, coloursinmylife, Craig Dingle, Creativa Images, criben, Daan Kloeg, Dabarti CGI, Daboost, Dana.S, Daniel Prudek, Danil Nevsky, David Litman, David Swindells/Pymca, Day Of Victory Studio, DC_Aperture, demidoff, Den Rozhnovsky, Denis Kuvaev, Det-anan, Dimedrol68, dowraik, Dusan Petkovic, EdBockStock, EDHAR, Ekaterina Kuchina, EpicStockMedia, EPSTOCK, ESB Professional, FabrikaSimf, Felix Mizioznikov, Feng Yu, fernanda photos, Filipe B. Varela, foodstck, Fotyma, FrameStockFootages, Frederic Legrand – COMEO, Frode Koppang, Gigra, Golden Pixels LLC, Gorodenkoff, Grzegorz_Pakula, Guaxinim, Halfpoint, Halfpoint, hin255, HomeArt, Hrytsiv Oleksandr, hxdbzxy, Iakov Filimonov, Igor Bulgarin, IhorL, Ingram Publishing (Superstock Limited), Ints Vikmanis, ivanfolio, Jacek Chabraszewski, Jan Faukner, Jaromir Chalabala, Jasmine_K, JeweBewe, Jiri Hera, Joe Techapanupreeda, joesayhello, John Kasawa, Jonas Petrovas, joo830908, JPagetRFPhotos, JudeAnd, Just dance, kana Design Image, karelnoppe, kate kultsevych, Kiarat Vidal, KKulikov, Kletr, koya979, Kris Jacobs, lazyllama, Lepas, lev radin, LightField Studios, Louis.Roth, Luca Luceri, Lucky Business, Lukas Gojda, Lurin, m_agency, Magdanatka, Maike Hildebrandt, marchello74, Marcio Jose Bastos Silva, Marco Rubino, margouillat photo, Maridav, Martina Vaculikova, Matt Benoit, maxpro, mazan xeniya, Merla, MetCreations, Michael Kraus, Michal Chmurski, Microstock Man, Mika Heittola, Mikbiz, mimagephotography, Moab Republic, Monkey Business Images, Monthira, Moolkum, Nadezda Cruzova, Navid Ibne, Nebojsa Markovic, Nemika_Polted, New Africa, NicoElNino, Nicoleta Ionescu, nikiteev_konstantin, nikkimeel, Nino Cavalier, Nopparat Khokthong, okimo, Oksana Mizina, Oleg Chernyavsky, Oleksandr Osipov, Oleksiy Mark, Olga Rusinova, OlhaTsiplyar, Oliver Hoffmann, oneinchpunch, Ongala, oorka, OzonE_AnnA, Pal2iyawit, Patryk Kosmider, Paul Vinten, Paulo Vilela, Pavel L Photo and Video, pcruciatti, Peshkova, Petr Vaclavek, photka, photo one, Photobac, Photographee.eu, photovideoworld, Pipas Imagery, pisitnamtasaeng, Pixelbliss, Plateresca, Popova Valeriya, Rafal Kubiak, Rawpixel.com, Red Confidential, rob3rt82, romiri, Romrodphoto, Ronald Sumners, Ruslan Kalnitsky, Sabphoto, Sahacha Nilkumhang, SamaraHeisz5, Santiago Cornejo, Sasha Ka, seligaa, Sergey Nivens, SeventyFour, Shazed Nirjon, shop_py, Shyntartanya, siamionau pavel, sibiranna, Sivakumar1970, Soho A Studio, Sorn340 Studio Images, speedimaging, sportoakimirka, Stephanie Frey, StepStock, stocksolutions, Su_Gus, Sunday Alamba/AP, Suradech Prapairat, Svitlana Sokolova, Syda Productions, Syrytsyna Tetiana, takayuki, Tapui, Tarzhanova, Tero Vesalainen, The World in HDR, Torgado, Travelpixs, TSpider, Tupungato, Twin Design, Twinsterphoto, Valentyn Volkov, Valerii Evlakhov, Venus Angel, VGstockstudio, VH-studio, Viacheslav Lopatin, Viktoria Kazakova, Vladislav Lyutov, vsl, Walt Disney Pictures/Kobal, wavebreakmedia, William Perugini, wizdata, wonlopcolors, YanLev, Yermolov, yoshi0511, zentilia, Zephyr_p, zhu difeng, Zurijeta).

Commissioned photography by: Gareth Boden pp.46–47, 72–73.

Commissioned illustrations by: Joanna Kerr/New Division pp.5 (icons), 10, 49, 56, 91; Mauro Marchesi/Beehive Illustration p.67; Geo Parkin pp.5 (bag contents), 14, 27, 56, 113, 125; Lee Teng pp.20–21.

Cover images by: Getty Images (basketball player/Henrik Sorensen); Shutterstock (DNA/Blackboard), (Barcelona/Nate Hovee), (violin player/Sunti).

Videos filmed and produced by: MTJ Media.

The publisher would like to thank the following reviewers for their helpful comments: Olga Kavkova, Gabriela Nátterová, Maria Fernanda Puertas, Michaela Sidová, Barbara Sillár